ADOLESCENCE

GUIDING YOUTH THROUGH
THE PERILOUS ORDEAL

A NORTON PROFESSIONAL BOOK

ADOLESCENCE

GUIDING YOUTH THROUGH THE PERILOUS ORDEAL

Miller Newton

W. W. NORTON & COMPANY • New York • London

Copyright © 1995 by Miller Newton

All rights reserved.

Printed in the United States of America

First Edition

Composition by Bytheway Typesetting Services, Inc.
Manufacturing by Haddon Craftsmen, Inc.
Book design by P.J. Nolan

Library of Congress Cataloging-in-Publication Data

Newton, Miller.
    Adolescence : guiding youth through the perilous ordeal / Miller
Newton.
        p.   cm.
    "A Norton professional book."
    Includes bibliographical references and index.
    ISBN 0-393-70194-8
    1. Adolescence.   I. Title.
HQ796.N516   1995
305.23′5 — dc20   94-42648   CIP

W. W. Norton & Company, Inc., 500 Fifth Avenue, New York, NY 10110
W.W. Norton & Company, Ltd., 10 Coptic Street, London WC1A 1PU

1 2 3 4 5 6 7 8 9 0

To Ruth Ann Newton, who has been a partner in my personal journey, family journey, and professional journey, for your love, criticism, and support on the journey and this book.

To my children, Johanna, Miller, and Mark, for the frustration and privilege of going through your growing up with reminders of my own adolescence as well as totally new experiences out of your individuality, all of which led to this book. Now I add to that my gratitude for our relationship as adults who remain connected in our family journey.

Contents

Acknowledgments

When you stop at a certain point in a human and professional journey to reflect on a dimension of that journey and then share your insights in writing, it is difficult if not impossible to detect all of the influences that have affected the route you have taken and the conclusions you have reached. I find this sad since many individuals who have influenced what is in this book will not be mentioned out of faulty memory rather than neglect. Nevertheless, this is my flawed but earnest attempt to say thank you to all of them.

As an avid reader, I am indebted to many individuals who have lived, learned, and then had the courage to express their wisdom and opinions on paper. I am appreciative for the influence of every one of them. In addition, many of them received a call out of the blue from someone unknown to them who wanted to pursue their wisdom beyond the written page. They have graciously talked to me on the phone, seen me in person, and shared out of their bountiful experience. Again, I am most grateful.

Over the last fifteen years, numerous families, out of love for their adolescents and a deep commitment to see those adolescents through the perilous ordeal into healthy adulthood, have shared their pain and joy with me in the process of treatment. Parents, siblings, and the primary patients have had the courage to open the intimate secrets of their families in order to pursue a healthier life. I am grateful to them for their commitment to family, their love for each other, and their pursuit of healthy life for the family and the individual.

E. M. Christine Kris, Ralph E. Tarter, Marsha E. Bates, Marsha A. Glines, David Sabo, and Don Shapiro all gave much time and a great deal of their personal wisdom and experience to me during the course of study that led to this book. In addition, they were all influential in shaping the outline and working with me on issues as well as the manuscript itself. I have also drawn upon the experience of Jan Krogh, Ulric Hermansson, Marleen McCormack, and Michael McCormack, who have worked with me in years past and remain a distant but intimate part of the professional family at KIDS of North Jersey, Inc. June Hayo and Tony Kozakiewicz have also contributed their ideas to the manuscript and have been part of both the peer counseling team and, later, the professional team at KIDS. Zisalo Wancier and George J. Carnevale also read the manuscript and helped with ideas.

To Mariana Pagliere, my assistant, who has not only been responsible for numerous editions of the manuscript but has also served as my first editor, shaping language, helping with clarity, developing the first generation of graphics, and sticking with this until she was ready to faint with fatigue, I am more than grateful. Also thanks to Pam Adelman for her assistance in some of the early generation of graphics and to Michelle Abbey for help with the final graphics.

To Susan Munro and Margaret Farley, my editors at W. W. Norton, who, with enthusiasm for the manuscript, have pushed me to deal with tough issues and questions that ultimately have made for a much better book, I say thank you.

ADOLESCENCE

GUIDING YOUTH THROUGH
THE PERILOUS ORDEAL

Introduction

A middle-aged woman calls to make an appointment with you for therapy, with a listless voice, a sad tone, and a sense of helplessness. She arrives at your office and begins to talk about her problem, which appears to be depression. It turns out to involve her sense of purpose as a woman. She experiences distance in her marriage and constant conflict with her husband. Her days of mothering are limited because her youngest child is "15 going on 30." As you sort through the presenting problems, it becomes quickly apparent that the teenager is at the vortex of conflict and depression in her life. Her rejecting teenager prevents her from experiencing the normal transition from the focal parenting period to the beginning of middle age. Her attempts to get support and help from her husband as a parenting partner result in criticism and conflict, since he joins the teenager in blaming her for the conflict with her daughter. Of course, she is depressed. She is the loser in this family system.

A couple arrive, having once had a successful marriage which is now in disarray. They seem to be in conflict about everything, from the content of meals to activity in bed. Several sessions grind by as they relentlessly blame each other and disagree on every conceivable issue. Slowly, from the shadows emerges an acting-out teenager playing "Let's you two fight, and get off my back."

A family is referred for treatment by their family practitioner, who suggests that there are real family problems. As the husband and wife and three children enter the room and take seats, the 16-year-old moves his chair back and takes an isolated conflictual position. As you attempt to make contact with each family member in order to learn about his or her concerns and what led to therapy, the teenager puts down every other family member with critical facial expressions.

Common to all three of these therapy situations is a troubled teenager. From a family systems viewpoint, we may explain this away by calling the teenager a symptom bearer, an identified patient, but the fact remains that this individual is tripping along a troubled developmental path to adulthood. This young person manages to stay at the center of the family storm. As you attempt to sort out the family situation, it is tempting to ally with the troubled teenager, blame the family, and lobby for more adult treatment and freedom. If you make this choice and are successful with the family, the complaint level increases as the teenager becomes more of a problem as a result of a wider arena of freedom. If you make the opposite choice, which involves strengthening the parent or parent dyad in order to effectively control the teenager, thus reducing the teenager to childhood status, the problems also increase.

What do you do?

The problem the therapist faces in this situation is lack of effective knowledge about the adolescent phase of development. You may have had a course in human development or child development. The child development course stops at the brink of adolescence and the human development course nods toward adolescence, then quickly moves into adulthood, leaving you blissfully ignorant about the adolescent developmental period and its problems. The result is you are forced to operate on personal experience, gut instincts, and some myths about adolescence that you have accumulated along the way. Ultimately, counseling problems involving adolescents become a nightmare because child and adult strategies consistently fail.

CHANGING ADOLESCENCE

Looking back from my early fifties to my own teenage years, I realize that much has changed about growing up. The last two decades have consistently romanticized adolescence as a life period until it has become the ideal time of life for most people. Adolescent music, dance, and dress are trend-setting for all the rest of us. We so idolize adolescents that they are convinced that they are the center of life for family, community, and nation. All normal adolescents have that self-focused quality, but it has run wild to the point where it dominates our culture and sets individual teens up for much difficulty.

A second societal trend in current adolescence is lowering the initial age for entering adolescence. For my generation, adolescence began someplace between 12 or 13, with the admission to junior high school and with male-female activities. Today, we find many parents pushing 10- and 11-year-old girls to wear makeup, teenage jewelry, and adolescent clothes, and to begin opposite-sex-oriented behavior. There is even a physical correlate to parents pushing kids to grow up too fast. Researchers call this the "secular trend" in which initial pubertal growth signs in boys and girls begin almost a year earlier than half a century ago, and menarche for girls comes significantly earlier than in the past.[1] In addition to pushing children into an almost adult phase of life, with the resulting confusion about identity and behavior, it stretches the half-child/half-adult period out by a year or two, making the agony of waiting for adult status more intense.

A changing economy and job market have also affected adolescence. The upper limit of adolescence has moved into the 20's, sometime between 22 and 24, due to increased knowledge and skill requirements for effective participation in the economy as a self-supporting autonomous adult. Many young people in their early 20's are either still in higher education with family financial support or are still living at home despite adult employment because they are unable to finance their own residence away from the family. Adding to the frustration of delayed adult status, the young adult is confused about what his or her status is in our society.

Related to the increase in age for autonomy in our society are confused messages about adult status. The law says an 18-year-old is legally an adult for voting and ownership purposes, yet the bank refuses to loan to 18-, 19-, or 20-year-olds on their own signatures for purchase of a car or housing. Separation of legal adult status from biological maturity contributes to the confusion. This ambiguous status as half-child/half-legal adult promotes a continuation of adolescent anger against authority. The adolescent often perpetuates the confusion by immaturely using this ambiguity for manipulative purposes.

Finally, the rituals of adult status have become fuzzy and vague. In my youth, graduation from high school and first job, marriage, or completion of four-year university signaled clear change in status from the preparation period of adolescence to acceptance as an adult. Today, none of those rituals necessarily confers adult status in terms of acceptance of the young person as an adult by other adults.

THE PERILOUS ORDEAL

There are some other troubling facts about adolescence. Historically, adolescence was the healthiest period and infancy was the most perilous. Given modern perinatal care and pediatric medicine, infancy has become relatively safe. Unfortunately, as infancy has become safe, adolescence has become increasingly dangerous for a growing minority of teens. Starting in 1970, there has been a gently progressing slope of increased adolescent deaths per 100,000 in the population. These new deaths are not the result of a new virulent and deadly disease but, rather, of violent causes from accidents, murders, and suicides. The second highest cause of death jumps back and forth between murder and suicide depending on the year.[2] All these forms of death not only indicate an unsafe period of life but suggest the fact that adult protection has been removed from adolescents going through that passage.

Currently, the 15- to 24-year-old age range has 102.1 deaths per 100,000 in the population. Of those deaths, 38.5% are from motor vehicle accidents, 15.4% from homicides, and 13.2% from suicides. Other accidents account for 11%; malignancies, 5.1%; diseases of the heart, 1.9%; and AIDS, 1.4%.[3]

To take one statistic, 30 years ago there were between 1,000 and 1,200 suicides in the 15- to 24-year-old age range each year. That number has now increased to over 5,000 per year.[4] Something is wrong with growing up when it becomes so troubled or sad that death is a better solution than working out problems in life. Violence, resulting in maiming injuries or homicide, is also a reality in the lives of many American teenagers. The recent run of shooting and knifing deaths in American high schools from the inner city to the wealthy suburbs indicates the presence of violence as part of growing up in America.

After years of encouraging "political" statistics about declining drug use among high school seniors, the National Institute of Drug Abuse announced an alarming rise in eighth graders' use of marijuana, inhalants, LSD, and cocaine. 27.9% of seniors and 13.4% of eighth graders reported binge drinking (a symptom of alcoholism) within two weeks of the survey.[5] Substance use continues as the plague of adolescence.

Looking at educational statistics, there appears to be a declining percentage of age cohorts who become and remain enrolled in the senior year of high school. For 18- to 19-year-olds, from 1960 to 1988, that figure has dropped from 28.5% to 25%.[6] If you go on to look at achievement of a high school diploma and graduation with passage of various state tests required to achieve the diploma, the rates are more discouraging. This is a particular problem in a society that is increasing its educational requirements in response to the complex technical nature of many jobs. Many young people are not prepared to function as adults in living tasks, such as filling out an income tax form, completing a driver's license test, and filling out a job application.

Another real concern is the increase in juvenile involvement in crime. According to U.S. Department of Justice, Federal Bureau of Investigation, Age-Specific Arrest Rates, between 1965 and 1988, violent crimes by 18-year-olds of both genders more than doubled and property crimes almost doubled. Weapons violations increased by three times.[7]

As more adolescents become involved in criminal and antisocial behavior, their ability to successfully complete adolescence and enter adulthood, as well as their ability to live through adolescence, declines.

Another alarming area is adolescent sexual behavior. The age of initial sexual intercourse has been declining for some years, more so for males than for females. With that decline in age of initial sexual experience has come an equal increase in the number of sexual partners for adolescents. At the same time, there is an alarming increase in sexually transmitted diseases. For example, the adolescent morbidity rate for gonorrhea in 1950 was 192.5 cases per 100,000. By 1989, it had become 295.3 cases per 100,000. Syphilis has grown from 6.7% to 7.9% per 100,000. AIDS, which did not exist as far as we know in 1950, occurred at the rate of 13.6% per 100,000 among adolescents in 1989, in spite of an incubation period from initial contact of 3 to 10 years.[8] To the disease rates, add the pregnancy rates among women aged 15 to 19, an increase from 96.2 per 1,000 to 109.8 per 1,000, with an abortion rate in 1973 of 22.8% per 1,000 almost doubling to 43.8% in 1985.[9] Adolescent sexual behavior is not simply free and fun, but involves serious disease consequences, not only for the current adolescents but for their adolescent-conceived children.

Another troubling characteristic of current adolescent development is the progressive resignation of parents from parenting during their children's adolescence. Parents in our society have increasingly turned over to public, social, and educational institutions the job of safety and guidance of children into adulthood. Our institutions have proved the inadequacy of public agencies in substituting for effective parenting during the adolescent passage.

The brief statistics cited above are the tip of a troubling iceberg. Adolescence in my growing up period was truly "Happy Days," the title of a TV show connoting the quality of this life period. We had bittersweet, but basically good, memories from this growing-up time. It was a safe period in which we grew physically, turned toward the opposite sex, stretched our minds and bodies, and grew up to take our place in the adult world. For a growing number of American adolescents, the teen years are no longer "Happy Days" but have become a painful, threatening ordeal involving violence, sex-related disease, unwanted pregnancy, and the sense of no meaningful life beyond age 21.

In anthropology, the term "ordeal" refers to a ritual set of tasks that young men negotiated in order to prove and demonstrate their adult male abilities. The completion of the ordeal resulted in a ritual of adult status. The tasks were challenging, perhaps ritually dangerous, but inherently safe and do-able. The tasks and mental preparation for the tasks were a form of learning and proof of one's ability to function as an autonomous adult in the society.

Adolescence today is no ritual ordeal. It has become a purposeless, dangerous, and threatening ordeal, which results in death for some adolescents and physical and psychological maiming for many more. For those of us who provide therapy and counsel, our job is to serve as a guide for troubled adolescents who face the perilous ordeal. If we do our job well, they will avoid the dangers, solve the problems, and emerge as recognized healthy adults.

PURPOSE OF THIS BOOK

As an individual who has worked with adolescents in a variety of frameworks, including religious institutions, colleges, and universities, as well as for 14 years in a long-term treatment program for highly troubled adolescents where I was both a clinician and clinical director, I offer this book as helpful information for a variety of practitioners who come in contact with adolescents. It is my hope that psychiatrists, psychologists, social workers, school counselors, teachers in junior high schools, high schools, and colleges, as well as pediatricians and nurses will find some helpful information here to increase their effectiveness with adolescents in the course of their practice.

I offer three kinds of information. First, the book refers to a number of theorists and studies representing current "state of the art" knowledge concerning adolescent development. In those cases, I cite the study or theory with a number in the text and a note at the end of the book for readers who are interested in pursuing the scientific and technical information.

Second, I use inference from technical studies and theories in order to provide practical information for therapists. These thoughts are several steps removed from scientific validity. We therapists cannot wait for closure in an area of scientific research to deal with an adolescent sitting in our offices today. We must use the best knowledge available combined with our therapeutic insight to infer the best course of action.

Finally, I offer information from my own experience of working with adolescents in a variety of educational and therapeutic settings. Hopefully, this combination of information will be helpful to many who have the opportunity to guide adolescents through the "perilous ordeal."

Part I of the book is designed to offer theory, overview, and foundation information. Chapter 1, entitled "Theories of Adolescence," reviews the theories of various experts on adolescent development. Chapter 2, "Childhood to Adulthood: A Rite of Passage," offers my own model for understanding the adolescent development period, using the "rite of passage" concept, which comes from my original training as a medical anthropologist. Chapter 3, entitled "Neurological and Cognitive Development," is a survey of neurological development and cognitive growth based on current knowledge in neuroscience and cognitive psychology. The brain is the directing center of the human body; therefore, what happens in the brain during adolescence is the foundation for what happens in the body, in behavior, identity, relationships, and other areas of growth. Chapter 4, "Pubertal Development," reviews current knowledge about the adolescent growth period. The first section addresses changes in growth and sexual hormone levels, which in turn trigger general physical growth, the focus of the second section. The third section addresses pubertal or reproductive system growth. Finally, Chapter 5, "Therapeutic Stance," develops a basic therapeutic stance for the clinician when approaching an adolescent. This stance is based on both scientific information complemented by my own experience working with young people.

Part II moves into specific tasks of adolescent development. Each chapter outlines basic information about that area of development and problems that may occur, followed by specific information about diagnosis, treatment, and/or referral. Chapter 6 addresses issues related to identity development. Chapter 7 deals with the development of spirituality and values. Chapter 8 discusses sexual identity and sexual behavior. Chapter 9 deals with family conflict, Chapter 10 with social relations, and Chapter 11 with educational and vocational processes and decisions.

Part III addresses developmental "traps" that teens face growing up in North America. Each chapter outlines the basic problem area, which is followed by specific suggestions related to diagnoses and treatment. Chapter 12 looks at aggression and violence, an increasing problem among adolescents in America. Chapter 13 explores the saddest phenomenon of adolescent development, the increase in adolescent suicide, what it is about and how to deal with it. Chapter 14 addresses the plague of our time, adolescent drug and alcohol use and dependence. Chapter 15 looks at the fact that drug and alcohol use, violence, sexual acting-out, delinquency, and suicide attempts tend to occur in a clustered pattern with the same adolescents. Chapter 16 deals with eating disorders, and Chapter 17 with adolescent depression. Chapter 18 looks at the special problems of adolescents with chronic diseases. Chapter 19, the conclusion of the book, offers three proposals for societal change to reduce peril in the adolescent ordeal, along with encouragement for the therapist to work with individual teens for personal change.

Part I

Foundations

Chapter 1

Theories of Adolescence

In approaching adolescents, it is important to answer the question "What is the adolescent developmental passage all about?" This raises the issue of a theory or hypothesis that not only makes sense in terms of what we know about the adolescent growth period but is also heuristic, that is, useful to clinicians in the process of therapy. Various theories have been proposed. However, compared to infant and childhood development, theories about adolescence are few. In this chapter, I briefly summarize theories developed by a number of individuals in seven areas.

First, some theories have looked at adolescence strictly from a biological viewpoint, explaining behavior and cognitive development as a direct result of physical change. Second is the group of psychodynamic theories that are one step removed from direct biological causation, but are nevertheless heavily focused on the development of the reproductive system with its resulting increase in sexual interest. Third are the cultural theories of adolescence resulting principally from ethnographic studies of non-Western cultures by anthropologists. Fourth is the interpersonal theory of development advanced by Harry Stack Sullivan, an American psychiatrist. Fifth are the developmental theorists represented by Erik Erikson and Arnold Gesell. Sixth are the cognitive theorists, Piaget and his successors, including Lawrence Kohlberg. In the cognitive area, Piaget and his followers have been criticized by a new group using information-processing theory as a basis for describing cognitive development. Seventh are a variety of social learning theories explaining pieces of adolescent development, rather than the whole adolescent period.

THEORIES OF ADOLESCENT DEVELOPMENT

Biological Theories

The beginning of the scientific study of adolescence was marked by the publication of G. Stanley Hall's two-volume text entitled *Adolescence* in 1904. Hall, one of the founders of American scientific and clinical psychology, was heavily influenced by Charles Darwin's work *On the Origin of the Species*. Hall's theory is clearly biologically based. He used the concept of "recapitulation," stating that the living history of the species became incorporated into the genetic structure of the individual.[10]

Hall believed that the development of the individual mirrors the development of the species through evolutionary stages. Infancy (from birth to 4 years of age) reflects the animal stage of human development with a focus on walking and sensorimotor skills needed for survival. The childhood stage (the years 4 to 8) represents a recapitulation of the hunting/fishing phase of human development. He saw this represented in various children's games. The youth stage (ages 8 through 12) reflects for Hall the life of savagery, in which rote-learned behaviors necessary for survival are acquired. The adolescent stage (beginning at 13 and extending into the mid-20's) corresponds to the cultural development period of rapid transition from primitive hunter/gatherer culture to urban industrial culture with a modern social order. Hall firmly believed that biological development has a direct influence on human behavior, which is not affected much by environmental conditions or social structure. Hall also characterized adolescence as a period of "storm and stress," which corresponds to the human evolutionary period of turbulence and transition to the modern world. "Storm and stress" is due in part to the rapid growth and change in the adolescent growth period.

David Ausubel, another biologically based theorist, focused on two major changes. One is the biologically based change in the reproductive system involving the increase in sexual drive that influences adolescent behavior in terms of sexual interest, relationship, and activity. The second change is based on the physiological growth from child to adult resulting in a behavioral drive to function as full adults in the society, independent from the caretaking family. Ausubel took cultural influences more seriously than Hall, but remained focused on these biological growth themes of adolescence.[11]

Psychodynamic Theories

The second group of theories are closely related to biological development. Sigmund Freud described human development in a series of stages based on sense and sexual areas of the body. The oral stage involves sexual activity by the mouth: feeding, weaning, and biting. Next, the anal stage deals with toilet training and control and release sensations. The phallic stage involves genital manipulation and the first oedipal conflict. With resolution of this oedipal conflict, the child enters the latency stage with repressed sexual drive. Finally, puberty produces the genital stage with intimacy and sexual relationships.

Freud and other theorists in the psychodynamic group saw adolescence as resulting from an increase in sexual drive that ends the latency period and forces a reopening of the oedipal issue involving the adolescent's attraction toward the opposite-sex parent and fear of reprisal from the same-sex parent. The reproductive system's growth, including hormonal increase, gives rise to a strong sexual preoccupation and urgency, which ends the repression of sexuality during the latency period, resulting in heightened sexual interest. Healthy resolution of the oedipal conflict is the directing of sexual interest outside of the family toward opposite-sex individuals in one's peer cohort. [12]

Anna Freud, the daughter of Sigmund Freud and the earliest psychodynamic theorist to be significantly involved with adolescent therapy, saw this physically based reopening of the oedipal conflict as "a developmental disturbance," the title of her chapter in Caplan and Lebovici's book *Adolescence: Psychosocial Perspectives*. [13] She saw rapid sexual maturation as causing disturbance in every area of the individual's life, including ego organization, object relations, and social relations. This description of adolescence as Strum und Drang sees entry to adulthood as resolution of the sexual drive-provoked conflicts.

Peter Blos, a contemporary psychodynamic theorist, stands firmly in the tradition of the Freuds with reference to adolescence. He owes some debt to Erik Erikson, a psychodynamic therapist whose theory of adolescence moved away from the primacy of the oedipal conflict. Blos sees the adolescent period as a second individuation from the family, provoked by sexual maturity. He sees pubertal growth triggering a replay of the oedipal conflict, breaking the

repressive boundary around the libidinal impulse that the first resolution of the oedipal conflict created. The healthy resolution of the
second oedipal conflict results in redirection of the sexual impulse
away from the family, toward individuals capable of intimacy and
appropriate adult sexuality. Moving from classic Freudian theory,
Blos emphasizes the social, cultural, and physical "surround" as an
influence on these two basic movements during the adolescent period. In so doing, he emphasizes the social and cultural dimension
of adolescent development. [14]

Louise Kaplan, another contemporary psychodynamic theorist,
also describes the basic drive in the adolescent period as the sexual
drive. Her work offers a detailed description of sexual maturation.
She interprets the sexual drive as a drive into "love dialogues," first
a narcissistic one with self in early childhood, subsequently directed
toward parent figures, and finally, because of intense sexual preoccupation, a drive toward "love dialogues" with opposite-sex individuals during adolescence. Her work is much more accessible and readable for the average clinician than Blos, who tends to be complex,
technical, and pedantic. [15]

Heinz Kohut, another psychodynamic theorist and clinician,
sees adolescence as involving resolution of drive balance as a result
of biological genital maturation and establishment of self through
narcissistic and object relations processes. Kohut's approach is called
self psychology. [16]

Cultural Theories

In the scientific debate about adolescence, Margaret Mead's study,
Coming of Age in Samoa, [17] was used as a weapon to debate the
concept of conflict or "storm and stress" proposed by biological and
psychodynamic theorists. Mead's study of adolescent female maturation in Samoa shows a portrait of a relatively conflict-free, easy
transition from childhood into adulthood. She highlights the absence of sexual conflict in adolescence. In addition, other cultural
ethnographers have given radically different pictures of adolescence
in non-Western cultures. These ethnographic studies were used to
contest the biological theories and the psychodynamic theories,
which proposed a relentless developmental process originating in
sexual maturation.

Some later anthropologists have questioned Mead's study, because she lived on an American military base and failed to learn the language, instead using translators for her inquiries into Samoan life. Critics, including later students of the Samoan culture, suggest that Mead was misled by informants attempting to "put their best foot forward" in terms of their descriptions of Samoan females growing up.

The Interpersonal Theory

Harry Stack Sullivan, an American psychiatrist who considered himself psychodynamic and Freudian in orientation, nevertheless developed a considerably different theory on development. He saw anxiety and the relief of anxiety as central to the development process. The infant, and later the child, learns to relieve anxiety in terms of interpersonal interaction with parents, in particular the mother. Subsequent interaction with other children at school spurs growth in interpersonal relationships in terms of accommodation and compromise. The prejuvenile era features the beginning of learned intimacy through a special same-sex friend. As the adolescent sexual drive develops, the adolescent turns the need for intimacy toward the opposite sex, struggling with issues of intimacy and lust until this is resolved in an adult intimate relationship. Sullivan saw the dynamics of interpersonal interaction as focal for development, including adolescence. [18]

Developmental Theories

Erik Erikson, a lay analyst who trained in Vienna but continued much of his professional life at Harvard University, turned development into a series of nuclear crises that needed to be resolved as a foundation for the next growth period. While these conflicts tend to arise again in the course of life, effective resolution of their first occurrence lays the foundation for resolving them again (See Figure 1.1).

Infancy deals with the crisis of "trust versus mistrust," which is worked out in relationship to the mother. The second crisis, which is loosely related to the anal or toilet-training stage, is called "autonomy versus shame and doubt," and has to do with refusal, temper tantrums, and the "yes-no" syndrome. The third crisis is called "initiative versus guilt" and takes place during the preschool years from

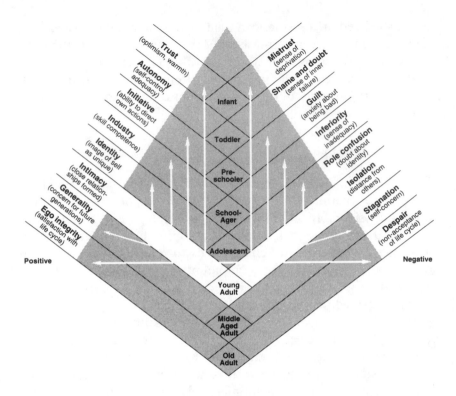

Figure 1.1: Erikson's Psychosocial Theory (Adapted from E. H. Erikson, 1963, *Childhood and Society, 2nd edition,* New York: W. W. Norton & Company, Inc. by Karen L. Freiberg in *Human Development: A Life-Span Approach, 4th edition,* Boston: Jones and Bartlett, 1992. Used with permission)

3½ to 6 years of age. This is the stage of rapid language development and involves locomotion and intrusion into space, intrusion into knowledge by consuming curiosity, intrusion into people's ears and minds by aggressive voice, and intrusion upon or into other bodies by physical attacks. The fourth crisis involves "industry versus inferiority." This is the apprenticeship period, which involves formal training, that is, schooling in Western societies. Erikson saw the adolescent period as a crisis involving "development of identity versus identity confusion or role diffusion." The search for identity involves establishing a meaningful self-concept and developing the ability to operate in an autonomous fashion as a recognized adult in the society. This lays the groundwork for the adult period, which involves the movement to "intimacy versus isolation."[19]

Arnold Gesell established a massive study of growth and development with children of suburban families in New Haven, Connecticut. His study resulted in a series of publications describing developmental milestones, including a general developmental profile and then developmental traits in a variety of areas. These areas include (1) "total action system," (2) "self-care and routines," (3) "emotions," (4) "the growing self," (5) "interpersonal relationships," (6) "activities and interests," (7) "school life," (8) "ethical sense," and (9) "philosophy."

The original study by Gesell and his associates took place in the 1950s. A subsequent study in the late 1970s resulted in revision of the books for republication in the early 1980s. Gesell and his associates refrained from overarching theories and stayed with descriptions of the developmental process with changing cognition, feeling, and behavior.[20]

Cognitive Theories

The principal cognitive theorist was Jean Piaget, who began as a biologist but turned his work toward developmental description of reasoning as a result of a job doing intelligence testing. Piaget's work involved a case study of his own children, subsequently validated by testing small groups of children in Switzerland on a series of developmental reasoning tasks. His theory is stage-based, with each stage becoming the necessary foundation for the subsequent stage.

Each stage involves a qualitative change in the nature of cognitive "schemas," which are mentally organized patterns of behavior. Each stage also involves an increasing repertoire of schemas for more mature behavior. Schemas are changed by two processes, assimilation and accommodation. Assimilation involves absorbing new information in current schemas. Accommodation is the process of adapting and adjusting schemas to new phenomena.

Piaget described four stages, which are subdivided into developmental phases. The first stage is the sensorimotor stage, which involves learning through sensorimotor action, and takes place in children from birth to age 2. The second stage of development, called the pre-operational stage, occurs from ages 2 to 7 and involves a transition from egocentric and motor-focused learning to early forms of social behavior. Use of language and mental images is the beginning of reasoning processes. The child learns to extract ideas from experiences. There is also intuitive thought and intuitive use of concepts. At age 7 or 8, there is a major change in the child's conceptual development, which Piaget called the operational stage of logical thinking. This is a period of basic logical and mathematical operations using concrete content. The child deals with tangible objects and problems that are tied to reality. He is now able to order things based on a variety of rules. Also, he develops the ability to categorize concrete phenomena. The fourth or final stage is called formal operations. Formal operations involves the ability to "think about thoughts" or to do abstract conceptual thinking.[21]

One area of study by Piaget was the development of moral or value thinking. Lawrence Kohlberg, an American, continued Piaget's work with a concept for stages of moral reasoning.

Kohlberg's theory describes three basic levels of moral development (see Table 1.1), each being subdivided into two stages. Level I involves the premoral or preconventional level of moral reasoning. This is the childhood approach that involves understanding behavior as "good" or "bad" in terms of obedience or disobedience to authorities and rules. Stage 1 of this level is an "obedience and punishment orientation." Stage 2 involves "instrumental relativism

Table 1.1 Brief Summation of Kohlberg's Stages of Moral Development

Brief Summation of Kohlberg's Stages of Moral Development

Level	Stage	Characteristics
Premoral	Stage 1	Punishment and obedience orientation
	Stage 2	Acts that are satisfying to self and occasionally satisfying to others defined as right
Conventional morality	Stage 3	Morality of maintaining good relations and approval of others
	Stage 4	Orientation to showing respect for authority and maintaining social order for social order's sake
Postconventional morality	Stage 5	Morality of accepting democratically contracted laws
	Stage 6	Morality by higher principles

(from Karen L. Freiberg (1992), Human Development: A Life-Span Approach, 4th edition, Boston: Jones and Bartlett Publishers) orientation." At that stage, children learn to distinguish the difference between physical damage and psychosocial intent. Level II, the conventional or morality level, involves acceptance of the existing social order and a clear recognition of the rights of others in the social group. The first stage of Level II is "interpersonal concordance orientation." This is an approval-seeking orientation where the individual behaves in ways to please or help others. The second stage in Level II is an orientation toward authority or duty. There is a strong belief that breaking the law is wrong and, in fact, produces guilt. Level III is the postconventional or autonomous level of moral decision-making, involving self-chosen moral principles. The individual now depends on autonomous universal principles of justice as a basis for decisions on moral issues. The first stage of Level III is the "social contract orientation" stage, recognizing that there is a mutual agreement or obligation between people in a society related to rights, equality, and human dignity. The second stage is described as "universal ethical principles orientation," in which an individual holds ethical principles even above the social contract and may practice, for example, civil disobedience in the name of a moral system higher than the existing law. [22]

More recent contributions to cognitive developmental theory have come from theorists with an information-processing orientation. Some of these theorists have focused on knowledge areas, describing acquisition of knowledge both in a structural and learning sense in a specific domain or area of knowledge. Others have described cognitive development as acquisition of critical thinking skills, which presumes a certain level of knowledge acquisition as well as abstraction skills related to questioning propositions. [23]

Social Learning Theories

Parallel to the information-processing theories related to cognitive growth is a series of social learning theories related to discrete areas of development. Theorists in this group tend to state theories about specific and limited areas of adolescent development. For example, Robert Selman's theory of social role-taking involves learning adult identity by experimenting with roles in relationship to various social settings, such as school, sports activities, and family and peer group during adolescence. [24] In addition, there is David Elkind's concept about the adolescent moving from egocentrism to sociocentrism as social learning.[25] They and other theorists in this group tend to focus only on their special areas of interest, often to the exclusion of other factors in adolescent development.

IS NORMAL ADOLESCENCE "DISTURBANCE"?

Stanley Hall, with his concept of "storm and stress," and the psychodynamic theorists, particularly represented by Anna Freud's article on adolescence as "a developmental disturbance," pose the idea that normal adolescence consists of rebellion, stress, conflict, and trouble. Many of us in counseling and clinical fields embrace this theory, because our view of adolescents is based on our experience with troubled adolescent patients. This view is reinforced by television and cinematic fascination with troubled teens. There has been a tendency on the part of therapists to see troubled adolescent development as "normal." One result of this belief is the limiting of our therapeutic intervention, rather than resolving adolescent problems and facilitating normal healthy development.

Several researchers investigating personality development in adolescence have painted an entirely different picture. In *Lives Through Time*,[26] published in 1981, Jack Block and his associates used two longitudinal pools of subjects to look at personality development over time. The results of their study showed five basic personality types among adolescent males and six types among adolescent females. Many of these personality types are relatively consistent over the developmental period from junior high through senior high to early adulthood. In being consistent, they fail to show the pathological or disturbed behavior that we consider to be "normal" among adolescents.

Subsequently, in 1984, Daniel Offer and Melvin Sabshin's work related to their study of adolescent development, in which they described three paths or styles of development, appeared. The first path is called continuous growth, in which the individual moves from childhood through adolescence into adulthood in a smooth consistent fashion with little conflict or trauma. The second path, called "surgent growth," involves some spurt periods with minor conflicts and difficulty. Only the third path, entitled "tumultuous growth," involves the "stress and storm" kinds of behaviors and problems that have often been considered "normal" by many developmental theorists. The "tumultuous growth" group tends to come from crisis-oriented families with some evidence of pathology.[27]

Based on the New York Longitudinal Study, Chess and Thomas see development as a complex, multi-factorial process. Temperament is seen as a basically stable structure that involves the individual's responses to environment. Resulting personality may be different than indicated by original temperament if the individual fails to find "goodness of fit" of his temperament in the developmental trajectory. This study, however, confirms that a number of adolescents who experience "goodness of fit" for their temperament go through adolescence in a relatively nontroubled mode.[28]

The work by Block, Offer and Sabshin, and Thomas and Chess states clearly that, for many adolescents, growing up is a relatively smooth continuous process. It suggests that disturbance and conflict are pathological rather than normal. Clinicians need to revise their view of adolescent development and treatment of adolescent problems in terms of healthy growing up as a baseline for evaluating the adolescents we see in counseling.

THE NEED FOR A WORKING THEORY OF ADOLESCENCE

Most classical theories of adolescence are marginally helpful at best. For those of us in "frontline" work with adolescents, the biologically based theories are clearly not accurate in terms of family, societal, and cultural influences on the adolescent development period. The psychodynamic theorists are so overfocused on the effect of sexual drive and sexual conflict that they ignore many other areas and dimensions of adolescent growth. Sullivan, with interpersonal dynamics as a factor in adolescence, Erikson with the identity quest, and Piaget's focus on reasoning all contribute good information about various dimensions but none gives us an overall conceptual framework for approaching the problems and needs of the adolescents in our offices.

Chapter 2 will present my own suggestion for a working conceptual framework to understand the adolescent patient. It focuses on normal paths through the adolescent period resulting in a healthy adult; at the same time the baseline gives us a criterion by which to determine disturbance, problems, and pathology. The theory will include a number of areas of adolescent growth in order to focus on the whole process of development from child to adult.

SUGGESTED READINGS

Dusek, Jerome B., "Theories of Adolescence," Chapter 2 in *Adolescent Development and Behavior* (2nd ed.), Englewood Cliffs, NJ: Prentice-Hall, 1991.
This is a brief, but good summary of theories of adolescence.

Muuss, Rolf E., *Theories of Adolescence* (5th ed.), New York: Random House, 1988.
This is a more extensive review of major theories about adolescence and various dimensions of adolescent development for the interested reader.

Chapter 2

Childhood to Adulthood: A Rite of Passage

Adolescence is the period and process of development from child to adult, involving multiple dimensions. First, the development involves maturation of neurological organization in the brain. This is reflected in mature cognitive processes, affective processes, and behavior. Second, it includes physical maturation of the body, involving growth in size and change in profile. Third, it involves maturation of the sexual/reproductive system, physically and behaviorally. Fourth, it involves a sense of self as an adult, that is, as an autonomous, self-directed human being. Fifth, it involves the acquisition of adult status in the social group or the culture. Sixth, it involves development of behavioral self-control in interaction in the community.

Adolescence is a growth process that moves the individual from childish dependence on parents to self-sufficiency or autonomy in various arenas of living. Autonomy involves economic self-support as well as sufficient knowledge and skills to negotiate the requirements of being an adult in society. It involves the ability to enter into social relationships with people in general and an intimate sexual relationship with another individual. It also involves the ability to function in a satisfying way in a variety of groups, from impersonal to family, in the society at large.

While adolescence is a developmental process for the individual, it takes place within the developmental process of the family. Family development is strongly driven by the developmental trajectories of the parents. Family life cycle, as it affects adolescent development, will be addressed in Chapter 9.

Many theorists have discussed the initiation of adolescence as either directly resulting from pubertal growth or indirectly resulting from pubertal growth mediated through expectations of family and rites of the culture.[29] I believe that physical growth and pubertal growth initiate the process of growth into adulthood, but that the physical triggers are mediated through cultural expectation and constructs.

Actually, the physical trigger for adolescence takes place in the brain. The human brain, as the directive organ for growth, life, and behavior, begins the process of adolescent development. It not only signals the body to grow and the reproductive system to mature but contains the imperative for the child to shed the dependent relationship and move toward maturity.

FACTORS IN DEVELOPMENT

Given my anthropological and psychological orientation, I believe that the adolescent process involves adaptive interaction between the individual and the environment. On the individual side, there are some predisposing factors, such as genetic constitution, temperament, and the general biological growth process. At the same time, environmental factors, including the physical environment, the immediate and extended family, and cultural institutions such as school, community, and peer group, all affect the developmental process. It is a complex multiphasic development process for each individual.

THE ADOLESCENT PERIOD

There are a variety of definitions and time schemas for the adolescent period. As mentioned in the Introduction, the age at onset of adolescence is becoming younger through parent expectation and the secular trend, which is earlier pubertal maturation. There is also a difference between maturation for males and females, with girls beginning physical adolescence a year or two earlier than males.

The adolescent period begins with interruption of preadolescence sometime in the tenth or eleventh year. The beginning of adolescence is the start of physical skeletal growth and the first signs of pubertal development, which involves change in breasts for females and the testes for males. These physical changes progressively disturb the equilibrium of preadolescence. New issues are forced into the awareness of the child, involving sense of and relationship to parents.

The upper end of adolescence has been extended because of the complexity of American society, the requirements of extended education, and the problem of developing financial independence. Adolescence ends when the individual completes educational preparation, moves out of the parental household, and establishes a financially autonomous life. This may occur anytime from the 20th year through the 23rd year for most adolescents.

Using these ages, it becomes apparent that adolescence has grown from a five- to six-year period (from ages 13 to 18) to the period from 11 to 22 during this century. This is a doubling of the preparatory and growth period. The longer period involves delayed expectation of adult status and rights. This delay produces insecurity and confusion for young adults and their status, expected roles, and behavior. It is a long "gray" period in terms of the meaning of adulthood.

THE RITE OF PASSAGE

Historically, most hunter/gatherer and herding cultures featured rituals marking the end of childhood and announcing adult status. Most cultural devices meet deep, primary human needs. The pubertal rites of passage across many diverse cultures suggest a fundamental need for some structure for the adolescent developmental period. Abstracting a general profile from many specific rites related to puberty and celebration of adult status points toward a structure for adolescent development. Rather than a single rite of passage, it involved a process that resulted in a ritual of adult status.

As the first menstrual period began, the female child would typically be taken away from family and village and isolated in a "menstrual hut." Various activities would take place during the period of isolation, some ritual and some instructional, all aimed at ending her identity as a child, celebrating her reproductive maturation and, most importantly, teaching her the behaviors and rules for an adult female in her culture. At the end of the withdrawal period, she would return to the village in a ritual ceremony celebrating her new status as a full adult woman in the society.

Young males, whose time of maturity was based more on physical than pubertal growth, would individually or as a group be initiated into adulthood. This usually involved isolation from the village with an instructional period by father, uncle, or some other male adult in the community in preparation for either a "quest" or a "ritual ordeal." The quest for a Plains Indian boy was the personal pursuit and killing of a buffalo. This process both demonstrated adult prowess and skills and served as a learning function about adult male behavior in his culture. Other cultures featured the "ritual ordeal" in which a young man had to go through a series of threatening tests, which themselves demonstrated adult male skill and prowess, as well as taught valuable lessons for adult male behavior. At the end of either of these processes, a ritual of adult status took place, often giving the individual a new adult name and serving as a reentry to society with full adult male status.

The processes described above involve recognizing physical growth change that ends childhood status. They involve a removal from the society as a child, with a period of preparation for learning information needed to function as an adult in the society. Finally, there is the reentry to the society with full adult status. This process offers a useful construct for the adolescent developmental period.

STAGES OF ADOLESCENCE

Preadolescence

The period from 9 years of age to the first signs of adolescent growth is usually called the preadolescent period. It is the culmination of the childhood growth and learning period. The individual has reached a point of mastery, comfort, and success as a child in family, school, and peer group. Socialization skills in peer groups, learned knowledge at school, and relationship with family all prepare the individual for the radical changes that come with the adolescent passage. A secure foundation, physically, cognitively, emotionally, and socially, must be built as a jumping-off point for the growth spurt and radical change of adolescent development. Preadolescence ends with the beginning of adolescent physical and pubertal growth.

Adolescence

For purposes of clarity, I divide adolescence into three stages. While these could be named in the traditional way as "early," "middle," and "late," I prefer to title these in process-functional terms based on the "rite of passage" concept.

Stage I: Withdrawal. The physical growth spurt and the first signs of pubertal growth initiate an instinctive withdrawal of the child from adults, particularly parents. This is represented by closed doors in bedrooms and bathrooms, and secretiveness usually initiated by self-consciousness about body change. The withdrawal, however, has a deep psychosocial purpose in terms of ending childish dependence on family. Without severing the psychological and social umbilical cord, the child has no chance of moving with tentative steps toward autonomy and adulthood. As the withdrawal progresses, the child develops secrets with best friends and subsequently a peer group, away from family and other significant adults, such as teachers. This new distance from family and adults is more psychological than physical. The whole withdrawal process is a precondition for exploration of identity, sexuality, and other facets of self as an adult.

Stage II: Isolation for Preparation. Early adolescents experience enlarged bodies and developing sexual profiles as discontinuities. In addition, they require space and time to come to terms with the new higher level of consciousness of self that occurs in brain development. This is a period of introspection and of interaction with peers, and concomitant isolation from parents and the adult world. The isolation period allows time for the child to integrate the enlarged adult body, the reproductively mature body, and the new sense of self into a unified person. This period is a time of lessened role expectation, allowing space for the individual to come to terms with the new body and growing sexual capability.

Children need new knowledge and new skills to function as adults in a society. For children in hunter/gatherer cultures, the skills and information were relatively limited and therefore could be acquired in a brief period of time. Now we live in a highly complex technical society, which requires years of preparation for adulthood. In many ways, school, sports, and extracurricular activities substitute for the mentor instruction in simpler societies. Peer group activities are also a major substitution for the "rite of passage" education.

There are, however, some serious problems in our society with the preparation period. We have moved with a vengeance to neutralize values in the public school system. Part of needed information for the emerging adult is knowledge of what is good and what is not so good in terms of adult behavior. It is as if our young people were handed a spear and a sling, rocks and arrows, and the mentor

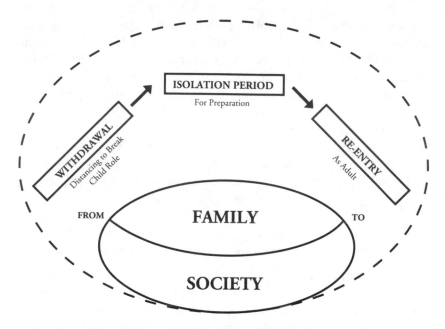

Figure 2.1 The Adolescent Passage

instructs them with detailed descriptions, but does not tell them how to use the tools or what the appropriate setting is in which to use them. In addition, the mentor fails to give them any help in finding appropriate targets for these hunting weapons.

A second problem is the total focus of adolescent peer culture on themselves and on two-dimensional media figures designed to cater to adolescent insecurity and fears. The mentors of my own childhood, often teachers, coaches, and activities sponsors, have virtually disappeared as significant bearers of adult wisdom of the society during this isolation period for American teenagers. Historically, the isolation-for-preparation period had movement and direction. Today, youth has become an end in itself, with no goal in terms of moving to a higher status in the society. Many young people desperately hold onto this period, as if it were the functional end of human life.

Peer idols in music videos and adolescent-oriented movies, as well as the local peer group, have become the teachers of values and adult behavior, pandering to adolescent fantasy. These sources are barren of helpful knowledge about becoming an adult.

Stage III: Reentry to Society as an Adult. Non-Western cultures celebrated reentry in a clear ritual of new status, often including change in clothes, jewelry, scarification, and name. In my own youth, completion of high school combined with first job, or completion of college combined with first job, marriage, and independent residence together constituted a ritual of adulthood in the society.

The rituals today have become less clear. Many young people waiting until later to marry or not marrying at all, an indistinct meaning of the end of education, and late entry to the work world with early access to voting all have blurred and confused the line between adolescence and adulthood. Many individuals have trouble finding a sense of self as an adult because there is no clear rite of passage recognizing adulthood. They drift into a pseudoadulthood period.

Pseudoadulthood

The last three decades have seen the evolution of a vague, confused developmental period for many young adults. During the period from 18 to about 23 years of age, individuals have been declared legal adults with the right to vote and to sign legal documents, but at the same time they are deprived of full adult status because of their continuing economic dependence on family and their need for further preparation and education for self-sufficient adulthood. This period is a confused one, encouraging childish demands of adult status recognition while at the same time evidencing immature patterns of behavior. The society tantalizes youth with hints of adult status, but at every turn reminds them of their limited role. For instance, even while liquor advertisers target young buyers, our society has found it necessary to move the age of alcohol beverage use from 18 to 21 due to the highway carnage that resulted from drunken driving.

The mixed ages at which one truly becomes a legal adult continue. Driving is legal at 16 or 17. High school is completed at 17 or 18 or 19. Voting and legal signatory rights begin at 18 and drinking at 21, but the ability to borrow money from a bank on one's own signature and to use a rental car occur at approximately 23. Marriage, once a marker of adulthood, is delayed until the late 20s for many young adults. The lack of a clear entry to adulthood and celebration of adult status sends ripples of confusion back through

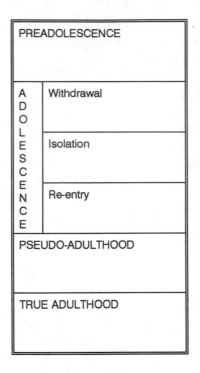

Figure 2.2 Adolescent Development Stages

the adolescent period. It suggests an eternal adolescence to budding young adults. Their attempt to continue youth and the peer-oriented isolation keeps them from earning true adult responsibility. This reinforces their continued adolescence.

MALE/FEMALE DIFFERENCES IN DEVELOPMENT

Carol Gilligan and her associates have pointed out real differences between male and female development. The beginning of the adolescent period with withdrawal from parents tends to be more competitive and conflictual for young males. Since the dominant parental figure is usually the mother, in order for the male to acquire adult identity, he must break the close tie and become different from the nurturing figure. The young female, on the other hand, can continue the close cooperative relationship with the mother as a role model and supporter for her own female development. This tends to result in a number of differences in development. Expectation for males involves competitiveness and achievement. Expectation for females involves nurture, relationship, and cooperation.[30] This appears to be changing for many young women as a result of the changing role of women in society. Involvement in career trajectories suggests increased female orientation toward achievement and competitiveness.

Most developmental theories describe human development, including adolescence, as if it were a singular process. The description is usually based on male development as opposed to female development. Gilligan's point reminds us that the world may look and be very different for a male and a female in the process of growing up. Since her initial work, there has been greater effort on the part of developmental experts to look at differences in developmental trajectories for females and males.

ETHNIC AND CULTURAL DIFFERENCES

Intellectual and political "correctness" standards in American academic and professional circles now require a strong affirmation of ethnic and cultural differences. This is a good and necessary correction from previous eras, when we tended to act as if there were a single cultural process in America. I believe recognition of and sensitivity to differences in cultural background are important.

While there are some differences in how African-Americans negotiate adolescence, Hispanic Americans grow up, and various specific Asian-American cultures deal with adolescence, I believe the rite of passage concept outlined above is applicable to each group and serves a useful purpose in understanding young individuals who seem to be having difficulty in one place or another of the growing up process. For African-American and Hispanic young people, differences are based not simply on coming from a different ethnic group, but on socioeconomic level and, for Hispanic young people, generation of entry to the United States. In other words, families in both of those ethnic groups who live in the same middle-income areas in cities and suburbs as white, Protestant, Catholic, and Jewish Americans produce adolescents with similar developmental patterns with different specific content. At the same time, low-income level African-American males tend to withdraw from family earlier by joining street culture, and newly immigrant Hispanics tend to reproduce the extended family and growing-up process of their former culture.

Unfortunately, most studies of minority adolescent development have focused on problems and problem youth. This leaves us with little information about normal development.

Developmental Detours and Traps

Treatment for adolescents and young adults is often occasioned by developmental problems. Human physical, mental, and emotional health requires operation in a range between two thresholds. Physically, temperature, blood pressure, and electrolyte amounts that are too high or too low are dangerous. Normal individuals have different profiles at various times but remain in the acceptable, healthy range.

For example, in the social relations development arena, the adolescent maintains a balance between peer affiliation and family influence. A teen who totally identifies with peers at the expense of family identification has crossed the threshold into unhealthy development. On the other hand, a teen who is enmeshed with family fails to develop healthy identity and socialization skills.

Generally, too much or too little of any aspect of adolescent development means problematic to pathological levels of impairment. Also, too early or too late development suggests impairment. Early or premature "foreclosure," which is closure on a developmental task before completion, spells impairment. Because problems are associated with the extremes, therapists working with adolescents need to have some contextual framework for normal and healthy ranges and ages for various tasks of adolescent development.

Chapter 3

Neurological and Cognitive Development

Until *At the Threshold: The Developing Adolescent*, edited by S. Shirley Feldman and Glen R. Elliott and published in 1990,[31] there were few references to brain development in books on adolescent development. As a matter of fact, even Feldman and Elliott have only one page describing adolescent brain growth in terms of weight and circumference. Until very recently, common knowledge among developmentalists limited brain development to the growth of new brain cells, which ends some time in the first two years of life. Since no new neurons developed, it appeared that brain growth had little effect on adolescent development. Most writers referred to unknown brain triggers causing areas of the hypothalamus to communicate via neurohormones to the pituitary gland, initiating physical growth and reproductive system maturation.

NEUROLOGICAL DEVELOPMENT DURING ADOLESCENCE

While no new neurons develop during adolescence, there is much growth, development, and change in the brain. That change will be described in two general areas. First, I will describe a series of discrete changes at cell synapse and morphological level. Second, I will move to the associational or systems level and describe a series of important systemic changes in brain function that occur during the adolescent period.

Both levels of change result in a creature with higher and more complex cognitive ability and behavioral repertoire.

Neuron Network Changes

1. Epstein describes a general increase in brain weight and circumference occurring in a series of peaks and troughs throughout childhood and adolescence.[32] He describes increases in circumference from ages 10 to 11 followed by a steep decline in rate of growth for girls and a more gradual one for boys. There is debate about his work and replication problems.

2. A second major neurodevelopmental process during childhood and adolescence is synapse breaking, that is, breaking connections between brain cells, which in effect breaks circuits and therefore functions. Synapse breaking occurs in two forms. First, some brain cells die, changing the pattern of brain circuitry as part of maturation. Second, other brain cells remain alive and viable but disconnect from adjacent cells. This changing neuronal circuitry impacts language, behavior, affect, and sensation areas.[33]

3. Synaptogenesis, that is, the forging of new synaptic connections, increases based on brain maturation. These new synaptic connections are influenced by three factors. First, there is a genetic factor involved in signaling an axon from one neuron to connect with another specific neuron. Second, these new connections are also experience- or behavior-driven. The individual engages in a new behavior, like attempting to walk, and it causes a network to be established based on synaptic connections between a subseries of neurons carrying that behavior. Repetition of the behavior solidifies the network by adding new neurons and connections. Third, axon connections with adjacent cells appear to be chemically guided, that is, the attraction between the two cells is based on a common neurotransmitter that ultimately communicates from one neuron to the next.[34]

4. With arborization (branching) of dendrites, there is a major increase in the number of dendrites per neuron. The potential for greater numbers of synaptic connections leads to increased complexity of brain networks.[35]

   Synaptogenesis and dendrite arborization reach a peak during the plasticity period of change in a skill or network. The number of synapses then decreases as the new network matures. One explanation for this decrease is "lateralization" of the new function, ending the need for nondominant-side intensity of synapses.[36]

The result of these processes is a reorganization of major systems and processes in the brain, based on changing neuron networks. The direction of this change is from a more generalized, diffuse, immature organization to a more specific organization in the mature brain.

5. This reorganization also involves the "connection" of previous "competitive" neuron networks in a large skill or control system. This process of absorbing specific networks into larger systems goes on throughout the adolescent development period.[37]

Continuing Myelination

A second major development in the child and adolescent brain is the continuing myelination of the axons on neurons. Myelin sheathing is the protein insulation covering the axon of the brain cell that facilitates faster and more efficient movement of electrical impulses. The result is more efficient operation of those cells and systems of the brain. Myelination is generally indicative of regional brain maturation. Areas involved with reflexes and with autonomic functions myelinate first; next, primary motor and sensory areas; then, the premotor areas and the limbic system. Last to myelinate are the associational areas and the neurons that connect cortical areas.[38]

Several researchers have documented the fact that myelination continues during the adolescent period, perhaps even into the 20's. The focal point of adolescent and early adult myelination is in the prefrontal cortex and related temporal and parietal areas. These systems are involved with executive functions of the brain: covert language, planning, verbal fluency, attention, regulation of behavior, and ordering movement or behavior in a time-sequenced set of events. This development represents maturation of the more cognitive functions of the brain.[39]

Reorganization of the Corpus Callosum

During childhood and adolescence, there is a change in synaptic connections in the corpus callosum. These are brain cells that connect the left and right hemispheres of the brain. These connections are the communication network between the two sides of the brain and, therefore, the two sides of the body. The reorganization of the corpus callosum involves breaking connections and networks that are more diffuse and general, and making new connections that are more specific in terms of function.[40]

Hemispheric Independence

Related to corpus callosum reorganization is the increasing ability of the two hemispheres to operate as relatively independent work stations. This hemispheric independence is facilitated by one hemisphere shielding itself from the other. Research suggests increasing development of hemispheric independence from age 10 to at least ages 14 to 16.[41]

EEG Wave Maturation

Thatcher has reviewed EEG studies and proposed five phases of spurt growth in the maturation of brain waves. Maturation is defined as an increase in coherence of frequency. Two of those stages occur in childhood. Stage 3 occurs between ages 11 and 13, Stage 4 between ages 14 and 16, and Stage 5 between ages 18 and 20. Brain waves mature in four cycles in a spiral staircase fashion. Cycle III comprises Stages 3 and 4 and Cycle IV is Stage 5. He speculates that these spurts in the maturity of brain waves represent increasing developmental neuron connections and networks that, in turn, increase the morphological density of brain tissue in those areas. A spiral staircase pattern involves development from left to bilateral to right. In the left hemisphere, short distance connections mature first, followed by longer distance brain cell connections. This reflects the linear and specific mode of the left. In the right hemisphere, long distance connections mature first, followed by shorter distance connections. This reflects the holistic mode of the right. Thatcher's study indicates that areas of the brain mature at different times, which agrees with myelination studies.[42] The chart in Figure 3.1 integrates the three growth spurts suggested by maturation of brain waves into the substages of adolescent development.

Specific maturation changes in the brain involve death of cells, breaking of synaptic connections, and making new synaptic connec-

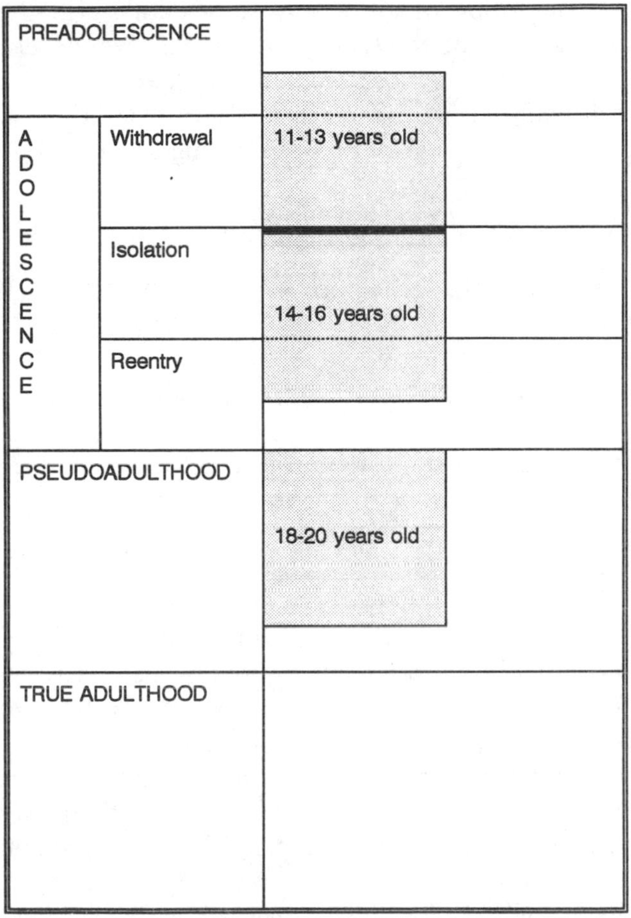

PREADOLESCENCE			
A D O L E S C E N C E	Withdrawal	11-13 years old	
	Isolation	14-16 years old	
	Reentry		
PSEUDOADULTHOOD		18-20 years old	
TRUE ADULTHOOD			

Figure 3:1 Brain Wave Maturation Based Growth Spurts

tions, thereby creating new circuits or networks in the brain that are more specific than immature generalized systems. Change from general to specific organization occurs throughout the brain, including the corpus callosum, which connects and coordinates the two hemispheres of the brain. In addition, myelination, that is, insulation of brain cells in the prefrontal cortex, continues toward completion in late adolescence. This increases the efficiency of communication of those cells, therefore increasing a variety of executive functions of the brain. This is confirmed by EEG brain wave studies that show maturation of brain waves, particularly in the frontal cortex, in spurts during the teenage years. The two developmental changes of specific, as opposed to generalized, circuits and mature executive functioning of the prefrontal cortex lay the foundation for a series of associational and systems changes in the brain.

SYSTEM OR ASSOCIATIONAL MATURATION

A series of system changes appears to occur in the brain during adolescence.

Development of Language as an Internal Tool

Brain maturation appears to focus on increased complexity of the language system in the dominant hemisphere of the brain during the teen years. For example, Dennis and Kohn suggest an increasing ability to understand complex syntax during the early adolescent period.[43] The left hemisphere is dominant for language in 98% of the general population. A special feature of this maturation is the increased ability of the adolescent to use internal language, that is, self-talk, to construct a symbolic representation in the brain of the outside reality system. This special use of language by teens is exhibited in the adolescent obsession with inventing slang, coming up with new uses of language to describe events in their lives and to categorize people, places, and behavior. The maturity of language as an internal self-talk tool is critical to a variety of mature functions, including the ability to formulate ideas, to test ideas, and to build systems of ideas, as well as to control behavior by cognitive process as opposed to feeling response. Dennis suggests a connection between language maturity and frontal lobe maturity, calling this frontal lobe function "social discourse."[44]

Increasing Working Memory

Related to both language and frontal lobe maturation is the increasing speed and capacity of working memory from 10 years to 19 years.[45] Increased working memory is a prerequisite for language and self-talk maturity, cognitive control of behavior, and "formal operations."

Maturity of Executive Function Skills

As a result of synaptic change and myelination, the prefrontal lobe of the brain reaches maturity. The prefrontal cortex has reciprocal connections between the sensory system of the posterior cortex, the effector components of the motor system, and the limbic memory system, which, in turn, involves regulating arousal, affect, and motivation. This involves maturity of certain executive function skills including attention, verbal fluency, covert (self-talk) language, goal setting, regulation of behavior, motor sequencing, and complex planning.[46] Dennis suggests a prefrontal language function, "social discourse," which involves inferential thinking.[47] These are necessary skills for deliberate and intentional behavior as well as increased maturity in behavioral control. Planning, self-monitoring, self-inhibition, and goal-directed behavior, which involves delayed gratification, sustained activity, and social behavior, are all based in the integrating function of the prefrontal cortex.

Cognitive Control of Behavior

Also, myelination, change in synaptic connections and networks, and the maturity of the frontal lobe executive system lead to a gradual change from emotional response control of behavior to a cognitive anticipatory control system for behavior. Feelings still contribute to the thinking process, but do not themselves control most behavior. Instead of responding to a situation impulsively, the maturing adolescent thinks about it and responds based on thoughtful analysis and potential consequences. This system is one of several key elements in mature human behavior.[48]

Cognitive Development

A result of frontal lobe maturity and executive function maturity is the development of cognitive maturity. Jean Piaget saw preadolescence as the time of "operational thought." As the brain changes in its capability, the individual begins to formulate ideas and theories related to concrete phenomena. This involves numbering, ordering, categorizing, conservation, reversibility, reciprocity, physical causality, spatial awareness, and time awareness. The ability to observe phenomena and come up with theories or rules to explain how events take place is one level of cognitive maturity.

The second level, which seems to occur between the fourth and fifth of Thatcher's stages of brain wave maturity, that is, between ages 14 and 20, involves what Piaget calls "formal operations." Formal operations involve the ability to "think about thoughts," that is, to use self-talk and internal images in a hypothetical way to rearrange and manipulate facts, events, and ideas in order to come up with new possibilities, new rules, and new courses of action. Formal operations include propositional reasoning, combinatorial analysis, proportional reasoning, and hypothetical reasoning. This is the movement from concrete to abstract thinking. [49]

Fischer, building on Piaget, suggests a four-level developmental process: reflexes, sensorimotor actions, representations (the equivalent of Piaget's "operations"), and abstractions (the equivalent of Piaget's "formal operations"). Each level contains four stages of development. The fourth stage of a previous level is the same as the first stage of the next level. These fourth/first stages are major transitions in cognition.

The transition to adolescence coincides with Level 4 (abstrac-

Table 3.1 Piaget's Four Stages of Cognitive Development

Stage	Substages	Characteristics
Sensorimotor period	Reflexes Primary circular reactions Secondary circular reactions Coordination of secondary schemas Tertiary circular reactions Invention of new means through mental combinations	The apparatus of the senses and of the musculature become increasingly operative.
Preoperational period	Preconceptual stage Intuitive phase	The child has the emerging ability to think mentally.
Concrete operations period		The child learns to reason about what he or she sees and does in the here-and-now world.
Formal operations period		The individual has the ability to see logical relationships among diverse properties and to reason in the abstract.

(from Karen L. Freiberg (1992) Human Development: A Life-Span Approach, 4th edition, Boston: Jones and Bartlett Publishers)

tions). At the first stage, young adolescents construct single abstractions about self, feelings, events, things, other people, and institutions. Next, the adolescent recognizes that one abstraction may be related to another. This second stage is called "mapping." At a slightly higher stage, the middle adolescent begins to discover that certain abstractions conflict with other abstractions, that is, that certain roles and traits exhibited to groups of people conflict with other roles and traits exhibited to other groups of people. In order to solve these conflicts, the young person develops the ability to organize a system of abstractions that fits together in somewhat paradoxical ways, but is functional for various arenas of his or her life. At the fourth and final stage, the young adult develops general principles for organizing systems of abstractions. [50,51]

While cognitive and information-processing theorists have questioned Piaget's paradigm, it is clear that adolescent thinking is different from child thinking. Adolescent thinking involves abstract rather than concrete representation, multidimensional rather than single-factor perspective, and relative rather than absolute conception of knowledge. [52]

Operational thinking is necessary for adult living in any society. Formal operational thinking is important for functioning in an urban, technological society.

Development of a Higher Level Awareness of Self

Awareness of self begins with the infant, who experiences self as the only reality. Other persons and objects are part of self. In time, the infant discovers otherness and then other people, particularly mother, and finally there is recognition of self in a mirror. Neurologically, the foundation of self-awareness is the proprioceptive system. This system involves awareness that various body parts are self and not other. When it is damaged, that awareness may be lost. In *The Man Who Mistook His Wife for a Hat and Other Clinical Tales*, Oliver Sacks describes an individual who tried to throw his leg out of his hospital bed, screaming for the nurse to get rid of this disembodied leg. He had sustained brain injury that damaged his proprioceptive system. He no longer recognized his own leg. [53]

As the individual grows, the level of self-awareness grows. Most children have a casual, easy acceptance of self. As adolescence begins, there is sudden bashful self-awareness. This awareness involves

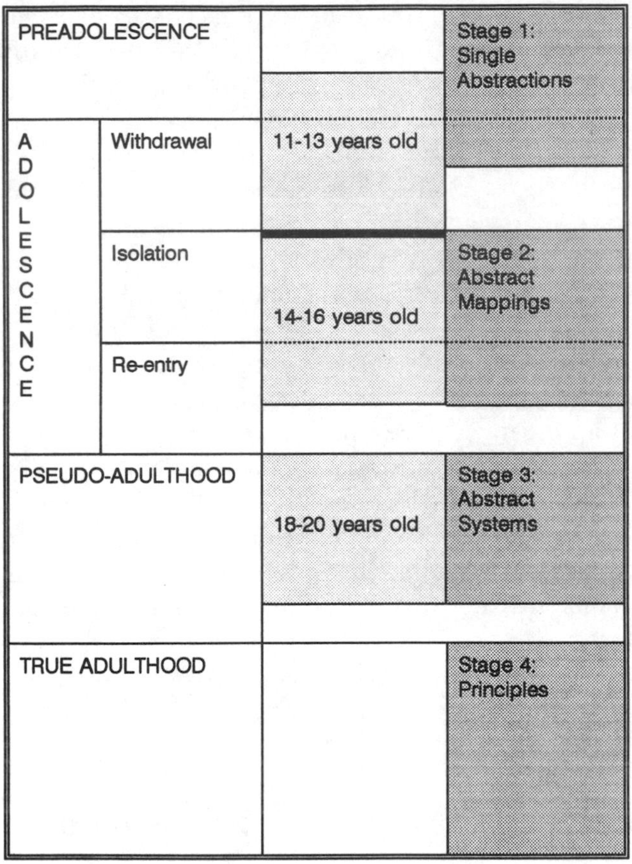

PREADOLESCENCE			Stage 1: Single Abstractions
A D O L E S C E N C E	Withdrawal	11-13 years old	
	Isolation	14-16 years old	Stage 2: Abstract Mappings
	Re-entry		
PSEUDO-ADULTHOOD		18-20 years old	Stage 3: Abstract Systems
TRUE ADULTHOOD			Stage 4: Principles

Figure 3.2 Brain Wave Maturation Based Growth Spurts And
Cognitive Stages of Level 4 Abstractions

concern with appearance, including pubertal change and awkward growth when feet, knees, hands, elbows, and noses grow first. Most important, the adolescent develops an ability to look at self from the viewpoint of others. He even performs alone as if there were an audience of peers watching. David Elkind calls this "playing to an imaginary audience."[54] This ability to see self from the viewpoint of others represents a radical increase in complexity of the neurological self system. Donald Stuss suggests that awareness of self is a complex system centering in the prefrontal cortex and its executive functions.[55] I think that a complex associational system connecting many networks of the brain to each other is involved in producing this level of self-awareness. It is a very high level cognitive system. This system of self-awareness is an important part of adult personality.

SEX DIFFERENCES IN THE BRAIN

By the third month of prenatal growth, the sex of the human fetus is clearly distinguishable. Several weeks earlier, a spurt of testosterone produces a male fetus, or the absence of that spurt continues the fetus as female. Since the androgens (male sex hormones) are in interactive feedback loops with the chemistry system of the brain, some sexual differentiation of the brain is suggested. Current research suggests that female brains tend to be more symmetric between the left and right hemispheres, while male brains tend to be more asymmetric. Some research indicates a difference between males and females in other specific brain areas, including the splenium, which is the back part of the corpus callosum connecting the two hemispheres.

The neurophysiological differences are reflected in some specific cognitive differences between males and females. These differences involve a tendency for more males to be at one end of the continuum on a specific cognitive ability, while the majority of females tend to be toward the other end of the continuum on the same ability, with some overlap between the two groups. For example, males tend to be more effective in visuospatial tasks, particularly mental rotation of objects or maps and using maps to find their way. Females, on the other hand, tend to be more effective in a series of language-related tasks, including identifying matching items, verbal fluency, and arithmetic calculations.

The sexual differences in brain physiology and intellectual function in no way suggest differences in overall level of intelligence. Two individuals may have similar overall intelligence, but have different patterns of abilities.[56]

SUMMARY

Briefly summarizing adolescent neurological development, a series of cells die, synaptic connections are broken, new synaptic connections are made, myelination is completed in the prefrontal lobe, and brain waves assume mature morphology. These developments involve a movement from simple, general neurological networks to complex specific neural networks. The results of these physical changes are: (1) higher levels of associational development involving use of language as an internal tool to construct reality and to think about concrete phenomena as well as ideas and concepts; (2) maturity of executive function skills; (3) development of cognitive control of behavior as opposed to emotional control of behavior; and finally (4) a high level of self-awareness. A number of these changes may be the neurological basis for what Piaget and other cognitive theorists describe as progression from concrete to abstract thinking.

SUGGESTED READINGS

Ackerman, Sandra, *Discovering the Brain*, Washington, DC: National Academy Press, 1992.
This book is based on a July 1990 symposium to initiate the "Decade of the Brain" proclaimed by former President George Bush in 1990. It is an excellent introduction to the current state of knowledge about the brain, imaging techniques, neurologically based diseases, neurochemistry, development of the brain, and various neurological functions, including perception, attention, learning, memory, recall, and thinking.

Brooks-Gunn, Jeanne, and Reiter, Edward O., "Brain growth," in Chapter 2, "The Role of Pubertal Processes," in S. Shirley Feldman and Glen R. Elliott (Eds.), *At the Threshold: The Developing Adolescent*, Cambridge: Harvard University Press, 1990, pp. 29–34.
This brief section of the book gives a hint of brain growth and then effectively summarizes the hypothalamus and releasing factors involved in initiating pubertal growth.

Chapter 4

Pubertal Development

Adolescence is a major physical growth period. This fact is based on observation of the changing size of the child into an adult. It also involves a second dimension, the changing profile from relatively undifferentiated body shape to a gender-distinctive differentiated shape for most adult males and females.

Many writers have treated adolescence as if it were a separate growth phenomenon, as opposed to a normal part of human lifespan growth. However, both physical growth and sexual maturation start with conception. From that moment on, there is a continuous developmental process, ending with death. Adolescence represents a period of increased rate and amount of growth, often termed the "growth spurt." It is a time when the human brain decides to speed up the process of the body becoming larger, sexually mature, and more male or female. As a continuous rather than discontinuous process, this growth period helps makes sense out of the psychological experience of the growing adolescent.[57]

Biological growth, initiated by the brain, involves three major areas. The first area is a change in the endocrinological system. Signaled by the brain, various glands, including the pituitary, the thyroid, the adrenal, and the gonads, radically increase hormone output. The second area of growth is general physical growth, which involves height, weight, bones, internal organs, and shape of body. The third area involves maturation of the sexual or reproductive system.

BRAIN CHANGES SIGNALING PUBERTY

The beginning of adolescent physical growth and reproductive maturation occurs in the brain. The hypothalamus, which is the brain center for one of the major brain communication systems to the body, generates a series of brain chemicals called neurohormones that signal the pituitary gland (the master gland of the body) to increase the release of hormones. In turn, these hormones initiate both the physical growth process and reproductive maturation. These neurohormones are called "releasing factors." Each neurohormone targets an area of the pituitary gland that, in turn, releases a specific hormone related to growth. The hypothalamic neurohormones are: (1) follicle stimulating hormone (FSH) releasing factor (FSHRF), which signals the pituitary to release FSH; (2) luteinizing hormone (LH) releasing factor (LRF), which promotes the formation of the corpus luteum; (3) corticotropin releasing factor (CRF), which signals the pituitary to release adrenocorticotropic hormone (ACTH); (4) thyroid-stimulating hormone (TSH) releasing factor (TRF), which signals the pituitary to release TSH; and (5) growth hormone releasing factor (GRF), which signals the pituitary to release growth hormone (GH), also called somatotropin. There is another hypothalamic chemical called somatostatin, which appears to have an inhibitory effect on the secretion of the growth hormone that is part of the control system for adolescent growth.[58]

The question has been asked as to the trigger for hypothalamic generation of the releasing neurohormones. This has not yet been decisively answered by research. However, it appears that the mechanism is an inhibitory one, inhibiting the release of the growth hormone and also inhibiting gonadotropin secretion. In other words, there seems to be a mechanism that restrains the signal to the gonads (which release hormones producing pubertal maturation) and to the growth hormone, preventing their release. Something seems to end the inhibition, allowing both of these systems to increase their effect, producing growth.[59]

ENDOCRINE DEVELOPMENT

Endocrinological development generally involves two signaling systems. The first signaling system is related to general body growth including height, weight, bone, muscle, and fat. This involves somatotropic hormones. The second signaling system involves maturation of the sexual reproductive system. The second system involves gonadotropic hormones. "Tropic" hormones turn on or maintain activity in other parts of the body.

General Growth

The pituitary, actually two glands designated as the anterior pituitary and the posterior pituitary, receives chemical signals from the hypothalamus and begins radically to increase the levels of secreted hormones. These hormones signal other parts of the body to take action related to growth. The pituitary secretes the primary growth-regulating hormone called somatotropin, which is produced by the anterior pituitary and often called the "growth hormone." Somatotropin is the principal chemical involved in growth in a variety of body areas, particularly bone growth. Allied to the growth hormone are two hormones produced in the thyroid, thyroxin and triiodothyronine, that increase based on a chemical signal from the pituitary (TSH).

Gonadotropins

Testosterone, estrogen, and progesterone, the primary gonadotropic hormones, also have a major role in general growth. Testosterone, for example, is particularly involved in growth of pubic hair and secondary adult body hair. The initial secretion of testosterone and estrogen occurs in the adrenal glands as a result of a signal from the pituitary. These modest amounts of gonadotropins join with other hormones from the pituitary to signal the gonads—that is, the ovaries in the female and the testes in the male—to raise their level of hormone secretion and begin the maturation process.

The anterior pituitary secretes several other gonadotropins. One is called "follicle stimulating hormone" (FSH) because it stimulates the maturation of ovarian follicles. This same hormone promotes maturation of spermatogenesis in males and is often designated as interstitial cell stimulating hormone (ICSH) in males. The second gonadotropin is "luteinizing hormone" (LH) since it promotes the formation of the corpus luteum during ovulation. These gonadotropins control production of the steroid hormones, that is, testosterone, estrogen, and progesterone.

The steroid hormones that are secreted primarily by the gonads, but secondarily by the adrenal gland, are the primary regulators of sexual and reproductive activity. They maintain the structure of the gonads by promoting their function, which is the production of sperm from testes and release of ova from ovaries. In addition, they have some relationship to sexual behavior. The relationship of testosterone to male sexual arousal is much clearer than the relationship of the steroid hormones to female arousal.

All three major steroid hormones, testosterone, estrogen, and progesterone, are present in both males and females from the time of sexual differentiation in fetal development to the time of pubertal development. Testosterone is the dominant steroid hormone in male sexual development and in male sexual behavior, but it is also present in females. Estrogen and progesterone are the dominant steroid hormones in female sexual maturity and ovulation.

The general hormone system operates on a negative feedback mechanism, so that as pubertal growth reaches its end the level of change in hormone and gonadotropin secretion signals the hypothalamus and pituitary to lower production to a level necessary for maintaining adult life and sexual function.[60]

GENERAL PHYSICAL GROWTH

The second area of biological development is general physical growth, which involves height, weight, and general body characteristics. The height spurt for females is the beginning of adolescent growth and occurs slightly after breast budding. The height spurt may occur anytime from 9½ to 14½ years of age and varies among individuals in the population. For males, the height spurt begins approximately a year later, beginning between 10½ and 16 years of age and concluding between ages 13½ and 19. Again, individuals vary in terms of initiation, completion, and growth duration for the height spurt. Height growth is based on bone growth. Bone growth involves not only lengthening as part of skeletal maturity, but also thickening to support a heavier body frame. Bones tend to grow until the ends of the bones fuse with the bone shafts (epiphyseal closure), signaling skeletal maturity.

Weight gain also spurts during the adolescent period and tapers off into adulthood. For males, this weight gain is associated with bone development and increase in muscle. Muscle and bone growth produces the broad shoulders characteristic of males. For females, the gain tends to be more associated with bone and fat growth. Fat growth occurs much more dramatically in the female than the male, contributing to breast development and broader hips, with fatty deposits in breasts, hips, buttocks, and thighs. These fatty areas are the basis of the female adult profile.

Internal organs, such as the heart, lungs, kidneys, liver, and pancreas, also go through a growth period during adolescence in order to accommodate their particular functions within the enlarged body. The heart doubles in size, with a resulting increase in blood pressure. The growth of internal organs tends to occur slightly later and to develop at a more even pace.

The growth pattern tends to be quite irregular, with peripherals such as hands, feet, and nose growing first, followed by the joints, knees, and elbows. Arms, legs, and face grow later and catch up resulting in normal adult body proportions. This irregular growth pattern creates an awkward appearance, as well as some difficulty in moving the body in a coordinated fashion. The irregular growth pattern often causes much distress for growing adolescents, who become preoccupied with large hands, elbows, knees, feet, or nose. They may become quite fearful about the outcome of their growth process.[61]

Patterns of Growth

Katchadourian[62] suggests six patterns for physical development:

1. Average children whose growth closely approximates the mean for height and weight of different ages.
2. Early maturing children who are tall in childhood because they are more mature than average children. Their adult height will be average, although their growth curve rises above the mean curves of average children.
3. Early maturing children who are also genetically tall. They are taller than average from early childhood and continue to mature rapidly. Not only will they become tall adults, but their growth curve also lies well above the mean.
4. Late maturers, with or without genetic shortness, whose growth curve lies *slightly* below the mean.
5. Late maturers, with or without genetic shortness, whose growth curve is *significantly* below the mean.
6. Those who find their way into the growth clinic because they start puberty much earlier or much later than expected. Their total growth life is either longer or shorter than average, and/or they may become much taller or shorter adults than would have been expected.

PUBERTAL GROWTH

Female Pubertal Growth

Female pubertal growth begins a year to a year and a half prior to male growth and tends to end at approximately the same time. The profile of female development tends to place females in a more mature general development profile and pubertal development profile than males during the early adolescent period. For girls, pubertal development begins with breast budding between 8 and 13 years of age. The breasts go through a series of changes, reaching maturity some time after 16. Pubic hair growth starts sometime later and reaches adult profile between 14 and 15. Changes in female genitalia occur somewhat later and are less noticeable because they are more internal. The ovaries mature in preparation for menarche, the uterus wall enlarges, and the vagina becomes larger with thickening walls. External genitals—labia, mons, and clitoris—become enlarged and more erotically sensitive.

Historically, cultures have treated menarche as maturity for young females. Menarche tends to occur midway through the pubertal development process for most girls. It may occur anytime from age 10 to 16½. There has been a trend, called the "secular trend," in which menarche tends to come earlier than in previous years.[63] Many studies cite 12.8 as the average age of menarche among American girls of European background. American girls of African background tend to have a slightly later onset of menarche. Early menstrual periods tend to be somewhat irregular until synchronization of FSH and LH signals synchronization in ovarian hormones controlling the monthly cycle. Fertilization and pregnancy may not be possible until hormonal and cycle synchronization occurs some months later.

Male Pubertal Growth

For males, pubertal growth begins with testes enlargement, which tends to be invisible because the testes are mostly enclosed in the body at the beginning of the development period. Testes growth may begin anytime from age 9½ to 13½, and continues to 13½ to 17½. Penis development begins later and occurs over a shorter period of time. This tends to be a more visible form of pubertal growth for males. Pubic hair begins slightly before penis growth, but does not reach full maturity until some time after the penis has reached its adult size.

For males, a loose equivalent of menarche is first ejaculation through a wet dream or early masturbation. It is more secret, less dramatic, and certainly not culturally celebrated as the beginning of adult fertility.

See the two schematics in Figure 4.1 for an age-related diagram of both physical and pubertal development.[64]

Factors Affecting Pubertal Growth

Genetic factors have been found to affect timing and age of onset for various pubertal characteristics. These genetic factors can be

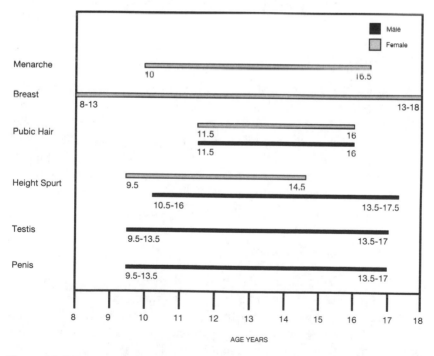

Figure 4.1 Schematic Sequence of Events at Puberty (from J. M. Tanner (1974), Sequence and Tempo in the Somatic Changes in Puberty. In Anne C. Petersen and Brandon Taylor, Chapter 4, "The Biological Approach to Adolescence: Biological Change and Psychosocial Adaptation," in J. Adelson, Ed. (1980), *Handbook of Adolescent Psychology*, New York: Wiley and Sons, p. 130)

traced to family patterns as well as ethnic group patterns. In addition, environmental factors may have some effect on pubertal development. Climate and season are variable in terms of onset of menarche for young women. Menarche seems to arrive later in colder climates than in warmer climates. Height seems to increase more in spring and weight in autumn. Nutritional deprivation, special problems, certain illnesses, and extreme emotional stress can cause delayed onset of both physical growth and pubertal growth.[65]

Amenorrhea

Failure to menstruate is called primary amenorrhea and may occur due to sexual infantism, ovarian malfunction, or genital tract abnormality. Secondary amenorrhea is cessation of menses due to a variety of causes, including nutritional factors, illness elsewhere in the body, use of drugs, pregnancy, anorexia, stress, and institutionalization.[66]

The Tanner Scale

A commonly used tool for assessing pubertal development is the Tanner Scale, developed by J. M. Tanner as part of his original study of pubertal growth in England. Table 4.1 is a graphic display of Tanner's concept. Stage 1 involves the mildest beginning of pubertal growth, while Stage 5 represents the mature or adult stage of growth. The chart includes genital development on the left for males, breast development on the right for females, with pubertal hair as a common developmental path for both males and females.[67]

Secondary Pubertal Growth

For both males and females, pubertal growth brings secondary growth features. This includes body fat in specific locations such as hips, breasts, and stomach for the female, enhancing the differentiated gender profile. Males develop broad shoulders, narrow waists, and Adam's apples. For both males and females, it includes body hair, with more for males. In addition, both males and females develop sweat glands that secrete body odors, which historically have had a variety of functions, including signaling interest in or readiness for sex. Males develop facial hair, at first silky and thin, but

Table 4.1 Pubertal Stages

Stage	Genital Development[a]	Pubic-Hair Development[a,b]	Breast Development[b]
		Characteristic	
1	Testes, scrotum, and penis are about the same size and shape as in early childhood.	The vellus over the pubes is not further developed than over the abdominal wall, i.e., no pubic hair.	There is elevation of the papilla only.
2	Scrotum and testes are slightly enlarged. The skin of the scrotum is reddened and changed in texture. There is little or no enlargement of the penis at this stage.	There is sparse growth of long, slightly pigmented, tawny hair, straight or slightly curled, chiefly at the base of the penis or along the labia.	Breast bud stage. There is elevation of the breast and the papilla as a small mound. Areolar diameter is enlarged over that of stage 1.
3	Penis is slightly enlarged, at first mainly in length. Testes and scrotum are further enlarged than in stage 2.	The hair is considerably darker, coarser, and more curled. It spreads sparsely over the function of the pubes.	Breast and areola are both enlarged and elevated more than in stage 2 but with no separation of their contours.
4	Penis is further enlarged, with growth in breadth and development of glans. Testes and scrotum are further enlarged than in stage 3; scrotum skin is darker than in earlier stages.	Hair is now adult in type, but the area covered is still considerably smaller than in the adult. There is no spread to the medial surface of the thighs.	The areola and papilla form a secondary mound projecting above the contour of the breast.
5	Genitalia are adult in size and shape.	The hair is adult in quantity and type with distribution of the horizontal (or classically "feminine") pattern. Spread is to the medial surface of the thighs but not up to the linea alba or elsewhere above the base of the inverse triangle.	Mature stage. The papilla only projects with the areola recessed to the general contour of the breast.

[a] For boys.
[b] For girls.

(from Anne C. Petersen and Brandon Taylor (1980), Chapter 4, "The Biological Approach to Adolescence: Biological Change and Psychosocial Adaptation," in J. Adelson, Ed., Handbook of Adolescent Psychology, New York: Wiley and Sons, p.127)

subsequently turning into the thickened hairs that constitute the adult male beard.

These secondary characteristics tend to develop at variable rates for different individuals. They are usually subsequent to primary forms of physical and pubertal growth, such as height, weight, breast development for females, testes and genital development for males, and pubic hair for both sexes.

ENDOCRINOLOGICAL GROWTH ISSUES

Normal height in America for males averages 5 feet 10.8 inches and for females averages about 5 feet 4.5 inches. Tall stature is 20 to

40% over normal range and short stature 20 to 40% under the normal range.[68] At 10 years, girls average 84% of their adult height. At the same age, boys average 78% of their adult height. At age 14, average girls have reached 98% of their adult height. Average boys reach 98% of their adult height at age 16.[69]

Much variability exists in adult height within the population. Growth timing and rates are also subject to great variability, due to a number of factors, including genetic messages, nutrition, and illness during growth.

Some individuals may have problems with growth outside the normal range. Dwarfism is abnormally low growth, more than 40% below the average. Sometimes slow development appears to be dwarfism; only a medical growth specialist can distinguish the difference. Dwarfism may result from different causes, some genetic and others environmental.[70]

Giantism is abnormally large growth, more than 40% above the average range. Like dwarfism, giantism may result from different primary causes.[71] Medical diagnosis is needed, particularly in early stages. Medical intervention is possible for many forms of giantism and dwarfism.

CHEMICAL TOXICITY

A number of chemicals that are toxic to the human body may affect the growth spurt. These include certain industrial chemicals, such as asbestos, as well as metals, such as lead and mercury. Exposure may be accidental or chronic, as in the case of lead paint or asbestos insulation in the home. Certain food products may also contain toxic levels of chemicals or metals.

The most common form of toxic chemical exposure for adolescents is mood-altering chemicals, including alcohol. While definitive study and replication have not been completed, there is enough hard research evidence to indicate concern. For example, Frank Diamond and associates conducted a study among a number of alcohol- and marijuana-using adolescent males. They discovered significantly decreased serum concentrations of luteinizing hormone (LH), follicle stimulating hormone (FSH), and testosterone. The average period of use for the group was 3½ years, and five of the six boys in the study showed a complete return to normal levels for all three hormones with 7 to 12 months of abstinence from use. Since

these hormones are not only involved in maturation of the reproductive system but also have some influence in the general growth
of the body, the study suggests real concern about use during the
adolescent growth spurt.[72]

Psychological and Behavioral Issues

Self-Consciousness about the Body

Pubertal and physical growth alone is cause enough for self-consciousness. Given growth in brain systems involving the ability to
see oneself from another's viewpoint, these changes cause the adolescent to become very self-conscious. Therapists often see early to
midadolescents who are obsessed with appearance because of their
irregular growth patterns. It is normal for a girl to have irregular
breast growth, with one breast slightly larger than the other. Simi-
larly, males may have one testicle larger than the other. This may
become a matter of great preoccupation, fear, and awfulizing. Other
adolescents become obsessed with large feet, hands, or noses. Still
other adolescents are frightened about the awkward appearance and
coordination of their bodies during the growth period.

Early Bloomers

Girls who are early bloomers tend to have more problems than
males. Male early bloomers tend to be the envy of their peers, since
they exhibit masculine characteristics and signs of maturity at an
earlier age. Males with mature bodies have more prowess at physical
tasks in sports, work, and defense. These changes give them a promi-
nent status among the male peer group. On the other hand, adolescent females who bloom early tend to be embarrassed and self-
conscious.

Both male and female early bloomers have the problem of mature expectations by peers and adults. Since they look older, they
are expected to behave in older ways. This is a particular problem
for the early bloomer female, who is expected to be more opposite-
sex-oriented than she may be psychosocially ready to handle at her
age. Research indicates that early bloomer females tend to become
more involved in dating, sexual behavior, smoking, drug use, risk
behavior, and delinquency than normal or late bloomer girls.[73] Male

early bloomers have fewer problems. However, they may be deprived prematurely of family nurturing due to expectation of mature needs and behavior.

Late Bloomers

Late bloomers have a different set of problems. While most of their peer group have an emergent adult profile, sexual development, and orientation toward the opposite sex, late bloomers find themselves in a childish state. This may result not only in problems with peer relations and self-concept but also in difficulty with childish treatment by parents and other adults.[74]

Work with early and late bloomers involves assurance, information, and cognitive restructuring. Reframing early or late growth with good developmental information is often enough. Work with parents and siblings about their treatment of the "bloomer" is important. Early bloomer girls should be allowed and encouraged by family members and the therapist to "go slow" in growing-up behaviors, including dress, makeup, activities, dating, and becoming involved with older peers. This allows time for self-concept and role-taking to catch up with physical and sexual growth. The therapist can help a late bloomer boy's family to be more sensitive to his fears and needs. The family can revise expectations to his age rather than his pubertal profile, thereby validating his maturing needs. Most nonendocrinological problems will be remedied by time and growth. The adolescent simply needs information and assurance in the interim.

Left-Handedness

Left-handedness, which Coren suggests is possibly a developmental deviant course due to prenatal or birth insult, creates a series of problems for growing adolescents. Left-handedness is a marker for several developmental problems, including learning disabilities, accident proneness, cross-eyedness, allergies, and other immune system problems.[75] In addition to the fact that they are not "normal"—that is, right-handed in such situations as writing in school, throwing a ball, or batting in sports—left-handed adolescents find themselves in a world designed for right-handers. It makes school activities, learning to drive, athletic prowess, and activity competence a problem. Slower and less graceful movement is a handicap in an environment designed for right-handedness. While this issue has not been mentioned or highlighted in much work with adolescents, it is a special problem left-handed adolescents have in dealing with an essentially right-handed world.

The issue has to do with degree of laterality (sidedness). Handedness is only one of several laterality preferences. Other indices of laterality include eyedness, footedness, and hearing dominance. Mixed sidedness is suggestive of increased developmental difficulty.

Anabolic Steroid Use

For at least a decade, 2% of adolescents have experimented with anabolic steroid use as a way to increase muscle mass, strength, and weight for athletic purposes. The need to be strong for males and the need for a competitive edge for both sexes pushes teens to use steroids. Originally this was a predominantly male activity; however, more females are now using steroids to increase athletic prowess. In addition to producing some dangerous personality changes, including angry and aggressive behavior, anabolic steroids may interfere with growth hormones and sexual hormones during the critical period of adolescent growth. For example, steroid use may masculinize adolescent females. Use of anabolic steroids is contraindicated for adolescents due to the danger of interfering with normal growth.

TREATMENT

For adolescents who are troubled by appearance, awkwardness, or abnormally large or small body parts, therapy should involve a combination of assurance and factual information. I suggest that the counselor not only explain the pubertal and physical growth processes to the teen, but also show him or her charts and diagrams so that the counselor's information is impartially validated. For counselors who are ill-equipped for this task, I recommend referral to the child's pediatrician. This referral should be accomplished by a phone call from the therapist to the physician explaining the child's fears and the nature of the current problem.

In cases of what appear to be abnormal growth or lack of growth, the indicated course is referral for pubertal growth assessment. The first station in the process is referral to the pediatrician by the therapist. If there are indications of abnormal lack of growth or excessive growth, then the pediatrician should refer the young person to an endocrinological growth specialist.

SUGGESTED READINGS

Katchadourian, Herant, *The Biology of Adolescence*, San Francisco: W. H. Freeman & Company, 1977.
This is a brief, but extremely detailed, description of physical growth, pubertal growth, and its endocrinological direction. The subsequent chapters on behaviorally related problems of adolescents are dated and not so relevant.

Tanner, J. M., "Growing Up," *Scientific American*, 229 (3), September 1973, pp. 34–43.
This is a brief, professional, but highly readable, article outlining pubertal growth by one of the seminal researchers in the area.

Chapter 5

Therapeutic Stance

While I would like to be able to recommend a comprehensive theory of therapy especially for adolescents, this is not possible, since adolescent problems occur in such a wide variety of areas and forms. However, I can suggest a special posture or stance for the therapist seeking to work effectively with teens. This chapter is designed to help you develop a therapeutic stance by addressing issues that are of central importance in working with adolescents. The concepts represent my long experience working with adolescent patients in a variety of settings. They are congruent with the concepts of adolescent development outlined in Chapter 2, and with information about adolescent neurological and biological development.

"A Caring Adult"

A good deal of research has investigated troubled developmental pathways. Many adolescents from highly troubled homes and highly stressed socioeconomic levels end up as troubled adults in terms of mental health, substance use, and criminal behavior. Yet, other young people from the same troubled environments and families move through adolescence in a continuous and healthy way, taking their place as basically healthy adults in American society. What makes the difference? A single factor accounts for the difference: the presence of "a caring adult" to provide support, responsibility, and advocacy for the young person.[76]

Your job, as a guide for an adolescent patient through the perilous ordeal of contemporary adolescence, is to be that strong, supportive, caring adult.

The emphasis here is on the *adult*. There has been a tendency on the part of counselors, therapists, and teachers to evaluate their effectiveness by their *popularity* with adolescents. Troubled adolescents will use this need for acceptance to manipulate the adult to achieve their own purposes. Ultimately, instead of appreciating the adult, they will dismiss that adult as failing to provide the strong, adult care that is needed to rescue them from mistakes and risks during adolescence. Your job is to be an adult whom the teen can rely on to protect him from his own manipulation and high-risk behavior. The adolescent needs "a caring adult," not a buddy.

DEVELOPMENTAL ORIENTATION

Most of us, as therapists, have approached adolescents as if they were adults with problems, resulting in a failure to make contact and to provide effective help. The key to effective work with adolescents is a developmental orientation.

First, this means having an understanding of the adolescent's developmental stage, including neurological development, physical development, pubertal development, and psychosocial development. Your initial contacts with the adolescent patient should help you assess where this individual is in the developmental journey in each of these areas. Location in these continua will shape how you go about communicating with the individual and how you provide therapeutic help. Lacking a developmental orientation, many therapists communicate in ways that simply miss the teen entirely. For example, waxing philosophical about issues misses the adolescent who is at the concrete operations level. She is thinking about very concrete and specific problems, not abstract, generalized issues; she will leave your office thinking about how smart you are, but without having received any real help.

Assessment of the level of cognitive functioning takes place in the initial conversation with the patient. The concrete operational level teen describes problems in very specific, concrete terms. The emotional level teen talks feelings as a basis for behavior. The early abstract level teen shows the ability to have and manipulate ideas about self, the problem, parents, school, and society. Operations include propositional reasoning, hypothetical reasoning (what ifs), and the ability to combine ideas and break them down into subunits. Finally, the higher abstract level teen has the ability to see conflicts between ideas and behaviors and to systematize behavior and thinking.

BLUNT, DIRECTIVE THERAPY

Remember that the adolescent is someplace in the process of neurological development, moving from diffuse brain organization to specified brain organization and moving from simple cognitive systems to more complex cognitive systems involving the ability to think abstractly in a variety of areas. Traditional therapeutic approaches, both psychodynamic and nondirective, presume a very high level of abstract thinking ability. The therapist who is nondirective, laidback, and highly conceptual often gets an accommodating response from the adolescent, who has no idea what the therapist is really saying.

My observation is that most adolescents in therapy are still in the concrete operations stage, communicating in black-and-white, either/or terms. I have found that effective therapy with most adolescents involves blunt communication and that fairly directive responses to questions and behaviors are more effective.[77]

At KIDS of North Jersey, we have developed a therapeutic approach based on the need for blunt, directive communication. At the beginning of treatment, the patient is encouraged to talk about problem incidents and behaviors in specific concrete terms. This involves starting recovery work at a developmental level of patient competence. The therapist directs the patient to expand talk into more difficult incidents, leading toward a reality-based picture of the problem or general lifestyle. Next, the therapist leads the patient to make connections between behaviors and resulting problems. This evokes feelings in the patient about various incidents. The therapist helps the adolescent tune into and experience the feelings, name the feelings, and understand the feelings' relation to the incident. Finally, the therapist directs the patient to explore alternative behaviors in similar situations and their consequences. Homework is prescribed involving experimentation with alternative behaviors. Therapy then involves discussion about the results of these experiments, leading to cognitive behavioral and lifestyle change.[78]

Initially, younger adolescents and troubled adolescents tend to be more concrete in their thinking and communicating patterns. As adolescents develop in healthy ways, their thinking becomes more conceptual and abstract. The therapist initially needs to communicate at the cognitive level of the patient in order for effective communication to take place. As the therapeutic relationship is established and progress occurs in problem areas, the therapist can "lead" and "push" the adolescent toward abstract reasoning skill. Concern with reasoning process, as well as with problem content, is the cognitive dimension of treatment.

COGNITIVE BEHAVIORAL THERAPY

A cognitive behavioral orientation is effective with children and adolescents with a variety of problems, as Donald Meichenbaum has reported.[79] This involves, first, helping the adolescent change her thinking about various current, salient, and emotionally arousing issues. Revised thinking will lead to different feelings and more effective behavior. Second, behavioral therapy involves homework and experiments with new behavior in the face of problems and situations. Behavioral experimentation is very concrete. Adolescents respond to behavioral experimentation with new ways to deal with peers, parents, and problems. Both successes and failures provide the grist for concrete reasoning together in therapy sessions.

Self-instructional training, one major cognitive behavioral therapy technique, involves teaching a patient to use self-talk in order to talk his way through a problem or behavior. Meichenbaum suggest four areas for self-talk: (1) problem definition; (2) focusing attention and response guidance; (3) self-reinforcement; and (4) self-evaluation coping skills and error-correcting options. Self-instructional training takes place in four phases. First, the counselor role models the self-talk process through the problem. Second, the patient does the new behavior with firm, normal, out-loud self-talk. Third, the patient goes through the process with quiet self-talk. Fourth, the patient repeats the process with silent self-talk.[80] Self-instructional training, which has been effective in many settings with children and adolescents, develops the use of language for cognitive control of behavior. Given the neurological development of self-talk as a means of behavior control during adolescence, this approach fits the developmental process.

Problem-solving therapy, closely related to self-instructional training, involves teaching the patient a five-stage process for addressing problems: (1) problem orientation; (2) problem definition; (3) generation of alternatives; (4) decision-making; and (5) solution implementation and experimentation.[81]

Other cognitive behavioral techniques include systematic desensitization, relaxation training, use of imagery, modeling, assertiveness training, mental rehearsal, and stress inoculation.[82,83]

MULTIMODAL THERAPY

The multimodal therapy concept, as developed by Arnold A. Lazarus, offers another important approach for adolescents. Lazarus suggests seven basic dimensions of personality: behaviors, affective processes, sensations, images, cognitions, interpersonal relationships, and biological functions. He provides a Multimodal Life History Questionnaire based on these seven dimensions. His approach is an excellent antidote for the therapeutic tendency to approach individuals through a single or standard modality, thereby missing important information in other areas of personality. The therapist's bias may miss a teen who is more oriented toward affective processes than cognitions, or biological issues than interpersonal relationships. This diagnostic approach helps determine the developmental stage and the issues of concern to the adolescent patient. Since the Life History Questionnaire is relatively long and at a high abstraction level, it may be necessary to revise it depending on the age and cognitive developmental level of the individual teen.

Lazarus goes on to use a variety of therapeutic approaches from various schools to initiate therapy in the area of primary concern for the individual patient. Entering the patient's life and problem areas through a single dimension, the therapist then moves on to related dimensions as they are involved in "here and now" issues.[84]

NEGATIVE COUNTERTRANSFERENCE

Freud and the psychodynamic school have highlighted the issue of transference in the therapeutic relationship. Transference involves issues with other people being projected onto the therapist by the patient in the present. Countertransference refers to all the therapist's reactions, often unconscious, to the patient. It can be an effective tool in therapy when the therapist emotionally senses something about the patient's mood, state, or problem. This information can be used to pursue a course of action with the patient that deals with issues beneath the surface.

Negative countertransference has to do with the therapist reacting to the patient in principally negative ways based on issues in the therapist's own life. Negative countertransference, which usually takes place out of the awareness of a counselor, is often harmful to the treatment process. It is critically important in dealing with adolescents to survey personal issues that may end up contaminating the therapeutic relationship.

First, adolescents often remind therapists of other individuals in their lives and pasts whom they liked or disliked. This like or dislike, in various intensities, tends to shape early interactions with the new adolescent patient. If the therapist is aware of the physical, behavioral, or emotional resemblance, he is able to control and discount this reaction, building a here-and-now relationship with the young patient.

Second, a number of us end up in therapeutic and helping professions because of our own youthful idealism, which began as part of our questioning and rebellion against the world of our parents' generation. Seeing their hypocrisy, we set out to build a better world. Many of us moved from social action into personal helping professions as a way to continue our commitment to helping others. Our own unresolved authority problems from our youth sometimes get transferred to our youthful patients, because we are still "covert adolescent rebels." In subtle ways, we encourage the adolescent patient to rebel toward parents, school authorities, and society in general. This negative countertransference problem actually increases the intensity of the young person's own problems with authority structures in the society—it is hardly helpful to him.

Third, there is a tendency on the part of adolescents who have not yet settled into adult responsibility to take risks and to pursue adventurous behavior for the emotional thrill of the experience. Some therapists who have regrets about responsibilities that prohibit them from daring, defiant, and risky behavior will tend to live vicariously through the risky behavior of the adolescent patient. They give implicit reinforcement and support for the adolescent to engage in risky behavior. This is a dangerous negative countertransference tendency, since 70% of all adolescent deaths are due to injury. The rate is highest for older teenage males. Many of these deaths and maiming injuries are due to risk-taking behavior, including a cavalier attitude about seat belts in cars and helmets on motorcycles.[85] Rather than reinforcing this kind of risk-taking, the therapist needs to encourage safe and responsible behavior.

Fourth, many of us come into the helping professions because of our own positive experience with a helper. Our self-esteem needs to be bolstered by our work experience with others. We have a tendency to need to be liked, especially by teenage patients. Adolescents are held up as the trend makers in our society. Therefore, positive response from an adolescent patient has a special value to therapists who need esteem-bolstering. This need to be liked sets the therapist up to be manipulated by the patient.

Fifth, most human beings, including therapists, tend to approach other people as if they shared the same basic human experience. This tendency to project self on others can seriously mislead the therapist in work with teens. First and most important are sexual differences. Males and females, particularly adolescents in the midst of self-conscious development of sexual identity, tend to experience life and relationships in different ways. In a cross-gender therapy situation (a male therapist with a female patient or a female therapist with a male patient), the therapist needs to be aware of the patient's different experience of life. This suggests fewer assumptions and more questions. Racial and ethnic differences are also significant in development and therapy. The African-American adolescent from a housing project in a major city or from a low-income, rural ghetto has a very different set of experiences from the adolescent in a professional or upper-income African-American family living in an integrated suburb. The third-generation Asian-American adolescent living in an integrated suburban development or urban condominium has a much different set of experiences than the Asian-American teenager whose parents immigrated to the United States and live in an ethnic community. Awareness of ethnic and racial differences poises the therapist to listen and learn rather than to assume.

Sixth, adolescents at the height of hormonal activity, sexual interest, and arousal tend to radiate high levels of sexual energy. Some therapists, who may be dissatisfied with their own sex lives, tend to use the sexual energy of the teen for personal gratification. While most individuals do not cross the line of sexual behavior with the patient, they tend to reinforce the teen, talking about driven and promiscuous sexual activity. This encouragement of out-of-control sexual behavior is another harmful tendency in therapy.

DIAGNOSTIC LABELS

Our current diagnostic system, the *Diagnostic and Statistical Manual of Mental Disorders (Fourth Edition)* (DSM-IV), has some adolescent categories, but is more focused on adult psychiatric pathology. In records from previous treatment, I frequently see cavalier assignment of adult diagnostic labels to troubled adolescents. Adolescent experimental behavior, including the use of conflict as a way to define oneself and one's own position, is easily misdiagnosed with a variety of adult diagnostic categories. I believe it is important to deal with the specific behaviors related to developmental paths without initially assigning a diagnostic label.

David Ausubel, in his book on adolescence, writes: "The chief problem in diagnosing the behavior disorders of adolescents is deciding whether the 'abnormal' behavior of a particular adolescent is merely an exaggerated expression of self-limited emotional instability characteristic of a transitional phase of development or whether it is reflective of a more fundamental personality defect rooted in childhood experience."[86] Ausubel gives excellent advice. I realize that we therapists need to assign diagnostic labels for third-party billing purposes and for the purpose of sharing information with other professionals. However, I believe it is important to keep personal stance, vis-à-vis the adolescent patient, open to the specifics of behavior, affect, and place in the development continuum.

TO MED OR NOT TO MED

We live in an era of magic faith in medicine. We have invented all kinds of effective medications and technologies for a variety of physical and mental illnesses. Unfortunately, there is a tendency to move to psychoactive medication too quickly in order to control behavior or to solve adolescent problems. When a specific drug at normal therapeutic levels fails to remedy the problem, the dosage may be progressively raised to several times the appropriate level. This controls the problem affect or behavior by reducing the teen to a walking semicomatose state. I will address this issue related to specific areas of concern in a number of chapters in Part III.

Neurological development is in major part based on the breaking of synaptic connections and the making of new synaptic connections in order to create new neurological circuits that convey a variety of new cognitive and behavioral competencies. One of the driving forces in the creation of the new neuron networks is the chemical attraction between cells in forming the synapse. Psychoactive drugs are analogs of the neurotransmitters. Whenever psychoactive medication is used with an adolescent, it interacts with the neurochemistry of the synapse and may interfere with development of a variety of new neuron networks and neurologically based competencies.

The bottom line: Avoid psychoactive medication except in the most extreme cases, such as adolescent-onset schizophrenia. In cases of problem behaviors, a variety of cognitive and behavioral approaches should be tried before considering pharmacotherapy. The prescribing physician should be a psychiatrist with experience in adolescent drug therapy and a reluctance to use drug therapy with adolescents.

GET INFORMATION

Adolescents are usually compelled into treatment, whether individual therapy or a therapeutic program, by an adult decision-maker. The decision-maker may be a parent, a school official, or someone in the criminal justice system. That individual is often the primary purveyor of information to the therapist. Since this person's reaction to the particular teenage patient contains not only reliable information but also personal irritation and often personal psychological threat, it is important to get other information.

I recommend that you as a therapist get permission to talk to as many significant adults in the adolescent's life as possible. This may include parents, teachers, school counselors, coaches, extracurricular activity sponsors, and adult siblings. Also contact the adolescent patient's primary physician. Some pieces of information may emerge from other significant adults, which may help explain the current problem or point to useful strengths that are not apparent from the primary complainer. You are looking for specific incidents and behaviors, not conclusions about the problem. It is crucial for the therapist to have as rounded a view of the adolescent patient as possible.

Some records may be useful as indicators of cognitive level and problems. I have found child study team reports, learning disability evaluations, and neuropsychological evaluations helpful. However, some child study teams cavalierly drop psychiatric labels on kids.

Other adults and professionals in an adolescent's life can be helpful with facts, specific behaviors, and incidents. Their conclusions about causes of problems may be erroneous, based on manipulation by the teen and/or faulty knowledge and premature closure. Your job in dialogue with the patient is to reach your own conclusions.

COPING STYLE

Preadolescence involves intense dependence on family and other adults for safety, security, and a variety of basic human needs. Early adolescence is characterized by a struggle between the need for autonomy and the need for security in dependence on family. The adolescent entering therapy usually brings with her this ambivalence about independence and dependence. Teens who enter the helping system are often reinforced in a process leading to "learned helplessness" and a victim self-identification, as explained by Seligman.[87] The victim mentality involves belief in personal helplessness in the face of powerful external forces and figures.

Personal coping styles are either externally focused, that is, based on information from other people such as parents or peer group, or internally focused, that is, skills for decision-making and dealing with issues come from within. Internally focused coping can either be emotion-based or cognitive-based. The adolescent neurological developmental system, involving development of frontal cortex executive skills, lays the foundation for the movement of focus and control of behavior from emotion to cognition.

An ongoing theme in adolescent therapy is helping the adolescent move cognitively and behaviorally from an external-focus style of decision-making and coping to an internal, that is, self-initiated, focus for coping and problem-solving. Within the internal focus, the therapist should encourage the adolescent to move from an emotion-focused style, which is a neurologically immature style that tends to be more impulsive and troubled, to a mature cognitive and problem-solving-based style. This theme should be constant in the mind of the therapist interacting in the counseling relationship with the teen: Healthy adult coping is internal and cognitive/problem-solving-based.

An internal cognitive coping style is based on taking responsibility for oneself and one's problems. The bottom line for the adolescent is taking responsibility for self, behavior and its consequences.

THERAPIST VALUES

Many of us identify ourselves as eclectic therapists, avoiding hard value decisions about health and illness, right and wrong. Unfortunately, this philosophy and style sets the therapist up to participate in the adolescent's self-destructive and high-risk behaviors by supporting many risk behaviors as a normal part of adolescence. It is crucial to good adolescent therapy for the therapist to make a decision or series of decisions about the nature of healthy development for adolescents. These value decisions become the framework and operating theory for the day-to-day work of evaluating and counseling teenagers as they face problem points in their development.

SUGGESTED READINGS

Ellis, Albert and Dryden, Windy, *The Practice of Rational Emotive Therapy*, New York: Springer Publishing Company, 1987.
An excellent introduction to the use of cognitive/rational therapy techniques in one-on-one therapy.

Lazarus, Arnold A., *The Practice of Multimodal Therapy: Systematic, Comprehensive and Effective Therapy*, Baltimore, MD: Johns Hopkins University Press, 1989.
This paperback book is an excellent introduction of a comprehensive approach to multidimensional diagnosis and treatment.

Maultsby, Maxie C., Jr., and Hendricks, Allie, *You and Your Emotions*, Lexington, KY: Rational Self Help Books, 1974.
This small book, using cartoon illustrations as well as text, is helpful with adolescents in learning to restructure their cognitions and beliefs.

Meichenbaum, Donald, *Cognitive-Behavior Modification: An Integrative Approach*, New York: Plenum Publishing Company, 1977.

This is an excellent book by one of the better-known theorists and practitioners of cognitive behavior therapy.

Persons, Jacqueline B., *Cognitive Therapy in Practice: A Case Formulation Approach*, New York: W. W. Norton & Company, 1989.
Another excellent introduction to the use of cognitive/rational therapy techniques in one-on-one therapy.

Part II

Developmental Tasks

Chapter 6

Identity

A moment comes in early adolescence when the young person becomes acutely self-conscious. "I'm me, and everybody's looking." Adolescents obsessively posture as a result of self-awareness. "How do I stand, smile, hold my head, walk, and talk?" This new self-awareness is the trigger for development of adult identity.

SOURCES OF SELF-AWARENESS

Adolescent self-awareness has several sources. Two neurological changes are critical for identity development. First is a higher level of self-awareness, in which the adolescent sees himself from someone else's viewpoint; this urgently presses the adolescent to construct *self*. Performing for the "imaginary audience" that is characteristic of most early and middle adolescents is, in large measure, a result of this higher level of self-awareness. Attention focuses on all aspects of self, including physical appearance, motor behavior, social behavior, language, and sexuality. Teens constantly perform for the "audience" in appearance, body movements, and talk.

The preadolescent tends to think of self and describe self in terms of concrete physical facts and competencies. Second, as increased abstraction and complexity are neurologically possible in thinking, the adolescent begins to describe self in more theoretical and abstract terms. As Fischer suggested, this period of formal development of self-concept begins with a series of different abstract self roles in different interpersonal settings. In middle adolescence, during the isolation period, the individual becomes aware of conflicts and contradictions between the different selves. In late adolescence, the "almost" adult begins to think systemically, and is then able to integrate a variety of aspects of self into a single abstract construct.[88]

SELF-CONCEPT

This single integrated construct is self-concept. Integration of aspects of self into a coherent whole is the necessary cognitive prelude for an adult sense of self. Susan Harter suggests that there are four major content areas for self-concept: (1) career choice and role; (2) spiritual and moral belief system; (3) a variety of social roles with relationship to peers, family, and other areas of society; and (4) sex role, involving intimacy and marriage.[89]

Self tends to be continuous from childhood into adulthood in spite of intentional and self-conscious development during the adolescent isolation stage. The basis of continuity is, in part, the influence of temperament with its genetic component. In *Lives Through Time*, Block looks at two major longitudinal studies and concludes that there are several personality types, most of which are relatively consistent over the developmental period from junior high school to high school and finally into early adulthood.[90] Thomas and Chess see temperament as relatively stable over time. However, temperament is affected by its "fit" with the environment of the individual. Change occurs as the individual responds to a "non-fit" environment.[91]

IDENTITY AS A JOURNEY

Murray Bowen suggests that the major step in identity development involves differentiation of self from the ego mass of the family. This occurs initially as physical separation from mother by birth and severing of the umbilical cord. Another step in differentiation occurs when the infant recognizes the difference between self and other.[92]

Adolescence represents a second major individualization phase, in this case from family.[93] This step in differentiation of self from family is the first substage of adolescence, involving psychological withdrawal from family. There are two bases for the urgent necessity of psychological withdrawal. Both are biological. The first, self-consciousness about physical change, that is, body enlargement and increasing secondary sex differentiation, requires the early adolescent to create distance from family in which he or she may be locked into a rigid child role. The distance allows space and time to come to terms with an enlarged body. It also offers the opportunity to return to family and adult world social relationships with a new status and role. Secondary pubertal development, with rising sexual interest and capability, also demands distance in order to come to terms with this new sexual body and ability. Closed doors provide the distance for the teen to come to terms with the body and genitals.

The second substage, the isolation phase, is the period of thinking about the enlarged, sexual body, and the beginning of thinking about various ways to express personhood through the new body. This is Fischer's first substage of formal operations. Isolation brings with it thinking about and experimenting with new roles. It is almost a play-acting phenomenon before family and peer audience, even when the audience is not present. Adolescents experiment with new hairstyles, makeup, jewelry, posture, walking style, music, interests, and even names. Some adolescents pick new nicknames or change to a first or middle name as an experiment with new identity and status.

Also during the isolation period, the adolescent is struggling with educational preparation for career and for adult performance in a complex technological society. Some role-taking experience in potentially new career areas is part of the experimentation. We will return to this in Chapter 11, "Education and Vocation."

Also late in the isolation period, the adolescent enters Fischer's

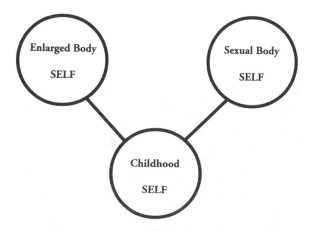

Figure 6.1 The earlier adolescent struggles with 3 selves

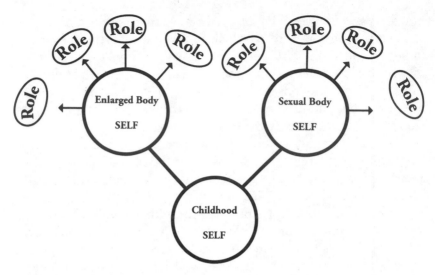

Figure 6.2 In process, the adolescent experiments with roles/images

second substage, in which he or she perceives conflicts and contradictions between various experimental roles in various settings. This creates an urgency to move toward integration and consolidation.

The final substage, reentry with adult status, is consonant with Fischer's third stage, which is systematic abstract thinking and involves integration of various specific roles into a single consolidated self-concept.[94]

Figure 6.4 fits the identity development process into the stages of adolescence.

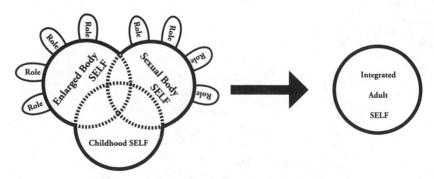

Figure 6.3 Late adolescent integration of identity

PREADOLESCENCE		• Child identity
A D O L E S C E N C E	Withdrawal	• Use of adolescent cultural devices to distance from family
	Isolation	• Experimenting with a variety of roles
	Reentry	• Sense conflict between roles • Initiate integration of roles
PSEUDOADULTHOOD		• Integration of roles into single self-concept
TRUE ADULTHOOD		• Autonomous adult identity

Figure 6.4 Identity Development

THE GOAL OF IDENTITY DEVELOPMENT

The adolescent separates from the family in order to pursue individuality. There appears to be a drive on the part of human beings, particularly during adolescence, to consolidate self in terms of uniqueness or distinctness. The child is an unself-conscious reflection of family ego. The adult is a conscious individual self. This final goal of adulthood involves two aspects. First, the adolescent moves into a "sense of self as adult." He really thinks of himself as an adult and feels mature. The second aspect involves family and social acceptance of this new consolidated self as an adult. It is truly the achievement of socially recognized adult status.[95]

The area of social recognition of adult self is somewhat problematic for contemporary American adolescents. The problem lies in the diffusion of clear adult rites for reentry into family and society with adult status. This diffusion perpetuates a half-adult, half-adolescent, ambiguous status, from age 18 until the early or mid-20's when one finally becomes independently resident and economically self-sufficient.

ADOLESCENCE AS A DIALECTICAL PROCESS

I see adolescent development of adult identity as a classic dialectical process. Childhood identification with and representation of family mass ego are the thesis. Neurological and physical change produces a distancing and a reaction, which form an antithesis. This antithesis involves the middle adolescent seeking alternative sources of information about self, religious and moral values, political values, education, and career choices. It is almost as if the adolescent defines himself in opposition to family values during a period of time. One problem with the antithesis (which is the isolation substage) for current adolescents is the absence of appropriate mentor role models. Historically, role models were teachers, coaches, activity sponsors, church and synagogue leaders, and other adults in special roles with youth activities. Not only did the person present in the formal role, but he or she was three-dimensional in terms of having other interests, roles, and a life beyond the immediate interaction with the adolescent. Most adolescents today do not affiliate with mentor-type role models. Rather, they affiliate imaginatively with role models through rock music videos and adolescent-oriented movies. Not only are these role models two-dimensional on the TV screen, but the deliberately contrived images by PR agents also convey a limited identity to adolescent fans.

The isolation period involves working through all of the contradictions in values and possibilities. While popular belief sees adolescence as substantially separated from family influence, research is clear that both parental and peer influences are potent throughout the isolation period. Parental values seem to be more influential in adolescent choices about education, career, religious beliefs, and political beliefs. Peer influence seems more effective in areas of music, extracurricular activities, appearance (including clothing, jewelry, and makeup), initial sexual behavior, and choices about substance use (including nicotine, alcohol, and illicit drugs).[96] Evidence of continuing parental influence during the isolation period, along with increased peer influence, supports the dialectical model as one way of seeing identity development and resolution.

Synthesis is the combination of thesis and antithesis in a new configuration. This is Fischer's third substage of formal operation involving the development of an abstract integrated role system. Synthesis is the immediate precondition for the reentry substage into family and society as a self-accepted and socially recognized adult.

GENDER DIFFERENCES

Psychodynamic therapists have pointed out that the process of identity development occurs in interaction with the same-sex parent and the opposite-sex parent. Children and early adolescents tend to role-model from the same-sex parent and learn how to be their own gender in male/female interaction with the opposite-sex parent.

Gilligan and her associates have pointed out the difference for male and female early adolescence at the withdrawal substage of development. The male's withdrawal involves severing closeness with mother, the primary nurturing parent, in order to be the opposite sex, the male. It is a movement of opposition and difference. This leads toward a focus on achievement and competition for achievement purposes. This pathway of identity development suggests autonomy and individuality. The female is able to move through adolescence continuing to identify with mother as the same-sex role model. While there is some distancing related to the new adult size and sexually capable body, it is still similarity with mother as opposed to separation that defines identity development for girls. The result is that females tend to interpersonally develop around issues of connectiveness, relationship, and nurture, as opposed to separateness, achievement, and competition. [97]

While Gilligan's work about female development centering around issues of connectiveness, relationship, and nurture holds true in a broad brush sense, young women today face new issues. Changing economics require both parents in many families to work. A changed political climate, emphasizing the rights of females to equal access in our society, poses new questions in the identity development process for young women. Young women are still attracted to the relationship focus of development, given role modeling by their mothers and the previous generation. But at the same time, many are now drawn to individual development around talents and career issues. This results in an internal conflict for many young women between the two foci of development. In addition, setting out on a trajectory of career development may result in conflict between mother and daughter over the daughter's independence, not only with reference to education and vocation, but also dress, moral rules, and other related issues. Some young women reach closure on this issue and pursue either marriage and family or career during the early decades of young adulthood. Often, these young women begin to question their choice in their late 20's and refocus their developmental trajectory around the opposite pole. Career-oriented young women marry and have children. Mothers return to education and career. A third choice involves attempting to do both, resulting in a whole series of conflicts around time allocation, personal relationships, and high stress. The third choice involves relationship stress because the society at large and males in particular have not gone through changed expectations about role and task in home and family.[98]

Males may conflict with fathers as well as mothers. If the father is an active influence in the family and in developmental goals for children, the young male striving for independence will conflict with the father's plan. This occurs when the father is involved in parental discipline and when the father has rigid goal expectations for his son that do not take into consideration the young male's talents, needs, and desires.

ETHNIC DIFFERENCES

Ethnic differences come in two major types. The first involves immigrant ethnic groups who are new to American culture and lifestyle. Young people growing up in these families find themselves in conflict between the traditional values and expectation of parents and the desire to successfully integrate into the culture of the new country. The intensity of these issues depends in some measure upon the age of the child at the time of immigration and whether the family lives in an enclosed ethnic community or in an integrated community among families who are currently functional in American culture.

The second area of ethnic differences involves groups that are currently established in America but for reasons of discrimination have been kept separate from full access. While some work has been done on ethnic differences in identity development, most of the work has been on African-American youth. The dynamic involved appears to be adaptation to socioeconomic situation. Middle and upper income ethnic youth tend to follow a similar trajectory of identity development, while the content of identity development for lower income minority youth is focused on adaptive protection in the face of limited options for adult roles.[99] For lower income African-American youth, the process of identity development is different in a small town in the rural South than it is in a large urban ghetto. The identity process is affected by limited options and by available gender roles in family, extended family, and community for adapting to the impoverished environment.

Youth in other ethnic groups face different trajectories of identity development. For example, Hopi, Pueblo, and Zuni males grow up in a world where identification with group, connectiveness, and cooperation are of paramount value. Therefore, individuality, competition, and conflict would not be part of a desired or rewarded path of development. Hispanic groups, while considerably different from each other, also share certain factors in the developmental process. "Macho" as a desirable quality for males is common to Mexican-American and Puerto Rican groups. Intense involvement in family and religion as a desirable female quality is also common to both groups. Unfortunately, most of the information available on development within ethnic subgroups is anthropological and qualitative. For the therapist working with minority youth, this descriptive literature is helpful in overcoming a cultural bias and understanding the context in which development of identity takes place for ethnic young people.

SOME FACTORS IN IDENTITY DEVELOPMENT

Effect of Birth Order

Walter Toman, Kevin Leman, and others suggest that birth order has some influence on identity development. The child distances during the withdrawal substage not only from parents, but also from older siblings and their roles. The need to be a distinct individual often influences a younger child to choose different roles than older siblings. First children are the subject of experimental parenting and parental demands for accelerated maturity. This may result in responsibility and leadership traits. There is a tendency for middle children to have a more ambiguous role in the family system, and for younger children to enjoy more freedom and fewer family expectations because of maturing parents and a "baby" role.[100,101] Birth order influence is variable with different individuals and families.

Efficacy Behaviors

While the adolescent in the isolation period is experimenting with new roles and behaviors, those behaviors that turn out to be efficacious or competent have a self-reinforcing effect. The behavior, receiving positive feedback, encourages more of the same behavior. As the behavior becomes regular and systematic, it shapes the content of the self-concept.

Conflict for Learning

Many adolescents use conflict as a dialogue technique in order to learn new information and to define self as different from authority figures. The conflict may be verbal or behavioral. It produces enormous stress for adult family members and for authority figures in youth-oriented institutions such as schools. Nevertheless, the conflicting dialogue is of great help in the abstract cognition process by which the adolescent defines himself.[102]

Fantasy and Reading

Many adolescents use fantasy as a tool for experimenting with potential new behavior and roles. The ability to fantasize is based upon increasing formal operational ability in cognition.[103]

Some adolescents use reading as another form of mental identity exploration. In this case, reading involves fictional and nonfictional stories about people whom they use as experimental role models.[104] In the age of television, fewer adolescents are using the written word as a tool for identity exploration. Rather, they are turning toward movies, television shows, and rock videos as a source of fantasy exploration. Two-dimensional images provide limited tools for imaginative identification.

SELF-ESTEEM

Self-esteem is the result of evaluating self-concept. Most adolescents develop an increasingly defined ideal self, which they compare to actual self. The result is a valuative finding of good or not-good about actual self as compared with ideal self. There is a tendency for self-esteem to be relatively low during early adolescence. During withdrawal and early isolation, teens are overly self-conscious and self-critical. During middle adolescence, fantasy, successful experimentation, and developing competency add to gently rising self-esteem. Experimentation with roles and efficacy behaviors leads to integration of selves into a coherent self in late adolescence. Self-esteem becomes stable.

SOME IDENTITY PROBLEMS

While a majority of adolescents moves through the developmental process either smoothly or with minor conflicts, some adolescents become troubled and even pathological in the identity development area.

Pseudoself versus Actualized Self

Some adolescents, in rigid family systems, fail to withdraw and distance themselves from the family mass ego. This results in a pseudoself, that is, an adult actualized *appearing* self that is in fact prescribed by family. The lack of choice and individualization involved suggests potential future difficulty.[105]

Relationship Dependency

Some young females in the identity development process foreclose individual identity by relationship dependency. They see a relationship with a male as adult identity and status. Instead of seeking an adult interdependent relationship, they become dependent on the male and the male's whims to define themselves. Tragically, these young females look to the adolescent male partner for instruction about self-as-adult female. Of course, the young male knows even less about female adolescence and adulthood than his partner does.

Some young males also fall into this developmental trap. The relationship becomes so demanding that family, same-sex friends, and activities are dropped. The capability of the young woman for intimacy potentiates this dependence since male peers may not meet this need.

Some girls go even further, having a baby for the purposes of creating autonomy and conferring adult status. Max Sugar suggests that adolescent pregnancy, while appearing to be a developmental step into adulthood, is actually arrested development for many teenage mothers.[106] Not only does it place severe limits on the teenage mother in terms of education, activities, and socialization, but it also results in troubled development for the infant and child, given the lack of mature maternal ability on the part of the mother.

TREATMENT

Therapy with an adolescent in the development process must be based on the teenager's location in the process from preadolescence to adult status. Working with a middle adolescent who is stuck in the withdrawal substage (that is, continuing to act out in order to create psychological distance between self and parents) is a different matter from working with an adolescent who is experimenting with various role behaviors, or with a late adolescent who should be in the process of role consolidation.

Recognizing where the adolescent is—or is stuck—in the identity development process opens the door to effective therapy. You can help the adolescent find ways to distance from family in the withdrawal phase without producing unnecessary conflict and alienation. You can assist the adolescent in productive role-taking as opposed to risky and dangerous role-taking during the isolation substage. Finally, you can work with the late adolescent in the reentry process by systematically exploring the various aspects of self involved in consolidation as adult self. This latter process is primarily abstract, cognitive therapy. Work on identity issues should always be focused on the consequences of various behavioral experimentation. It is important to help the adolescent move from rigid, single-concept thinking to multidimensional thinking, assessing good and bad results from any role or behavior.

Therapy with identity development involves helping the adolescent sort through various issues around "Who I want to be." The therapist helps the patient identify which roles are coherent with his or her own temperamental traits and personal goals and which are noncoherent. Some noncoherent roles have developed in response to the peer group and others have developed in order to produce distance from the family. Patiently, the therapist helps the adolescent to give up roles and behaviors that do not fit and to develop traits and roles consistent with self and goals.

It is particularly important in working with an adolescent female to help her develop individual identity separate from relationship dependence. While recognizing her relationship and connectiveness orientation, the therapist can help her understand the difference between dependent connectiveness and adult interdependent connectiveness. For young females who are driven toward pregnancy as a way to distance from family and achieve adult status, it is important to help them understand what it will be like, in terms of life changes, to be a mother and to have total responsibility for an infant.

Another important task involves pointing adolescents toward young adult and older adult mentor figures who can provide three-dimensional role models as alternatives to family values and views. Use of two-dimensional media is very limiting for most adolescents in the developmental process. Putting the mentor back in the isolation substage is genuinely healing for many youth. Mentor figures can be found in many settings including school, extracurricular activities, community programs, and employment settings.

SUGGESTED READINGS

Harter, Susan, "Self and Identity Development," in S. Shirley Feldman and Glen R. Elliott (Eds.), *At The Threshold: The Developing Adolescent*, Cambridge: Harvard University Press, 1990.
This is an excellent, though technical, description of concepts related to adolescent identity development.

Gilligan, Carol, *In a Different Voice: Psychological Theory and Women's Development*, Cambridge: Harvard University Press, 1982.
This is the book that opened the issue of differences between male and female adolescent development.

Erikson, Erik H., *Identity: Youth and Crisis*, New York: W. W. Norton and Company, 1968.
This is a collection of several papers on identity. Chapter 3 on "The Life Cycle: Epigenesis of Identity" is a good source of Erikson's crises. Other chapters focus on dated issues of the period.

Chapter 7

Spirituality and Values

Allied to identity development for adolescents is the spiritual quest for the meaning of life. Most children at preoperational levels simply accept, in a concrete way, the meaning framework of their family. The child lives in a world of meaning based on the authoritative word of parents and other adults.

With the neurological and cognitive capability for operational thinking, the preadolescent begins to question why things are as they are. This may involve moral rules, the existence of deity, religious practice in the family, and in particular, death.

The 10-year-old imagines God as an individual man, but the 11-year-old, moving toward more abstract thinking, regards God as "a spirit."[107] There is a slow process, including ages 11 and 12, when the early adolescent begins to think a great deal about God, religion, and other basic issues in life.

CRITICAL THINKING ABOUT MEANING

The 13-year-old takes the first step toward questioning values in the family. The development of critical thinking about the meaning of things is based upon neurological maturity, which is the foundation for the ability to think systematically on an operational level and to think abstractly at a formal operations level. Without the ability to question propositions, the adolescent would probably continue with the family's belief system.

The Withdrawal Stage

During the stage of withdrawal, which involves distancing self from mental and emotional control by the family, the adolescent begins to question authority-given belief about everything. One of the areas of question is morality. The adolescent begins to question the behavioral rules promulgated by parents, school authorities, and religious institutions. In addition, as courage grows for independent thought, the adolescent questions the foundation propositions of religion. This process grows with knowledge base and intellectual activity through high school into college. While this is healthy cognitive development for the teen, it is very difficult for many parents.

OTHER SYSTEMS

At some high schools, but certainly at most colleges and universities, the adolescent becomes exposed to different religions and alternative value systems. These alternatives become material for a growing

PREADOLESCENCE		• Acceptance of family beliefs and values
A D O L E S C E N C E	Withdrawal	• Questions authority given roles, beliefs and values
	Isolation	• Exposure to other systems or moral values and religious beliefs • Conflictual dialogue about values and beliefs
	Reentry	• Some experimentation with other values and beliefs • Develops personal meaning as synthesis of family/new values
PSEUDOADULTHOOD		• Synthesis value system skewed toward other belief
TRUE ADULTHOOD		• Balanced synthesis between family and other values

Figure 7.1 Spiritual Development

antithesis belief system in reaction to the family belief system. The adolescent will provocatively announce questioning of sacrosanct moral values and religious beliefs of parents and other important adult authority figures. He is seeking the conflict dialogue in which he will explore new beliefs and define himself as different from his parents.

SYNTHESIS AND REENTRY

As the mature adolescent approaches adulthood, the influence of family, which has never disappeared, becomes more important again. The "anti" stance gives way to a blended belief system in the young adult anxious to join other adults, including former authority figures and parents. The young person begins to develop a personally owned system of meaning, which incorporates much of the family religious and moral system. Family members become more comfortable with this new, responsible young adult, a young adult who has adopted personal, yet acceptable, religious and moral beliefs.

KOHLBERG'S STAGES OF VALUE DEVELOPMENT

Lawrence Kohlberg, former professor of human development at Harvard, began where Piaget left off in the area of values development. Kohlberg proposed a construct involving a series of levels that contain stages of development of moral values.[108] This system of progressive development was based on Piaget's structure of logical reasoning.

Level A: The Preconventional Level

Stage 1. Punishment and obedience, in which children determine right and wrong as literal obedience to rules and authority in order to avoid punishment and to avoid doing physical harm.

Stage 2. Individual instrumental purpose and exchange, in which the individual begins to serve her own and other people's needs by seeing correct behavior in terms of "fair deals." Following a rule is in one's own interest because others have to follow the same rule, thereby creating a just and fair system for all. This is still a very concrete individualistic perspective.

Level B: The Conventional Level

Stage 3. Mutual interpersonal expectations, relationships, and conformity, in which the reasoning involved in correct and moral behavior has to do with an understanding of early interpersonal relationships. One plays a good role because it involves loyalty and keeping trust with other people. A concrete "golden rule" of a sort governs behavior. The young person is not yet looking at a generalized system of right and wrong.

Stage 4. Social system and conscience maintenance, in which the young person begins to realize that, for the social order to serve everyone's welfare, one has to, out of duty, behave in the correct way. This is a more systemic interpersonal view of moral decision-making.

Level C: The Postconventional and Principle Levels

Stage 5. Prior rights, social contract, or utility, in which the individual has reached the point of abstract thinking and recognizes basic rights, values, and legal contracts of a society, even when they conflict with the concrete rules and laws of one specific group. This is the normal adult perspective about morality and values.

Stage 6. Universal ethical principles, an extraordinary stage, in which one behaves by perception of universal ethical principles that all of humanity should follow. This is the kind of perspective that would cause Mohandas Gandhi and Martin Luther King, Jr., to accept consequences for law violation in order to force the issue of universal justice and to initiate change of an unjust law. This ideal form of morality is characteristic of exemplary, mature individuals. Some late adolescents reach this stage as they embrace idealism in the desire to create a better world out of their antithetical stance toward the world created by their parents' generation.

Kohlberg conducted a number of experiments, as have his followers, using moral dilemmas with various age groups in order not only to see the conclusion the individuals find for the dilemma, but also to study the process of reasoning that led to the conclusion. In addition, Kohlberg and associates experimented with a number of free or experimental schools in terms of using democratic decision-making as a technique to help adolescents move up to higher stages of reasoning about moral values. These experiments resulted in some success. With help, some adolescents can move a single stage higher in moral reasoning.[109] Moving to a higher stage means more effective reasoning about values in general and healthier decisions about specific behaviors. Adolescents should reach at least Stage 5, where their behavior is based on the concept of human rights and the social contract.[110]

PROBLEM BEHAVIOR

Many adolescents who show up at the therapist's office have problems related to value development. These are based in several developmental problem areas.

First, many troubled adolescents remain immaturely self-centered. They have not yet recognized the effect their behavior has on other people. They are still at the stage of obeying rules because of authority figures and from fear of punishment. Given the current climate of permissiveness in the school and criminal justice system, these young people quickly learn that they can break the rules, take other people's property, and harm other people physically, with little or no consequences.

A second problem area is the young person who, in his or her withdrawal and isolation stages, becomes affiliated with a peer group that is antisocial and criminal. This is reinforced by some pop figures in the media world, such as "rappers" and heavy metal rock music figures who endorse violence, hostility toward the police, property destruction, sexual aggression, and drug use. For impoverished and ethnic minority youth, disregard for laws and rules may seem justified by experiences of real injustice and discrimination. The consequences of these behaviors are not justice, but often loss of family, education, and freedom.

Third, there are a group of young people whose involvement in alcohol and drug use creates systemic neurological insult, to the point where they are cognitively impaired in thinking processes, which influences how they relate to authority, rules, law, justice, and other people.

A HIGHER POWER

Adolescent egocentrism and the "me first" orientation of our culture result in many teens becoming stuck in infantile self-centeredness.

Maturity involves awareness of other people, family, community, nation, human rights, the ecological relationship with nature, and the need for a "higher power." A "higher power" is simply a larger-than-self framework in which to test one's own motives and values. The "higher power" concept of Alcoholics Anonymous is a good framework for the therapist to use in helping adolescents tame egocentrism and develop a spiritual orientation for living.

TREATMENT

There are two basic types of therapy with adolescents who are breaking the rules and the law. First, for drug users, it is critical that they become drug-free so that therapeutic dialogue with them is possible. Second, for those rule breakers and other adolescents with behavior problems, it is critical to manage the consequence system so they begin to experience the results of their behavior. As they begin to have difficulty with the consequences of behavior, it becomes possible to talk about the reasoning involved in the decisions that led to the behavior.

Many young people who are not behaviorally troubled or using drugs, but are struggling with questions of meaning and religion, become counseling cases through parents' fear about the young person's journey away from traditional religious behavior and belief. The therapist needs to assess the cognitive processing level of the individual and then begin to help her work through the religious and moral issues. Cognitive processing level is determined by analyzing reasoning as either concrete or abstract. The focus on working through needs to be not only about ego satisfaction for the individual, but also about how her critical thinking and its resulting behavior will affect relationships with people who are important to her. The patient needs to decide what beliefs and practices are worth serious relationship problems. The teen needs to learn how to disagree without rejecting people who hold different beliefs.

There is always the temptation for the therapist to be led on a tangent of philosophical and intellectual games, rather than keeping the discussion focused on the relationship consequences of belief, moral values, and the resulting behavior. Most adolescent value conflicts are not issues of serious danger to self and others. The counselor needs to deal with critical thinking, values development, and family or authority conflict resolution, rather than the philosophical correctness of belief. However, some value stances involve physical danger or psychological peril. Cult membership, carrying weapons, sexual promiscuity and aggression, and substance use are clear examples of this category. The therapist has an obligation to help the adolescent patient change dangerous beliefs. This is one example of how important it is for the therapist to have a personal belief system about healthy adolescence.

Finally, the therapist should help the adolescent patient discover limits on self and the need for others, including a "higher power."

Chapter 8

Sexuality

Adolescence brings with it surging gonadal hormones, enlargement of the body, maturation of the reproductive system of the body, and most important, rising sexual feelings. Physical development presses on the budding adolescent an urgency about sexual orientation and others. Sexuality is continuous, literally, from the fetal period when a surge of testosterone occurs, or does not occur, producing respectively male gender and female gender. Puberty represents a radical increase in development of the sexual system and related feelings.

Preadolescent children, although different in appearance because of the gendered cultural trappings of clothes, hairstyle, and body movement, are nevertheless relatively alike in general profile. The development of the reproductive system during puberty brings with it related secondary sexual characteristic growth, such as broad shoulders for males and expanded hips for females. These changes cause a dimorphism in body appearance that is designed to encourage sexual interest and, ultimately, reproduction with its ensuant perpetuation of the species.

The beginning of sexual development involves the hypothalamus, followed by a triggering of pituitary hormonal release. In turn, the gonads increase their production of gonadotropin hormones, directing growth of the sexual parts of the body and the ability to behave in an adult sexual way.

Louise Kaplan points out an interesting fact about human beings. In humans, alone, the brain and the sexual system mature at virtually the same time,[111] that is, the higher functions of the brain, including the prefrontal cortex and its executive skills, mature at the same time as sexual capabilities. Sexuality in human beings not only is physical and instinctual, but also involves the intellect, including cultural channeling of the sexual drive.

There is some evidence that children as young as 2 years of age are aware of their own gender. Most children continue to develop a sense of self-gender as well as appropriate behaviors related to the meaning of gender difference in their culture. The physical changes in adolescence initiate a serious developmental period for the meaning of gender, that is sexual identity, and its related behaviors toward other individuals. Cultural expectations play a major part in the development of dress, appearance, hairstyle, and behaviors, which express gender in a way that makes sense to same-sex and opposite-sex individuals in the same society. Physical sexual maturity is channeled through cultural expectation to produce sexual behavior.

PERSONAL EXPERIENCE OF CHANGE

Adolescent males and females appear to have different experiences of the pubertal process. Increasingly, girls have preparatory knowledge for breast budding and menarche. Sex education and parental freedom to communicate about body change give the girl a sound enough foundation so that her first period is neither frightening nor repugnant, as experienced by some females in the past. Girls who reach puberty on normal-to-late schedules in general have positive feelings about the maturation of their bodies with reproductive potential. Research indicates that girls communicate at a much higher level than boys, particularly with their mothers, about issues to do with their own growth and change.[112] Many girls have expectant and positive feelings about pubertal maturation.

Compared to females, male adolescents have less preparation and are less communicative with parents about their body changes. Early maturation conveys status on young males, both in terms of body size and genital growth, as evidenced in the physical education shower room. Males seem to continue to rely on "dirty" stories for most of their information about pubertal growth and sex. This form of information, laced with humor, is often woefully inadequate in terms of accurate facts about sexuality.[113]

"Early bloomer" girls seem to be embarrassed by the development of their bodies, while "late bloomer" boys have the same problem. Both are subject to teasing by family and peers, which contributes to real difficulties with pubertal change and sexual identity development.[114]

The meanings of pubertal change, body image, and sexual identity are influenced by a variety of responses to physical change. Positive responses by family and peers encourage healthy development of new identity, including gender. Negative responses, some of which appear positive, such as expectation of sexually oriented behavior from early bloomer girls, have negative effects on the development of growing sexual identity and behavior.

SEXUAL IDENTITY DEVELOPMENT

Part of the process of sexual maturation is the development of sexual identity. Peter Blos suggests that this begins in the interaction of the small child with the same-sex parent as well as the opposite-sex parent. Early development involves identifying with, and copying the role model of the same-sex parent and by learning to act one's gender with the opposite-sex parent. Blos and other psychodynamic therapists have described this process, beginning with the first oedipal period and continuing in a milder form during latency until sexuality blossoms again during the pubertal period. [115]

I suggest that, particularly during the latency period, siblings play an important role. The individual develops same-sex modeling not only from parents, but also from older same-sex siblings. In addition, there are overtones of opposite-sex flirtatiousness and communication with opposite-sex siblings.

During the late childhood period, most children develop a special relationship with a same-sex friend. This intense relationship, as suggested by Harry Stack Sullivan, is a learning experience leading to the possibility of opposite-sex intimacy during adolescence. The special friend is a practice relationship, in which the child develops relationship and communication skills in preparation for later life. [116]

NORMAL INTIMACY DEVELOPMENT

Mark Schwartz of the Masters and Johnson Institute describes six steps in the development of heterosexual intimacy and behavior:

1. *Pubertal change* initiates interest in self as a sexual person as well as interest in the opposite sex.
2. *Recreational contact* in late childhood and early adolescence is the beginning of contact with the opposite sex. Teens play games involving physical contact. They pick at each

other in classrooms and push each other during activities, all of which is part of the initial contact process.

3. *Cognitive process*, involving fantasy and much thought about several individuals or a particular individual of the opposite sex, prepares the way for actual communication in a relationship.

4. A *spiritual process* begins in which early communication establishes that two particular individuals have much in common in terms of values, goals, and interests.

5. An *emotional ability to share feelings* develops as a result of the spiritual process. The sharing of feelings is the beginning of true intimacy. Emotional sharing feels intimate.

6. *Sexual contact* begins in terms of hand-holding, touch, kissing, and petting contact, leading ultimately toward sexual intimacy based on feeling and spiritual intimacy.[117]

Wendy Maltz, a noted sex therapist, describes the stages of normal sexual development:

1. Feeling physically safe and protected from overt sex.
2. Feeling love for oneself.
3. Enjoying touch and sensations.
4. Developing sexual curiosity.
5. Initiating social relationships.
6. Establishing meaningful friendships with nonsexual forms of intimacy.
7. Based on this foundation, the individual chooses to become sexually active with an intimate partner.[118]

Both constructs describe an interest in sexuality based on physical change, moving slowly toward sexual intimacy through a variety of relationship stages. The stages include thinking about the other person, discovering interests and goals in common, becoming emotionally intimate and, based on safety and closeness, beginning to touch. In this process, individuals discover the meaning of their gender identity in interaction with the opposite sex.

Figure 8.1 fits the sexual identity and intimacy development process into the stages of adolescence.

PREADOLESCENCE		• Same-sex special friend
A D O L E S C E N C E	Withdrawal	• Same-sex peer group and physical/game interaction with opposite sex
	Isolation	• Dating with mental, emotional, and physical contact
	Reentry	• Relationships replace group as primary • Beginning of intimacy
PSEUDOADULTHOOD		• Serious intimate relationships
TRUE ADULTHOOD		• Adult committed and intimate relationship

Figure 8.1 Sexual and Intimacy Development

SEX AS A ROUTE TO INTIMACY

One of the tragedies of our time is that adolescents put the sexual cart before the horse. Instead of first developing intimacy, then becoming sexually active, they get lost in a maze of physical sex with many resulting problems.

Historically, males and some females masturbated, but most young females delayed sexual intercourse as an important milestone of adulthood. For many girls, first intercourse occurred in the framework of a commitment to be married. Since the late 1960s, more adolescents have become sexually active at younger ages. A recent study reports 12% of boys and 6% of girls at age 13 have had their first intercourse experience. Currently, by the age of 18, 67% of boys and 44% of girls have sexual experience, and by age 20, the figures go up to 80% for males and 70% for females.[119] Unfortunately, this sexual experience is not necessarily limited to dating relationships. A growing minority of young people is promiscuous, in the sense that, in limited periods of time, they have sexual relationships with several different partners. Among 15- to 24-year-old women who began sexual intercourse before the age of 18, 75% had two or more partners, and 45% reported having four or more partners. Fifty-seven percent of males have had two or more partners and 47%, four or more partners by the age of 19.[120] This has resulted in proliferation of sexually transmitted diseases and later difficulty with development of intimate relationships.

Several problems result from earlier and more promiscuous sexual activity. First, the lack of coherent adult identity makes many teenagers vulnerable to sexual dependency. The moment of orgasm represents a dissolving of self into unity with another person. For those young people who do not have firm identity, this moment of self-dissolving may lead to confusion and dependency, because it occurs without the frame of reference of structured, self-conscious adult identity. Second, sexually active young people begin to see sex itself as the end and purpose of the experience. Individuals who follow the more mature paradigms outlined by Schwartz and Maltz see sex as part of a wider comprehensive relationship with another individual. Those young people who attempt to find intimacy through sexuality often develop something like drug tolerance with their sexual behavior. They attempt to raise the ante by varying sexual behaviors, ultimately leading to hurtful and sadomasochistic practices. When this fails, they vary behaviors in terms of more individuals and different combinations, all of which undermine the possibility of future intimacy.[121]

DRUGS, ALCOHOL, AND SEX

A number of recent studies implicate drug and alcohol use with initiation of sexual activity and with the development of sexual promiscuity. My own study of 273 adolescents in treatment at a drug and alcohol rehabilitation program in 1983 found that 47% were under the influence of a mood-altering substance at the time of first intercourse. This figure was an average of 53% for females and 42% for males. Their increase in substance use paralleled their increase in sexual activity and promiscuity.[122] Irwin and Schafer refer to a number of studies that show a high correlation between at-risk sexual behaviors and high levels of alcohol and other substance use.[123]

FACTORS IN INITIATING SEXUAL BEHAVIOR

Irwin and Schafer go on to outline a number of influences on the beginning and the course of adolescent sexual activity.

1. Biological factors in terms of the timing of pubertal development.
2. Sociodemographic factors, including race, as a strong predictor of early sexually activity, with African-American male adolescents at the earliest end of the continuum.
3. Parental behavior, particularly the relationship between mother and daughter.
4. Peer behavior in terms of attitudes of the immediate peer group, especially best friends.
5. Psychological factors, including high self-esteem, which delays initial sexual behavior, and cognitive functioning — high achievers tend to delay initial sexual behavior and low achievers tend to develop earlier sexual behavior.
6. Regular religious participation, which tends to delay the beginning of sexual activity. [124]

LACK OF KNOWLEDGE

Notwithstanding earlier, more frequent, and more promiscuous sexual behavior by increasing numbers of adolescents, they continue to be ignorant about sexual development, sexual activity, and intimacy. Katchadourian states: "One would expect American teenagers to be quite knowledgeable about sex. Generally though, they are not, even about the elementary facts. It is this ignorance combined with widespread sexual activity that is alarming."[125] It is the combination of increased sexual activity with continuing ignorance about one's own body, sexuality, and sexual behavior that spells increasing problems for young adults in America. The problems include difficulty developing adult intimacy, increasing sexually transmitted diseases including AIDS, teenage pregnancy, and the inability to establish stable families, thereby affecting the next generation.

PREGNANCY AND ABORTION

Free adolescent sexuality has brought with it a number of problems. First and foremost is the problem of unmarried teenage pregnancy.

Twice as many African-American females as white females become teenage mothers. Hispanic adolescent girls have the lowest pregnancy rate at 6%, as compared to African-Americans at 24%.[126]

While birthrates for early adolescents remain low, they have increased by 225% since 1960, going from 0.4 per thousand births to 1.3 per thousand births in 1987.[127] Within the 15- to 19-year-old category, there are some interesting trends. The rate has gone down from 35.7 per thousand to 31.8 per thousand, and the rate for 17- to 19-year-old females has dropped from 120.3 per thousand to 80.2 per thousand. This is explained in part by the legalization of abortion in 1973. There has been a dramatic rise in the abortion rate among young females in America. For example, the abortion rate has risen by 15% for 19-year-olds with all races combined.[128]

Adolescents who become mothers are more likely to drop out of high school, to be on public assistance, to marry young (but with less stable marriages that end in divorce), have more children in a lifetime (particularly unplanned, unwanted children), and to be unemployed.[129]

Early pregnancy forecloses normal development into mature adulthood through school, friendship, and dating activities, as preparation for intimacy and childbearing. Not only does this create a group of adults with serious problems that require ongoing support from the society, but it has an effect on the next generation because the mother (and father, if present) is unprepared in terms of maturity to provide healthy nurturing for the young child.

CONTRACEPTION

Decades ago, two proposals were forwarded to solve the problem of adolescent pregnancy. First, many experts proposed sex education through the public schools. While some schools are reluctant, most schools include sections on reproductive system development, pregnancy, and childbearing in health education classes. Education has had little effect on the rate of adolescent pregnancy.

The second solution has been to make contraception available, with or without the knowledge of parents and at little or no expense to adolescents. Adolescents have tended not to use contraceptive devices in their sexual activity. They talk about contraception devices such as condoms, diaphragms, and foams as interfering with the spontaneity of the sexual process. This cavalier attitude expresses the impulsivity of emotional rather than cognitive control of behaviors. In the high achievers survey, most of the high school students rejected condoms based on lack of spontaneity in sex. As one student put it, "If it were there when I needed it, I'd probably use it." He was not referring to availability through the local high school, since most kids don't have intercourse in the high school corridors or restrooms. He was referring to someone standing by with a condom available, in the back seat of the car or in someone's bedroom, whenever he decided to have sex. [130] The impulsiveness of adolescents with regard to sexuality, allied with adolescent self-consciousness, works against use of birth control as a means of preventing adolescent pregnancy and sexually transmitted diseases. By and large, the few teenagers who have used contraception have been females who are on birth control pills at the instigation of parents. The continuing high level of adolescent pregnancy and the dramatically increasing level of sexually transmitted diseases suggest that our current approach to adolescent sexuality is a failure.

SEXUALLY TRANSMITTED DISEASES

A roaring epidemic of sexually transmitted diseases exists among adolescents in America. There are rising rates of gonorrhea and syphilis, after many years of effective control by public health measures. Other not so well-known diseases, such as chlamydia trachomatis, genital herpes (HSV-2), human papillomavirus (genital warts), are all increasing at a dramatic rate. [131] There appears to be a higher rate of increase in all of these diseases among adolescents, particularly from ages 15 to 19. There are also sharply increasing rates among the 20- to 24-year-old young adult group.

While the HIV and AIDS rate is low among adolescents, a long incubation period before detection is possible may be deceptive in terms of actual prevalence. [132] Teens may be far more infected than we now know.

Again, the liberalization of American sexual practices has reaped a crop of debilitating diseases that predict a variety of long-term problems, including impaired reproductive process for young females. The attempts to prevent this by sex education and distribution of condoms have apparently failed. Using education as a basis for behavior is often premature, given the immature levels of cognitive control in many adolescents. The ability to plan for subsequent behavior is also a skill based on development of the prefrontal cortex and executive skills that are not necessarily mature in most early adolescents. Our society needs to find a better strategy for managing teenage sexuality.

SEXUAL ABUSE

Childhood and early adolescent sexual abuse is a reality. It brings with it a series of psychological sequelae, including problems with identity, self-esteem, and sexuality, which require attention on the part of therapists. While sexual abuse occurs in all kinds of settings, incest is the most common form. Older male to younger female appears to be the most common form of incestuous abuse, with abuse by a stepfather the most prevalent. Older female to younger male, male to male, and female to female appear to be much less frequent.[133] Whites and African-American families appear to have approximately the same rates of incestuous abuse. Hispanic families tend to have higher rates. Asian-American and Jewish families tend to have lower rates.[134]

Childhood sexual abuse has profound effects on the development and mental health of the individual. Adult survivors of sexual abuse tend to seek treatment for a variety of disorders, including depression, anxiety, eating disorders, substance abuse, dissociative disorders, somatization disorders, and explosive disorders.[135] A series of factors influence serious aftereffects of sexual abuse. These include:

1. duration and frequency of abuse
2. type of sexual activity, whether touching or invasive
3. use of force and aggression
4. age at onset, with younger onset often causing more damage
5. age, gender, and relationship of the perpetrator
6. passive submission or willing participation on the part of the child
7. overt and disclosed incest with lack of assistance
8. parental reaction to disclosure
9. institutional response to disclosure[136]

In my clinical experience, I have found early sexual abuse leads to one of two common adolescent patterns. First, I have worked over the years with a number of girls and young women whose early and continuing sexual abuse has produced early sexualization. These individuals experience all of life as sexual. They are preoccupied with sexual thoughts about every individual with whom they have contact.[137]

A second result is phobic fear about sex. Having been physically invaded, traumatized, and hurt, the individual sees all sexual approach as threatening. She may even see nonsexual encounters as sexually threatening. Fear about sex for this individual interferes with socialization skills and activity in many arenas. This interferes with the normal adolescent development of opposite-sex orientation and early exploration of relationships leading to the potential of intimacy and healthy sexuality.

SEXUAL ADDICTION

Patrick Carnes has pointed out that some individuals become so hooked on sexuality that sexual behavior becomes addictive.[138] Many of us working with adolescents have seen patients in the early or middle stages of sexual addiction. This involves compulsive practice of self- and other-sex, sometimes with violent and aggressive overtones. Sexual addiction tends to produce progressive dysfunction in every other area of life, just as alcoholism and drug dependence do.

ALTERNATIVE SEXUAL ORIENTATION DEVELOPMENT

Homosexuality is a sensitive and difficult issue at this time in American society. Social and political action around issues of injustice and discrimination toward gays has resulted in a variety of ideological positions with regard to homosexuality, some helpful and some harmful for therapists working with adolescents in the process of forming sexual identity.

Initial gender awareness appears in early childhood, roughly between 1 year and 2 years of age. Gender awareness is expressed in identification with the same-sex parent and attraction to the opposite-sex parent. Gender differences in preschool children are often apparent in play activities. In psychodynamic theory, the oedipal period brings with it major identification with the same-sex parent and attraction to the opposite-sex parent, which reaches a temporary resolution leading to the latency years. Reproductive system spurt growth in adolescence brings another period of intense involvement with gender identity, orientation, and sexuality. Given the structure of American society and delayed access to full adult role and status, these issues of gender identity and sexual orientation may reach closure as late as the adolescent reentry period or the pseudoadult period.

A variety of influences seems to shape gender identity and sexual orientation. Early childhood experiences of a remote or abusive same-sex parent interfere with identification. A strong, dominant, and/or protective opposite-sex parent may become the object of identification instead of attraction.[139] Many adolescents with gender identity confusion and apparent homosexual orientation have experienced sexual abuse during childhood.

A biological foundation theory is advanced by some as a definitive explanation for homosexual preference. We are discovering in many areas of human behavior that behavior is influenced by biological predisposition, but that it requires environmental factors to trigger the actual behavior. At this time, research about the biological theory appears to be equivocal.[140] Horgan, writing in *Scientific American*, reviews several genetic and neurological studies about homosexuality and finds them to be less than definitive.[141] There are a number of defective gender chromosome-based disorders. In the overwhelming majority of cases, those individuals with defective genetic messages about gender nevertheless behave comfortably according to the gender appearance of their bodies. For example, an individual with a defective male chromosome, involving lack of sufficient testosterone, will develop a female appearance and behave according to the female appearance.

Homosexuality is too complex a system of behaviors to be ascribed to a simple or single cause, whether genetic, neurological, or psychological.

Another theory proposed in the media by gay activists is lifestyle choice. I believe this is an inadequate explanation although, given the psychological distancing of early adolescence and the attraction to role models who produce conflict with family values as part of the individualization process, gay activists have some attraction for young people just as civil rights leaders and peace activists did in an earlier era. The strong role of homosexuality in art, theater, and music is also a potentially attractive role model for oppositional behavior to family. My own clinical experience suggests the influence of environmental factors during childhood and adolescence. For example, I have worked with a number of young people, confused about sexual orientation, who have been involved in normal same-sex experimentation in late childhood that has carried over to middle adolescence due to a general developmental lag in their own personal trajectories. Compared to the increasing opposite-sex involvement of many of their peers, their delayed same-sex experimentation, and the same-sex special friend attraction, they have been confused about their own sexual orientation. A second and similar group consists of young people who do not conform to the very rigid gender role expectations of the more popular peer groups in their school and community. These young people, who may, in interests and behavior, be more androgynous, find themselves confused because of their peers' definition of masculinity and femininity.

Another group of young people have been seduced, either as childhood sexual abuse victims or under the influence of drugs and alcohol, by a slightly older homosexually- or bisexually-oriented adult. Since the genital stimulation felt good, these young victims became confused about their sexual orientation. This confusion leads to questions about possible homosexual orientation. With those patients, I have been able to help them understand the process they went through, and tune into their own sexual thoughts and fantasies about the opposite sex. Through good information, they were able to recover their own gender orientation in sexuality. A few young people remained for whom this was not possible. This may be based on a variety of causes. These patients will move on to become adult homosexuals.

Frederick Berenstein, in *Lost Boys*, describes the case called "Benjamin L." in which a 12-year-old believes he is homosexual. Berenstein, in gentle psychodynamic therapy, works through issues related to a threatening father and a strong, warm mother, as well as experimentation with homosexual pornography. Gentle analytic work helps Ben to explore his own identity and slowly move toward an acceptance of himself as masculine and heterosexually oriented. Berenstein stays with the case through early adult sexual activity into marriage. This is a case example of another therapeutic modality dealing with the issue of sexual orientation and helping an individual who is ambiguous as a result of disturbed family object relations into mature heterosexual orientation.[142]

Adolescents' initial gender assertions should not be accepted at face value. Exploration of gender orientation by the therapist should take place around the above issues.

GENDER CONFUSION

The DSM-IV contains a section related to gender confusion on the part of children, adolescents, and adults. Sometimes, gender confusion is mild dissatisfaction with activities and dress of one's own gender and attraction to the activities and dress of the opposite gender. This may resolve itself in the course of adolescent sexual identity formation. It may lead to cross dressing. Sometimes, the gender confusion leads to a desire for sex change operations. Adolescents with whom I have worked, who identify with the opposite sex either through dressing or through internal emotional process, have often experienced severe abuse in early childhood. Fathers who are aggressively driven, violent, or drug dependent will scapegoat a male child with verbal, emotional, and physical abuse. In this troubled sea of aggression and violence, the child finds warmth, nurture, love, and positive things only in the mother. Many young males have trouble developing a normal male identification with the violent father who serves as a role model for maleness. Consequently, the gender identification with the mother creates a desire to be more like the mother than the father, resulting in a desire to be female rather than male. Gender confusion is one of several possible outcomes of this family pattern. Many therapists choose to leave this issue alone. I have found that long, patient work on the abuse and the family issues allows the gender-confused patient to reach acceptance of his own physical gender and to define a comfortable identity and behavior style with his physical gender. I recommend pursuing this slow, patient course rather than early foreclosure and movement toward sex-change surgery.

DELAY OF INITIAL SEXUAL ACTIVITY

Healthy development of personal identity, sexual identity, social skills, and self-esteem is best served by delaying initial sexual intercourse as long as possible into the late teens or early 20's. Blos suggests that early sexual intercourse causes developmental problems for adolescents.[143] Early sexual activity may involve several different traps that result in foreclosure of adult sexual identity and intimacy. Our experiment with adolescent sexual freedom has been a disaster. Diseases, early pregnancies, and unhealthy development have followed. It is time to recognize our failure and change our expectations about teens and sex. Adult constraints, such as discussion and education as well as limit-setting in dating activities, can make a difference. Our kids deserve the chance for healthy adult intimacy and sexuality.

TREATMENT

Treatment related to sexual issues is divided into a number of different approaches depending on the primary problem.

First, dealing with adolescents who are sexually acting out, that is, engaging in compulsive and/or dangerous sexual behavior, often requires primary treatment for drug and alcohol use, which disturbs the ability of the cognitive processes of the brain to control behavior. No effective therapy with sexual acting out will take place until the drug and alcohol dependence has been resolved.

Second, adolescents who are promiscuous or compulsive about sex should be helped into an abstinence period in which there is no sexual activity while they sort out their own sexual identity and the results of their sexual behavior. Then they need to construct a value system related to sexuality and intimacy. My experience is that, as long as the individual is involved sexually, it is difficult to think therapeutically about the issues. Also, promiscuous teens should be referred to a physician for examination and screening for sexually transmitted diseases, including herpes, chlamydia, gonorrhea, syphilis, human papilloma virus, HIV infection, and possibly hepatitis B (HBV).[144]

Third, for those individuals who have been sexually abused, whether they are highly sexualized or sexually phobic, the abuse issue needs to be addressed. Treatment for sexually abused adolescents begins with the development of a trusting, secure relationship with the therapist. Safety and security are necessary for the sexually abused patient to begin disclosing and dealing with issues. The therapist who suspects sexual abuse, given behavioral and affective symptoms, should gently pursue the possibility of childhood and/or early adolescent sexual abuse. If abuse is disclosed, the therapist needs to explore the adolescent patient's willingness to deal with the issue. Once the teen makes the commitment to explore the issue, abreactive work begins. Abreactive work focuses on reprocessing the events of abuse with feelings. Reexperiencing the overwhelming affective experience of the abusive event is necessary in order to detoxify it so it can drift into the past. The terrifying feelings of these events make it necessary for the patient to have containment strategies and safety devices for use during abreaction. The therapist helps the patient develop a fantasy of a safe place to retreat or a safe area of the therapist's office. Abreactive work should be modulated to a pace that the patient can handle. This work may go on for some months until all of the significant events of abuse are dealt with, experienced, and resolved. At the end of abreactive work, defective beliefs and cognitions about self and sexuality are explored in order to develop reality-based and healthy beliefs. The therapist works with the adolescent patient to develop healthy sexual behavior in the present, including boundaries that help the sexually compulsive patient not act out and the phobic patient to experience normal human sexuality. Finally, the therapist works with the adolescent patient to repair damage in related developmental areas such as identity, family relationships, social relationships, and education and career trajectory.

If abuse is current, the therapist must take appropriate action to stop the abuse and develop protection for the adolescent. Also, a moratorium on all sexual activities is an important condition for effective therapy.

While not a universal rule, gender of the therapist may be important. Adolescent females tend to be self-conscious about their bodies and sexuality and extremely self-conscious about issues related to sexual behavior. A female therapist may be necessary in order to provide sufficient safety and security for pursuit of incest and sexual abuse issues.

For those counselors and therapists who have not had experience in this area, it is important to refer the patient to a therapist who is experienced in sexual abuse therapy. If a referral is not possible, then you should proceed carefully, cautiously, and under the supervision of a therapist experienced in this field.

Fourth, for all sexually compulsive patients, not only is a moratorium on sexual activity necessary, but often attendance at one of the 12-step groups for sexual addiction is helpful. For some adolescent patients who are so compulsive that they are unable to stop acting out, it may be necessary for them to go into a program that treats sexuality as an addiction. A structured program will help them stop compulsive behaviors (see Treatment References below).

Fifth, potential homosexuality or bisexuality should be explored in a calm, gentle, nonjudgmental way. For many adolescents, their supposed orientation is based on a developmental lag, lack of knowledge, and/or a seduction experience. The therapist, in helping them sort out the beginnings of their homosexual or bisexual experience, may be able to help them reach resolution about same-gender sexuality. Many young people are pushed into homosexual identification based on confusion about a developmental lag or seduction experiences.

Sixth, for gender confusion, again, gentle work around the origins of gender identity and early childhood abuse may be helpful. Identification with an opposite-sex parent in early childhood because of revulsion toward a same-sex parent is usually the foundation of gender confusion. Sexual abuse and biological predisposition may also be factors.[145] Gentle work with origin, as well as help finding same-sex persons who are not so threatening, is helpful for role model purposes.

Seventh, stopping sexual activity and returning to the earlier developmental task of building intimacy is the foundation of good therapy for sexually troubled adolescents.

SUGGESTED READINGS

Black, Claudia, *Double Duty: Sexually Abused*, New York: Ballantine Books, 1990.
  Claudia Black, a well-known codependency therapist, makes real sense out of early sexual abuse experiences and the results in the life of the abused person.

Carnes, Patrick, *Out of the Shadows*, Minneapolis: CompCare Press, 1983.
  This is the first book defining sexual addiction and suggesting a 12-Step approach. It is good, readable material.

Carnes, Patrick, *Contrary to Love*, Minneapolis: CompCare, 1989.
  In this subsequent book, Carnes suggests techniques of therapeutic work with a sexual addict.

Courtois, Christine A., *Healing the Incest Wound: Adult Survivors in Therapy*, New York: W. W. Norton, 1988.
  Courtois writes a comprehensive book on incest and its treatment, includ-

ing references to the work of most significant researchers and treatment theorists in the field.

James, Beverly, *Treating Traumatized Children: New Insights and Creative Interventions*, Lexington: Lexington Books, 1989.
This is an excellent practical book on treatment techniques for children who have experienced trauma due to natural catastrophe, accident, surgery, physical abuse, and sexual abuse. The author does refer to adolescents often in the book, which gives excellent treatment suggestions for experienced clinicians dealing with young traumatized patients.

Maltz, Wendy, *Sexual Healing Journey: A Guide for Survivors of Sexual Abuse*, New York: Harper Perennial, 1991.
Maltz, originally a sex therapist, writes a book about her techniques for helping abused individuals return to satisfying sexual behavior and relationships.

Sugar, Max, *Atypical Adolescence and Sexuality*, New York: W. W. Norton, 1990.
Sugar edits a book of contributed chapters, some of which are of real use to the therapist dealing with adolescent sexuality.

TREATMENT PROGRAMS

The following treatment programs treat adolescents for sexual trauma or compulsions. Some of them also treat other addictions as well.

Cottonwood de Tucson
P.O. Box 5087
Tucson, AZ 85703
Phone: (602) 743-0411
Length of stay: varies, approximately 35 days

KIDS of North Jersey, Inc.
P.O. Box 2455
Secaucus, NJ 07096-2455
Phone: (201) 863-0505
Length of stay: individual

Masters and Johnson Sexual Therapy Center
1525 River Oaks Road W.
Harahan, LA 70123
Phone: (800) 733-3242
Length of stay: adolescents: 6 weeks; adults: 4-6 weeks

Southwood Adolescent Services
330 Moss Street, Chula Vista
San Diego, CA 92011
Phone: (800) 544-2673, (619) 426-6310
Length of stay: varies, 3 days to 3 weeks acute care, then day treatment, outpatient treatment, or residential treatment for 2 weeks to 6 months

The following treatment programs treat young and older adults for sexual trauma or compulsions. Some of them also treat other addictions.

Cottonwood de Albuquerque
P.O. Box 1270
Los Lumas, NM 87031
Phone: (505) 865-3345
Length of stay: varies, approximately
30 days

River Oaks Psychiatric Hospital
1525 River Oaks Road W.
Harahan, LA 70123
Phone: (800) 733-3242
Length of stay: average is 4 weeks

Sierra Tucson
16500 North Lago del Oro Parkway
Tucson, AZ 85737
Phone: (800) 624-9001
Length of stay: 5-30 days

Chapter 9

Family

Adolescent development takes place within the context of family development. A number of family theorists and family therapists see the life of a family as a developmental trajectory. Lee Combrinck-Graham suggests that family life is actually a spiral in which the continuum is various generations going through the seminal events of human life and family life. Combrinck-Graham sees those seminal events as (1) childbirth, (2) middle years of childhood, (3) adolescence, (4) courtship/marriage, (5) childbearing, (6) settling down, (7) 40's reevaluation, (8) middle adulthood, (9) grandparenthood, (10) plan for retirement, (11) retirement, and (12) late adulthood.[146]

Betty Carter and Monica McGoldrick see the stages as (1) leaving home: single young adults (a valuable addition to the staging of family development), (2) the joining of families through marriage, (3) families with young children, (4) families with adolescents, (5) launching children and moving on, and (6) families in later life.[147] Death should be added as a stage.

I would suggest that the family development process is a spiral of at least three parallel lines that interact with each other through the forward moving process. Each of the lines represents a generation of the family. For example, the senior line would become grandparents at the time that childbearing occurs in the middle line and birth occurs for the youngest generation. Which events are parallel will depend upon some decision-making at adult family levels as well as the timing of births. For example, adolescence for the youngest generation might occur at the reevaluation stage in the middle generation or at a later adult life stage, depending upon the age of the parents at the birth of the child. How the three streams of the family trajectory interact affects, for example, the ability of an adolescent to go through individuation at the appropriate time. Combrinck-Graham suggests that certain events pull a family closer together, such as the birth of a child or a marriage, which brings two separate families together in the union of the couple. Other events, such as 40's reevaluation and launching of the younger generation, would have the effect of pulling away from the center of the family. The first effect, pulling to the center, is referred to as centripetal. The distancing and pulling outward is referred to as centrifugal.[148]

Taking into account the direction of certain developmental

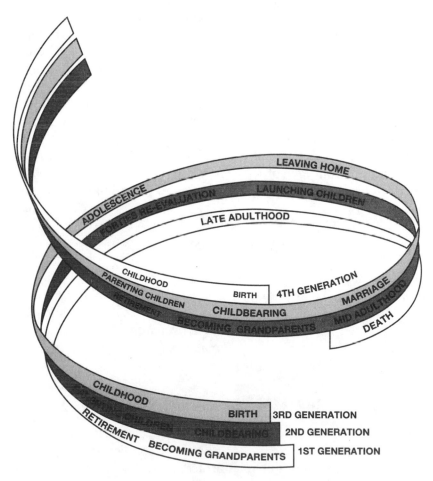

Figure 9.1 Family Development Trajectory

events, those events may work together in a complementary fashion. For example, parents who are still rooted in family building and family maintenance serve as a secure pad for adolescents in the launching stage. Adolescents vacillate back and forth between the need for distance from the family and the need to come rushing back for family support to deal with growing up issues. If, on the other hand, one or both parents is in the midlife reevaluation phase, which involves a very self-centered introspective stance, the launching is not so secure, since the parent is distancing at the same time that the adolescent is going through the distancing/closeness vacillation of growing up.

Other events, such as divorce and remarriage, which may occur at any place along the parental and grandparental trajectories, may affect the substages of adolescence in a variety of ways. Untimely parental or grandparental death will also have an effect on the trajectory of the youngest generation in adolescent and launching stages.

To summarize, adolescent development takes place within the framework of a changing family. Family development is like a spiral with three generations growing and developing in parallel interaction with each other, sometimes pulling closer, sometimes pulling further away from each other, depending upon the particular phase of development that each generation is going through at the moment.

FAMILY CONFLICT

Some teenagers go through the adolescent passage with minimal family conflict. These young people tend to handle their distancing from family in quiet and cooperative, as opposed to overt and conflictual, ways. They are always cited by parents as a pleasure in comparison with other teens who make family life misery during the adolescent years.

NORMAL FAMILY CONFLICT

A second group of teens, still on a normal developmental trajectory, go through adolescence with healthy family conflict. First, they produce conflict in a series of small irritating ways over curfew limits, use of the family car, hairstyles, dress, and other day-to-day issues.

PREADOLESCENCE		• Close and open
A D O L E S C E N C E	Withdrawal	• Gravitation to peers • Secrets • Closed doors
	Isolation	• Life with peers away from family • Conflicts over privacy
	Reentry	• Initiation of family participation in new adult role
PSEUDOADULTHOOD		• Ambiguous family relationship
TRUE ADULTHOOD		• Relation to family as autonomous adult

Figure 9.2 Family Relationship

They use these issues to distance themselves from the mass ego of the family as part of their withdrawal phase.

Second, this group of teens use conflictual dialogue as a technique for defining self in the individuation process. Conflictual dialogue is typical of more verbal, outgoing teens. Arguing over moral values, religious issues, dress, music, politics, and a variety of other issues helps these teens develop their own positions on issues and their own identity as separate from the family.

Teens in this group, notwithstanding the difficulty and irritation for parents, are on a healthy pathway toward adulthood. Their disagreement and debate form the basis for subsequent synthesis of the family's values and their own independently developed values.

Unhealthy Conflict

Unfortunately, there is still another group of teens who go through the adolescent passage or get stuck in the passage. This group tends to be conflictually involved with family in a pathological way. Pathology is defined as crossing a line between healthy conflict and unhealthy conflict. Unhealthy conflict is family conflict that produces serious problems in one or more areas of the developing adolescent's life.

SOURCES OF FAMILY CONFLICT

Family Systems Conflict

A series of family systems issues may cause conflict beyond healthy boundaries. These conflicts may arise as a result of individual issues in the family or systems problems in the family.

One common source of family conflict is the attempt by a panicky parent to overrestrict the last child in the family. A mother whose identity is solely wrapped up in parenting may experience growing anxiety as the last child begins the withdrawal phase. The healthy withdrawal of the teen proposes loss of role and esteem for the mother. The mother will react by overrestricting, finding problems with the child, and overnurturing. This attempt to maintain enmeshment causes the child to increase the intensity of withdrawal and distancing.

A second profile of family conflict occurs when the teen is scapegoated by the family system. In this case, another pathological problem exists within the family. The problem is sufficiently threatening to the family that denial is necessary. Denial brings with it misdirecting of blame to another individual in the family, in this case a teenage family "scapegoat."

Another troubled family system is one in which there is a practicing alcohol or drug dependent individual. The very nature of chemical dependency means unpredictable behavior on the part of the user and, therefore, instability in family relationships and a high level of anxiety on the part of each family member. This family profile is likely to produce ongoing conflict between various family members around attempts to control the alcoholic by manipulative behavior. Teens are often blamed for not being quiet enough or for not swallowing their own issues in an attempt to please the user.

Birth order of both parents and children may result in conflict. Gender and rank (birth order) are factors. Toman describes two types of relationships. One is *identification* between two individuals who share the same or similar roles. Second is *complementation* where the roles involve interactive fit, for example, an older sister who has nurturing and leadership traits with a younger brother who is in a baby role. Fewer than three years between siblings may involve competitive conflict, particularly between same-sex individuals. More than three years between siblings tends to produce more complementary roles. Parents' sibling role may affect their relationship with their children. For example, a parent with no opposite-sex siblings may have difficulty relating to an opposite-sex child.[149]

Problem alliances between a child and one parent are sources of family conflict. For whatever reason, one parent distances from the parent-couple dyad, and forms a close, almost couple-like, relationship with a child. This inappropriate parent-child enmeshment provokes conflict between the child and other siblings and between the child and the excluded parent.

Several sources of family conflict relate to the high level of divorce and remarriage in American society. Divorce and the breakup of a family represent a loss to many adolescents, with an ensuing period of mourning and grief. The neediness of a newly single parent may conflict with the teenager's need to distance from the family. Often a newly single mother wants to recover the fun and excitement of the adolescent dating period. She abdicates the mother role and attempts to become a sister or friend to her teenage children. Her dress, hairstyle, slang, and behavior become more adolescent, much to their embarrassment. Her evident sexuality may produce problems and conflicts, particularly for a teenage daughter.

Remarriage often causes conflict between a teenager and the stepparent. The stepparent is seen as replacing the adolescent in closeness with the custodial parent. Unresolved with the parental split, other teens resent the stepparent replacing their absent "real parent." Single fathers tend to remarry younger women. This presents another conflict for the adolescent for whom the new wife is almost a peer. In addition, the existence of divorced parents with new partners brings with it intense loyalty conflicts. Stepfamilies offer difficulty for the children who must adapt to new step-siblings.[150]

Finally, some parents, responding to the cultural emphasis put on adolescents as being mature, expect to be freed from the constraints of parental responsibility when their last child reaches his teens. This expectation of freedom from parenting duties results in much disappointment as their adolescent children hit snags and difficulties along the path to adulthood. Teens in this situation will often cause crises in order to provoke the security of parental supervision and responsibility.

Developmental Problems

Adolescents with developmental problems may be a source of conflict for the family. Learning disabilities, both detected and undetected, may cause conflict between the adolescent and parents or between parents. Early and late blooming may be the subject of family conflict between the adolescent and siblings, between the adolescent and parents, or between the parents.

Parent Loss

Rutter et al. document the difficulty for adolescents who have lost a parent some time during their childhood or early adolescence to divorce, death, or imprisonment.[151] The effect is more profound the younger the child is at the time of loss. In addition, lowered income, parental absence due to the necessity for the remaining parent to work, and potential institutionalization of the children all add up to serious problems for teens.

Adoption Issues

Adoption issues may give rise to conflict during the adolescent period. In my own clinical experience, there are two pathways for adopted adolescents. Some adolescents I have seen in treatment as patients, or as siblings of the primary patient, have no issues related to adoption. They view the adopted parents as their only parents, have bonded with them, and have no desire to pursue natural parents.

A second group, however, have an urgent desire to resolve their identity by finding natural parents, in particular the mother. Often, the pursuit of the natural mother is a fantasy kind of solution to current problems in their own life. This desire to resolve family issues produces a tendency to remain "in family" as opposed to normal and healthy distancing as a prerequisite for individualization and adult independence.

Maughan and Pickles, in reviewing studies on adopted children, find that adopted boys may be more vulnerable to difficulty than girls, and that early infant adoptees seem to have lower rates of difficulty than other children from similar birth circumstances.[152]

In KIDS of North Jersey and previous clinical experience, I have seen a larger percentage of adopted children as patients than occurs in the general population. This suggests that issues related to adoption are sufficiently troubling for some adolescents that they move onto the pathway of problem behaviors, including drug/alcohol use, sexual precocity, delinquency, and violent behavior.

Substance Use

Common to many substance users are high levels of family conflict. A difference in values about drinking and drug use, as well as other antisocial behaviors that seem to arise in correlation with adolescent drug and alcohol dependence, cause escalating family conflict. Attempts by parents to supervise and control teens in response to their increasingly troubled behaviors lead to high levels of conflict. The conflict may escalate from argument and defiance to violence, initiated either by parent or troubled teen.

Codependency

Allied to the substance use problem is the issue of "codependency." Codependency is the term used in the substance abuse field to describe reactive family disorder to a primary alcohol or substance dependent individual. Reactive disorder means disturbed emotions, behavior, and cognition as a result of family system adaptation to the user. In Chapter 14, I will describe the roles that children often use to cope with chemical dependency in a family. Those roles in themselves may produce various forms of family conflict.

Many codependent young people develop anger or rage, not only toward the primary user, but also toward the enabling parent. The enabling parent, preoccupied with the user, is not available to others in the family. Some adolescents carry rigidified codependency roles and anger toward the using parent or the enabling parent into adulthood. This continuing reference to family of origin may produce dysfunction in adult life.

A number of codependency groups propose to deal with this

issue, either from a 12-step perspective or other viewpoint. As long as the group assists the individual in facing his or her issues with an alcoholic family of origin, it is helpful. Sometimes the groups meet the need of angry individuals for a peer group to restimulate anger toward a parent. This reinforces the stuck position of the individual in his or her codependency role.

Codependency also involves loss of one or both parents for developmental purposes. This loss needs to be acknowledged and grieved. Then therapy and self-help group process becomes developmental "reparenting."

Problem Peer Group

Some adolescents cross the line from normal to pathological family conflict due to norms in a deviant peer group. This overlaps with the problem of substance use as a source of family conflict. Intensity of the peer group enmeshment as well as its anti-authority values may be a major source of conflict with parents.

RUNNING AWAY

Another phenomenon of our time is the runaway older child or adolescent. Much has been made of children who are refugees from family physical or sexual abuse. These young people certainly need institutions that provide alternative family support as well as therapy for their abuse experiences. However, there are large numbers of other young people who run away from families in a pathological move toward withdrawal in the isolation period. This may be triggered by adolescent drug and alcohol use or some other problem behavior that produces fear of family consequences. [153] Before allying with the runaway, therapists should be careful to discover the true nature of the problem. Therapists need to discover the profile of the family and its willingness to deal with the troubled adolescent. Quick closure in labeling the family may avoid the strongest resource for dealing with the troubled youth.

PARENTING AND FAMILY STRENGTH

With reference to the research cited in Chapter 5, McCord documents the fact that the presence of a strong, caring, parental figure provides stability for adolescents going through the developmental period in a highly stressed family.[154] This research is suggestive of the importance of strengthening parenting for adolescents involved in conflict with family and a troubled developmental pathway.

Maccoby and Martin have developed a paradigm of effective parenting style as it affects the trajectories of adolescents growing up. They find three parenting styles to be less effective or harmful. *Authoritarian* parenting, which involves strict rules and harsh consequences without discussion or explanation, is one harmful method. Second, *indulgent* parenting, tending to spoil children and clean up the consequences of their behavior, is another form of nonhelpful parenting. Third, some parents, preoccupied with their own lives, show *indifference* to their children.

The style that appears to be most helpful to children and adolescents in the developmental process is called *authoritative* by Maccoby and Martin. Authoritative means structured rules that are sensible, explained to children by parents, and enforced in a consistent nondiscriminatory way. This approach to parenting involves intelligent explanation of the reasons for rules as well as reasonable enforcement.[155]

This research suggests that the therapist needs to diagnose the parenting style of the family. Then, family therapy would include assisting parents to change parenting styles from one of the three harmful approaches to the authoritative approach.

TREATMENT

Family treatment is clearly the recommended mode of therapy for family conflict. The only exception would be adolescent patients exhibiting the clustered behaviors of drug/alcohol use, sexual promiscuity, delinquency, and violent or aggressive acting out. These individuals often require intensive, long-term treatment, in addition to family therapy.

One of the major reasons for family therapy is that, notwithstanding peer affiliation, the family remains a major influence throughout adolescence. The fact of family influence requires that the family be involved in the therapeutic process. Murray Bowen suggested that family therapy may take place in a variety of forms. The preferred modality is to see the entire family in weekly sessions. Participation in a family therapy group may be also helpful. In the absence of the ability to see the entire family, Bowen suggested that family therapy is possible with a partial family, that is, those family members who are willing to participate in treatment. It is important to see the teenager and other family members, parents or siblings, who are the source of primary family conflict. Finally, Bowen stated that therapy is possible with an individual from a family systems perspective. You may be able to deal with family issues in an efficacious way with only the individual as long as your perspective is that individual's interaction in the system. [156] This means discovering the patient's role and interaction patterns in the family and helping the patient to be aware of system issues.

Collect as much information as possible about the ages and situations of parents and grandparents of the primary patient. Then, construct a spiral diagram of three parallel lines, one for each generation of the family. Locate the major stages of development for each generation in relation to the other two. This will provide a visual reference of the family context of your adolescent patient.

Family therapy about conflict must preserve the individuation process for the adolescent. Work should focus on learning to resolve conflicts in constructive ways. The therapist needs to be careful not to ally with parents to reduce the adolescent to preadolescent or child status in the family. Also, the therapist should not ally with the adolescent against the family. This would increase conflict and support the adolescent's unrealistic fantasies about independence.

SUGGESTED READINGS

Carter, Betty, and McGoldrick, Monica (Eds.), *The Changing Family Life Cycle: a Framework for Family Therapy* (2nd ed.), Boston: Allyn & Bacon, 1989.
This is an extensive edited volume with a number of important theoretical concepts and practical suggestions for family therapy in the context of family development. Chapters on "Transformation of the Family System in Adolescence" and "Launching Children and Moving On" are particularly helpful.

Napier, Augustus Y. with Whitaker, Carl A., *The Family Crucible*, Toronto: Bantam Books, 1980.
This is an excellent description of therapy with a single family by Napier and Whitaker. The principles of family therapy are described between transcripts of sessions.

Visher, Emily B., and Visher, John S., *Step-Families: A Guide to Working With Stepparents & Stepchildren*, New York: Brunner/Mazel, Publishers, 1979.

This is an excellent and highly practical approach to working with stepfamilies including parents and children. It includes a number of specific strategies and techniques.

For therapists interested in pursuing family therapy, the following authors are recommended:
Salvador Minuchin
Jay Haley
Carl Whitaker
Murray Bowen

Chapter 10

Social Relations

Much to the frustration of parents and other adults, early teenagers appear to be totally self-centered. A higher level of neurological self-awareness is one source of self-preoccupation. The growth spurt, involving exaggerated feet, hands, ankles, elbows, and nose, as well as developing sexual characteristics, also contributes to pre-occupation with self. One of the major themes of adolescence is developing social relationships and adult social skills.

FROM EGOCENTRIC TO SOCIOCENTRIC ORIENTATION

David Elkind suggests that, as cognitive development occurs through the Piagetian stages, the nature of self-awareness and egocentrism changes. Higher egocentrism is a developmental process of decentering. [157]

Elkind goes on to outline stages of egocentrism related to cognition:

1. sensorimotor egocentrism (birth to age 2)
2. preoperational egocentrism (age 2–6)
3. concrete operational egocentrism (age 7–11)
4. adolescent egocentrism (age 11 to adulthood) [158]

Early adolescents are focused on their own behavior, body changes, and physical appearance. The early adolescent feels that others, particularly peers, are watching and are as critical, con-cerned, and admiring as himself ("an imaginary audience"). [159]

Arnold Gesell describes diminishing self-awareness in the six-teenth year on the part of males and females. He sees the 16-year-old adolescent as more willing to see another's point of view. [160]

This interest in others' view of self is the beginning of a more sociocentric orientation. Others' opinions are more important. Now, social reality is perceived.

USE OF PEER GROUP FOR SELF-EVALUATION

While the early adolescent has a general self-focus and performs to "an imaginary audience," she tends to use the peer group as a social form of self-evaluation. The importance of others in evaluation of self is the beginning movement toward significant adult social inter-

PREADOLESCENCE		• Special friend (same sex)
A D O L E S C E N C E	Withdrawal	• Adolescent egocentrism • Same sex peer groups as "audience" for self
	Isolation	• Mixed groups • Special relationships (opposite sex)
	Reentry	• Intimate relationship • Organized group activities
PSEUDOADULTHOOD		• Adult social relationships
TRUE ADULTHOOD		• Social responsibility

Figure 10.1 Social Maturation

action.[161] This focus on peer group as a standard for self-evaluation is part of the isolation period, during which the adolescent sees self as other than part of the family mass ego. Social importance of a group is a developmental milestone on the way to adult interdependence.

PREADOLESCENT SPECIAL FRIEND

Sullivan suggests that the first step toward adult relationships is the development of a special same-sex friend during the preadolescent period.[162] Not only is this preparation for later opposite-sex intimacy, but it provides learning about the nature of special social relationships in adult life. Later friendships are based on the learning done during the preadolescent period with a special friend and continued into early adolescence with same-sex friends.

PEER INTERACTION AND JUSTICE

During the isolation period, the peer group becomes increasingly important. The adolescent identifies with a particular peer group, including slang, dress, and hairstyle, as well as interest in music, extracurricular activities, and other middle adolescent pursuits. This experience with strong group identification is an important process in terms of learning how to interact with people outside the family.

During the same period, most adolescents develop a strong sense of comparative justice. Conflictual dialogue with parents often has to do with fair treatment as compared to treatment of friends by their parents. In addition, justice becomes an issue in comparing parent treatment of self and siblings. The concept of fairness and justice is another piece of mature social relationships.

Some adolescents become stuck in peer group dependence in middle adolescence. These young people are often involved in peer groups whose values have to do with delinquent behavior, stealing, and running away. These young people experience intense family conflict as the family attempts to protect the individual from the negative effects of his or her peer group. Peer group membership based on delinquent behavior is unhealthy foreclosure of normal adolescent social development.

PURSUIT OF INTIMACY

Early adolescent peer activity involves same-sex friends in a peer group. These same-sex friends offer a sounding board for a series of issues in which peer influence is more important than parent influence. These included sexual information, hair and dress style, extracurricular activities, and other issues.

As adolescence unfolds, interest in the opposite sex leads toward mixed-sex peer groups. The mixed-sex peer groups facilitate maturation toward dating and intimate relationships.

As the adolescent approaches adulthood, the importance of peer group diminishes, leaving an intimate opposite-sex relationship and some special friendships as primary. This healthy development in socialization corresponds to the increasing individualization of the adolescent and his comfort with adult identity.

SOCIAL ROLE-TAKING

Role-taking, or experimentation, is important in a variety of arenas for the developing adolescent. As mentioned in Chapter 6 on "Identity," role experimentation contributes to the development of adult identity. Role-taking or experimentation is part of learning social relationship. Not only does the adolescent experiment with deliberately constructed roles in the same-sex peer group during early adolescence, but he also experiments with roles in mixed groups and dating. Finally, the adolescent experiments with role-taking as a member of a variety of adolescent social groups and activities. Selman describes these in a variety of domains: (1) the individual concepts domain, (2) the friendship concepts domain, (3) the peer group concepts domain, and (4) the parent-child concepts domain. [163]

ORGANIZED GROUP PARTICIPATION

Learning to be part of a variety of group-based activities is another important developmental activity during adolescence. Being a student at a middle school or high school, an athletic team member, a club member, or an activities participant requires increasing ability to deal with others in structured social settings. Preparing for a driver's license examination, taking the test, and becoming a licensed driver involve another learning process about social structure and social participation. Healthy adolescence involves a variety of activities leading toward social skills for adult living in a complex society.

SOCIAL PROBLEMS

While temperament and personality development lead individual adolescents in different directions in terms of social learning and participation, healthy development requires learning basic socialization skills. Some adolescents function better in smaller interest-based peer groups with a limited number of good friends. Other adolescents do better in diverse groups. This depends on their level of extroversion/introversion.

Some individuals cross the line at either end of the extroversion/introversion continuum into pathological behavior. One type of adolescent becomes so peer group oriented that he or she fails to develop sufficient individualization as a person. This individual has difficulty being alone and is dependent on the peer group for all values. This pattern becomes more evident as the adolescent moves into middle and late adolescence.

A second pattern involves the loner, who fails to develop friendships or the ability to negotiate group participation. This individual will have difficulty later in life with the social dimension of a variety of settings necessary for adult living, including higher education and work.

Gangs

Teenage gangs are one form of pathological peer orientation during the isolation period. Although gangs are spreading to small cities and suburbs and among white males, they are more frequent in large cities, among African-Americans and Hispanics, and among low socioeconomic status youth. Gangs represent an extreme identification with a peer group at the price of diminished family influence on behavior; the gang becomes the family. Gang members tend to begin delinquent careers at younger ages and are more violent than non-gang delinquent youth. [164]

Unfortunately, gangs are portrayed in movies, television, and even cartoons as using action and violence to solve problems rather than talk and negotiation. This promotes violence as the solution to threat. Also, this results in early foreclosure on the development of self-talk as a tool for cognitive control of behavior.

TREATMENT

Treatment for adolescents with socialization difficulties is usually individual, although group process can help some individuals learn to function in social settings. The feedback of group members can help the individual to assess and change his or her own behavior. Overly selfish individuals can learn how their behavior affects others in a group.

Loner individuals should be assisted in joining "safe groups" with reference to special interests either in or out of school. These highly activity-focused, relatively nonthreatening settings encourage the loner to begin developing socialization skills.

Some individuals have special handicaps in terms of appearance or physical limits that inhibit their participation in adolescent peer groups. Adolescent peer groups tend to exclude individuals who are "different." Again, the therapist can help the individual to accept his or her difference and to find peer settings that are not so "popularity-oriented," but are more activity-oriented. Often religious groups are less rejecting than popular school activities.

For those individuals who are peer group dependent, both family and individual therapy need to take place. The therapy in this case is focused on helping the individual to move through the group dependence process to a more mature stage of individual interests and personality. Therapy should focus on issues where the individual is uncomfortable or hurt by conforming to the peer group.

Gang members should be isolated from the gang as a necessary precondition for therapy. Therapy should focus on developing discussion as a tool for resolving conflict and self-talk as a tool for behavior control. Self-instructional training is a useful technique with these patients.

Therapy about social skills and relationships involves helping the teen to learn how to read other people's intentions and behavior. Also, it involves learning to forecast the effect of one's own behaviors on others. Recognizing the needs and rights of others is the necessary foundation for relationships. Balancing the needs of self and others is the basis of healthy interaction.

Therapy related to social skills is based in large measure on cognitive skills. The therapist needs to assess the cognitive processing level of the individual adolescent patient, and to work with the individual at the appropriate level of cognitive processing. Dealing with social issues is one arena in which the therapist can lead the patient into slightly higher levels of reasoning.

Chapter 11

Education and Vocation

David Ausubel states that "the interpersonal environment in the school impinges upon many of the developmental tasks of adolescence—emancipation from the home, the acquisition of primary status, and the achievement of greater volitional independence in dealing with adults."[165] Ausubel's point about the major function of the school as a location for adolescent development is very important. During the relative isolation period of middle adolescence, most teens use the school as a site for primary developmental tasks. They experiment with future vocational interests in the classroom and in extracurricular activities. They find peers to establish as a peer group for social development, and they use the pool of opposite-sex individuals to begin the dating and intimacy development process.

Dusek, in his textbook on adolescent development, sees two functions of the school. The first, the "maintenance-actualization function," provides a larger arena for the student to grow socially and emotionally. Second is "the skills-training/cultural-transmission function" of the school. In this case, he is talking about the primary teaching/learning tasks of schools and the related transmission of cultural values and rules.[166] Of late, the political pressure on schools to become neutral in terms of moral values has gutted the schools' cultural-transmission program. Instead of serving as a surrogate mentor or trainer during the isolation period for those skills necessary to function as an adult in the society, the school has become a neutral giver of facts and information. As a result, we see many adolescents ending the isolation period and reentering family and society as adults without adequate preparation in the rules of adult behavior in society.

School Problems

Many experts cite the elementary to middle or junior high school transition as problematic for preadolescents; they point to the junior high to high school transition as another point of potential developmental difficulty. In both cases, the "late bloomer" may be ill prepared physiologically and socially to enter the more complex school institution and the older age group. A variety of problems occur, including fear of peer contact, difficulty with learning, and often a desire not to attend school. Another problem may be inability to connect with a peer group, causing social isolation and loneliness.

School Fit

Jacquelynne Eccles and her colleagues suggest person-environment fit problems where the characteristics of the individual and the particular school do not fit. Junior high school usually introduces a change in size of socialization group, expectation of student initiative, class size, discipline, teaching style, and participation expectation. These changes may not fit the developmental status of the individual adolescent.[167]

Attendance and Motivation

Attendance and motivation is a problem for some students after transition to a higher level school. Current lack of attendance controls, allied with an inability of certain adolescents to achieve efficacy in school, causes avoidance of the classroom. Some students skip selected classes. Others miss entire days. Drug and alcohol use or a delinquent peer group may be a factor in skipping school. Avoidance of homework is another sign of motivation problems. Sometimes developmental lags, learning disabilities, or information gaps cause adolescents great frustration in a learning environment.

Cheating

Cheating has become commonplace in middle, junior high, and high schools. According to Kiell, "cheating is an infantile manipulative level of adaptation to the environment."[168] Most adolescents in America accept cheating as a fairly normal school practice. Occasionally, individual students are caught by teachers who are serious about learning as opposed to simply passing.

Behavior Problems

Other students run afoul of the disciplinary system of the school in terms of behavior problems. Some of the problems are violent behavior, truancy, and peer resistance to authorities of the school. Some students with learning disabilities or drug/alcohol-related cognitive deficits will act out as a defense mechanism to cover up feelings of inadequacy and shame. Behavior problems occur for a variety of reasons.

Learning Disabilities

While the concept of learning disability is widespread in American society, most parents and many therapists do not have a clear concept of the various problems. First and most important, there is no single learning disability, but many different specific types of learning disabilities. Information gaps in reading, writing, and mathematics are not learning disabilities, though they may seriously impede current grade-level performance, since they are part of the foundation for the current level of study.

Second, learning disabilities are not low intelligence. Many learning-disabled teens have high I.Q.'s, notwithstanding problems learning in one or more specific areas. The conflict involved in being intelligent, yet having trouble expressing that intelligence is painful to the individual. This is complicated by untrained people who see and react to the learning-disabled person as "stupid."

Learning disabilities involve a developmental failure in terms of specific neurologically based systems. These systems involve language, attention/concentration, mathematics, visual/spatial abilities, motor coordination, and concept formation. Many learning disabilities can be remedied if properly diagnosed and then treated with effective cognitive training.

Attention-deficit/hyperactivity disorder. DSM-IV currently defines this as a single disorder with variations. In fact, there appear to be two specific disorders involved. The ICD-9-CM, which is the accepted international diagnostic classification manual, cites two disorders, attention deficit disorder and hyperkinetic disorder. The first disorder has to do with problems in attention and concentration in which the child or adolescent cannot attend or sustain attention over a period of time. There are several theories about the specific neurological problem involved. The second is hyperactive disorder, in which the individual is overactive and therefore unable to be calm and still in group or classroom settings. Stimulant medication like Ritalin may help some hyperactive children calm down and function better in a learning situation. There is mixed opinion about use of stimulants with adolescents.

Auditory disabilities. These disabilities involve hearing and processing difficulty in receiving incoming verbal information.

Language-based disabilities. There is a great variety of language-based disabilities, some involving reading, others involving writing, and still others involving verbal communication. Dyslexia has generally been used as a term to cover a number of forms of reading disability. One group of disabilities involves the mechanics of reading. Some of these involve reversed letters, others involve scrambling of letters in words, and still others involve grammatical construction difficulties. Another disability area involves comprehension of read material. There is not one but several dyslexias. Evidence is emerging for a left-hemisphere brain impairment basis for the dyslexias.[169]

Mathematical disabilities. There are two basic learning disabilities in mathematics. One is calculation difficulty, and the other is difficulty with mathematical reasoning.

Visual/Spatial disabilities. There are a variety of disabilities in the area of visual/spatial perception. Adolescents may have a number of distorted or missing areas in visual/spatial perception, such as figure/ground discrimination difficulty, orientation of figures and letters in space and sequence.

Motor disabilities. Again, depending upon the specific motor function, there are a large number of different motor or movement problems that could underlie a learning difficulty. These include problems with mixed dominance for hand and foot preferences, and incomplete lateralization.

Learning and memory disabilities. Some kids have problems in processing, retaining, and recalling information. These disabilities may be in the verbal area, the visual area, or the motor area. Often individuals with these disabilities have contradictory Verbal I.Q. scores and Performance I.Q. scores.

When a therapist works with a patient who has school difficulties, whether behavioral or cognitive, and the therapist sees attention deficits or hyperactivity, language, motor, or other problems in counseling sessions, he should suspect a developmental disability. First, substance use must be ruled out as a possible cause of learning difficulties. Chemical insults to the brain mimic learning disabilities, such as the effect of regular marijuana use on new learning and memory. Neuropsychological evaluation is the next step in providing specific help for a learning disability.

Facilitating success in class and school activities is crucial to motivation for learning.

VOCATIONAL IDENTITY DEVELOPMENT

Related to school activities is the growing concern of the middle to late adolescent about career and career identity. One of the preparatory tasks during the isolation period is the development of skills, knowledge, and credentialing for a job. During high school, this may simply be choosing a higher education track, or a trade or vocational track. Nevertheless, it is an important concern of most high school students.

Figure 11.1 describes vocational identity development in the phases of adolescence.

There appear to be a variety of influences on middle adolescents in career track choice. First and probably most important is the influence of the family, including the kinds of jobs and careers it values. "Early foreclosure" in terms of carrying a family mantle — a specific profession, job, or business — may cause serious developmental difficulties for some adolescents.

Second is gender influence. For many adolescents, the appropriateness of various career tracks for males and females remains an influence. However, in recent decades, change in female access to a number of vocations has opened the door for many teenage girls. This has been a positive influence in terms of wider career choices for American adolescent females. Some girls, however, still feel conflicted between a future mother role and excitement about a particular career track.

PREADOLESCENCE		• School for itself • Imaginary vocational goals
A D O L E S C E N C E	Withdrawal	• School for itself • Vocational goals based on distancing adolescent culture
	Isolation	• Specific subject competency at school • Beginning of serious vocational exploration
	Reentry	• Choice about educational track • Preliminary choice of vocation
PSEUDOADULTHOOD		• Completion of educational preparation OR • First job
TRUE ADULTHOOD		• First career job

Figure 11.1 Educational/Vocational Development

Peers, while not as influential as parents, are a factor for many adolescents making vocational choices. More dependent teens will follow perceived peer leaders in certain vocational tracks. Others will steer away from desirable career tracks because of a negative attitude by their peer group. Peer influence, however, is not a determining factor, but rather an influencing one.

Most adolescents experiment with areas of career interest in school classes, extracurricular activities, and part-time jobs and activities. Some work experiences open to high school students offer no more that supplementary income. However, some high school students are able to connect with business or professional ventures that allow them to experience and experiment with that professional or vocational role.

A good example of an outside school activity offering a chance to explore a vocation is a nursing-trainee program for teenagers in Cherry Hill, New Jersey. The program trains and employs 16 students from eight South New Jersey high schools and two community colleges as certified nursing assistants. These students take a 90-hour preparatory course, half in the classroom and half in clinical experience. They then are employed up to 24 hours per week at minimum wage as health-care workers in nursing homes in the area. Not only do they supplement the existing staff, but they have an opportunity to explore nursing and health-care related professions. The training program is known as "TNT, Teen Nursing Trainees."[170] Counselors who work with adolescents need to have a number of resources like the TNT program as potential job role-taking experiences for teenage patients.

For those teenagers who connect with mentors, either teachers in school, activities sponsors, or bosses on part-time jobs, the mentor influence can be very important in looking toward a future career. The commitment and excitement of the mentor about the job, as well his or her willingness to steer the teen into a preparatory track, are most helpful.

Unfortunately, many teens drift through the isolation period with little or no idea about future career. They are unable to connect with an area of excitement or interest in which they can develop competencies. As they approach adulthood, panic sets in. This panic may result in indifference toward school and a period of lethargy at home. These particular teens need help in exploring their interests and learning how to experiment with interests as preparation for adult employment.

EVALUATION

When a therapist discovers learning-related problems, expert evaluation is critically important. A variety of evaluation protocols are available. If the problem appears to be hearing or oral language, a speech/audiological evaluation by a specialist is in order. If the problem appears to be in another learning area, evaluation by a learning disability specialist is needed. This may take place privately, since there are many fine learning disability practitioners and clinics available to families in almost every American community. Many schools have relatively expert child study teams comprised of a school psychologist, a school social worker, a learning disability specialist, a consulting neurologist, a consulting psychiatrist, and a speech/audiologist. Evaluations by these groups are mixed, but this may be the preferred route for families with limited resources.

A higher level of evaluation is a work-up by a neuropsychologist. A neuropsychologist will use an initial screen to determine cognitive and performance areas of dysfunction. After determining general areas of dysfunction, the neuropsychologist pursues specific cognitive and behavioral problems through very specific instruments.

TREATMENT

The therapist has a variety of roles in treating individuals with school and vocational problems. Assurance and information for primary patients and parents is the foundation for dealing with learning, school, and vocational choice-related problems. Often, the therapist serves as a general practitioner using a variety of specialist referral resources for testing and evaluation for specific kinds of treatment. For example, vocational testing may be used as a way to assist a confused adolescent in considering career options. The therapist may continue general work in helping a teenager resolve school problems while using a learning disability specialist for specific remediation of a deficit.

Behavior and authority problems may be addressed with a cognitive-behavioral approach. The adolescent is helped to accept the facts of a system and its rules. Then, he or she is helped to learn problem-solving techniques, to try alternative behaviors, and to assess their outcomes.

The goal is to help the teenager reach a competent level of performance at school and a foundation for adult skills in general living and then a specific job or career.

Part III

Developmental
Traps

Chapter 12

Violence

A while ago, I visited a New York middle school in order to talk to two classes about adolescent drug abuse. While I knew about metal detectors at the entries of many urban schools in America, it was different to experience it personally for the first time. Metal detectors have entered the public schools as an attempt to deal with growing violence by guns, knives, and other weapons in our schools.

We continue to see on television and read in the newspapers about elementary, middle, and high school kids who shoot teachers, knife peers, and otherwise engage in promiscuous violence. Growing-up has become a "dangerous ordeal" for many American young people.

Many of us dismiss the headline stories as events that happen to other people in other communities. Recently, however, a high school student in Pinellas Park, Florida, near my original home, walked into school and shot the principal. Pinellas Park is a small, generally middle- and working-class community on the west coast of Florida. It is far removed from the great urban centers of America, which are normally characterized as violent. Violence has become part of the daily currency of growing up in America.

STATISTICS ON VIOLENCE

Among major developed nations in the world, the United States leads the world in homicide rates for young men aged 15 to 24. In 1987, the United States had 21.9 killings per 100,000 men between 15 and 24. The second highest rated nation was Scotland with 5.0 per 100,000.[171] Handguns are a major problem in homicides in America. Again, we led the world in 1985, and since, with 8,092 handgun deaths, as opposed to Japan, with 46.[172] Our cities have the highest rate; according to 1988 statistics, Detroit led the nation with 68.6 homicides per 100,000, followed by Washington, D.C., with 60.0 homicides per 100,000.[173] A 1990 national crime survey report found close to 1.2 million violent crimes had been committed against adolescents that were not reported.[174] In 1990, Christoffel reported that 12- to 19-year-old males experienced violent crime at a rate of 80 per 1,000, nearly double that of female rates.[175]

If the above numbers about violence were not sad enough, in 1991, a survey of the elite of our high school young people conducted annually by Who's Who Among American High School Students found that 33% of the male students in this group had access to handguns. Of these students, 41% have been exposed to a violent incident at their school, and 45% of these young people know someone who has brought a weapon to school.[176] Violence threatens the life, not only of the troubled student and the average student, but also of the high achiever.

VIOLENCE: NOT EQUAL OPPORTUNITY

The facts about violence and teenagers in America show that this is not an equal opportunity problem. First and foremost, young American males are far more vulnerable to violence and death as a result of violence than are females. As a matter of fact, the indications are that the violent crime rate experienced by males is at least double that of females.[177] A second fact is that minority males are more subject to violence and death as a result of violence than are white males. For instance, the homicide rate for white males aged 15 to 19 was 9 per 100,000, as compared to the rate for African-American males, which was 79 per 100,000.[178] Latino males of the same age have the second highest group risk for death by violence.[179]

Finally, white females have the lowest death rate per hundred thousand. A 1991 report showed that white females in the age range of 15 to 19 had approximately 4 deaths per 100,000 as compared to African-American females with 11 per 100,000.[180]

African-American males, Hispanic males, and white males, in that order, are at risk for death by violence. In addition, the same groups rank in the same order at risk for violent episodes short of death, which may result in physical or psychological impairment as well as interruption of the development process, including educational activity. While females are not as highly at risk, white and African-American females are exposed to far more violence than should occur in a developed country. Some research suggests that when controlled for socioeconomic class, ethnic and racial differences in violent behavior almost disappear.[181]

VIOLENCE PORTRAYED

Whether it is Clint Eastwood, Chuck Norris, Arnold Schwartzenegger, or some other super hero, the final scene in many action movies shows the macho male standing with smoking guns or karate-toughened hands, with smoke clearing and bodies strewn all over the ground. The movie moment is dramatic and powerful, showing the hero with a sense of accomplishment. However, the real moment is far more sad. The adolescent male has triumphed over an enemy by violence only to find himself in a poignant moment of ruin. What follows is apprehension by authorities and the eerie feeling that always occurs when one human being has taken the life of another. The young aggressor experiences a moment that foreshadows legal trouble, jail, and ruin. His expectation of triumph is shattered by the reality of his violent act.

Therapists and counselors find themselves face to face with a growing number of young people, principally male, who are in trouble because of aggressive acts. Some are already in the criminal justice system and see us as part of dealing with trial, case disposition, or rehabilitation. Others see us at an earlier stage where their acts of violence have created difficulty for school authorities and family. Many of us approach these young patients with a sense of apprehension because of their previous aggressive acts. This chapter is designed to make sense out of teenage aggression and violence.

FIGHT OR FLIGHT

Human beings have evolved a safety or defense mechanism over thousands of years in response to living in a wild setting. An axis, involving the hypothalamus in the brain, the pituitary master gland, and the adrenal glands, goes into action in response to a perceived threat or danger. This system provides a fast and intense arousal of the body in order to fight the danger or to flee rapidly to avoid the danger. This human brain-based system was very adaptive for human beings faced with danger from carnivorous animals, who included human beings in their diet or on their list of intruders in their territory.

Today, we live in an urban society in which fighting is nonadaptive. Violence between human beings in a close living setting often sets up a long chain reaction of counterviolence by friends and families of the victim, who in turn are victims of the next round of counterviolence.

Also, many threats in modern society are more psychological than physical. Either a fight response or a flight response may be totally nonadaptive and inappropriate in the face of psychological threat. In spite of the inappropriateness, our body turns on a system that arouses us to fight or flee. This system is the basis of violence and the aggressive response on the part of many young people in our society. As a matter of fact, this particular system is more prevalent in the male, who was the defender of women and children in the group. Today, in America, we see senseless fight responses to perceived threats by our young people.

Neurological Substrate

Elliott describes in great detail the neurological or brain basis of aggression and violence. He suggests that it includes a great variety of areas in both hemispheres of the brain. The activity, which is connected to the hypothalamus, is both excitatory-arousing and inhibitory. The inhibiting mechanisms limit the excitement toward aggression from becoming more intense and violent than necessary under the circumstances. Elliott describes violence as a result of failure by the inhibiting system to control the aggressive impulse.[182]

A situation occurs that contains within it physical or psychological threat. The individual's perception of threat ignites an arousal of the brain. While the arousal is going on, the individual thinks about the situation and cognitively evaluates the meaning of the threat. If the threat is perceived as likely and imminent, the inhibiting controls of aggression are reduced in the brain, resulting in violent action toward the source of threat.

Elliott goes on to describe the three types of violence based on his neurobiologic analysis. First is "episodic dyscontrol," meaning the individual loses control and becomes violent once in a while.

The second he describes as "psychopathic," which means that the person has a continuing, psychotic behavior problem that results in violence toward others. Third, he describes "compulsive violence," which suggests an addictive type of behavior to become aggressive and violent in many settings. [183]

Violence appears to be a result of action in the brain, based on the historically developed fight or flight response to danger, and on environmental factors that influence thought and behavior with reference to threat and violence. For example, individuals whose families encourage young males to fight to defend themselves, or whose peer group is "into" violence as proof of manhood, tend to act more on perceived threats than others. [184]

BASIC CAUSES OF VIOLENCE IN YOUTH

Having worked with large numbers of young adults who have been involved in violent activity, I see two basic causes for adolescent aggression and violence. First, many adolescents act out and become violent in response to physical or psychological threat. Some kids live in a world in which physical aggression is a part of day-to-day existence, at school and on the street. They find it necessary to use violence to deal with frequent threat in their lives. Other kids psychologically perceive threat due to low-threshold paranoia. They are almost constantly suspicious of adult authority figures and peers. This results in their use of aggressive threats and acts of violence as tools for psychological self-protection.

A second source of adolescent aggression and violence is based on personal power needs. Many young men, and some young women, feel impotent in many areas of their lives. Their parents are often authoritarian and violent, their teachers insensitive, and their peers aggressive. The only technique they see as useful to defend self and to feel personally powerful is violence. Within this group that uses violence for power is a second group of young people who become hooked on the feelings of rage in connection with violence toward others. These teens literally become "violence addicts" as a result of subjective perception of a "high" in the feelings of anger and rage.

Connected with both causes of adolescent violence is impulsivity as a result of failure to develop mature cognitive control over behavior. These young people continue to respond emotionally and, therefore, impulsively, toward perceived threat or the need for personal esteem and power. The normal inhibitions on impulsivity that occur as a result of development in the prefrontal cortex and cognitive executive control over behavior appear not to develop in this group.

SUBSTANCE USE

There is a high correlation between young men who are daily drug and/or alcohol users and those who engage in violent behavior. Mood-altering substances influence violent behavior in a variety of ways. Our society contains within its cultural value system an expectancy that individuals under the influence of alcohol or drugs tend to be more impulsive, angry, and violent. In addition, there appears to be a distorted serotonin substrate underlying both alcohol and aggressive behavior. Alcohol seems to serve a disinhibiting function, allowing the intoxicated individual to behave in ways that would normally be inhibited.[185,186] On the other hand, some evidence exists that amphetamine (speed) and cocaine intoxication stimulates aggressive behavior.

Of the students surveyed in 1991 in the Who's Who Among American High School Students, 95% thought that illegal drugs were the most important cause of violence in their world. Twelve percent of these highly successful young people have personally witnessed incidents of drug-related violence at their schools.[187]

THE TYPOLOGY OF VIOLENT BEHAVIOR

There appear to be several types of violent behavior. The typology and classification system below is a heuristic one based on my own clinical experience.

First, there is *provoked* violent behavior. In this situation, physical aggression either occurs or is threatened toward the individual. The source of threat is clear and provocative.

Second, in other situations, we see individuals who become violent in *apparently unprovoked* situations. In exploring these situations with the patient, we may discover that this adolescent was provoked in ways not visible to adult authorities at school or at home. Or, we may discover that this individual cognitively perceived a threat that was not visible to others. This perceived threat may result from distorted perception or belief about the motives and/or behavior of the other person.

A third type of unprovoked violence is *truly unprovoked*. That is, the individual has acted aggressively toward someone else without any provocation. This situation usually points toward use of violence to enhance personal power. It may be an occasional power-based form of aggression, or it may be one incident in a series of violent incidents that point toward "violence addiction."

Finally, there is *intoxicated* violence, which is based upon loss of personal, cognitive, and behavioral control as a result of expectancy, chemical inhibition of behavior control, or stimulation of aggression related to intoxication by alcohol, marijuana, cocaine, or other substances.

There are alternative ways of viewing violent behavior and its motivation, including racial bias, gang violence, sexual violence, economic motives as in drug dealing, and inaccurate cognitions about other people.

NEUROPATHOLOGY

In some cases of violent acts and violent patterns for which no physical threat, psychological threat, or power need can supply an explanation, the counselor needs to look toward physical pathology. A variety of neurological conditions, including tumors, epilepsy, and head injuries through accident or previous violence, may result in damage to the inhibiting system in the brain. Insult to the prefrontal cortex often results in aggressive behavior. Fuster and others suggest

Provoked by	Aggression
	Threat
Apparently unprovoked	Invisible provocation
	Perceived threat
Truly unprovoked	Occasional power acts
	Power addicted
Intoxicated	

Figure 12.1 Typology of Violent Acts

that prefrontal insult releases the cortical inhibition of limbic system-based aggression.[188] Subcortical areas, including the septal area, the head of the caudate nucleus, the lateral amygdala, the anterior lobe of the cerebellum, and the fastigial nucleus are also involved in the aggression system. For example, stimulation of the lateral amygdala suppresses aggression.[189] While most epileptics are not violent, there appears to be an association between aggressive behavior and some cases of temporal lobe epilepsy. Interictal attacks are not uncommon.[190] The above conditions may give rise to neuropathologically based violence. In these cases, the therapist should look to the neurologist for an adequate evaluation.

VICTIMS AND WITNESSES

Perpetrators are not the only individuals involved in therapy due to violence. Victims and witnesses are also seriously traumatized. The effect of being in a situation where violence takes place, whether alone, in the family, or in a public place, produces a clinical disorder called post-traumatic stress disorder (PTSD). Conceptualization of PTSD arose around problems of Vietnam veterans. As the symptoms of the disorder became commonly accepted, it was apparent that the disorder applied to many individuals who have been the victims of or witnesses to human violence in other settings.

Symptoms include numbing, which may involve diminished interest in activities, as well as a feeling of detachment from others, and a limiting of emotional range. Another symptom is a decreased sense of having a long-term future. A third symptom is heightened arousal, resulting in sleep disturbance, hypervigilance, and an exaggerated startle response. Many PTSD patients also have repetition symptoms, such as disturbing dreams, flashbacks, and distressing recollections accompanied by intense psychological distress. This particular group of symptoms produces another symptom, fear of losing one's mind. Finally, some patients appear to have "psychogenic amnesia," which involves inability to remember certain aspects about the traumatic event or, in the case of ongoing physical or sexual abuse, loss of memory for detail and events themselves.[191] The primary symptoms of PTSD for young witnesses and victims of violence give rise to developmental pathology. Most devastating is the sense of insecurity that undermines all development. The numbing effect with loss of interest in activities affects educational development as well as identity development through role experimentation in a variety of activities. A decreased sense of having a long-term future impacts dreaming about and setting goals for adult stages of life. Heightened arousal involves health problems as well as interference with normal relationship development during adolescence.

TREATMENT

Treatment strategies are chosen based on assessing the cause of the individual's violent behavior.

First, if the violent behavior is based on perception of threat, the therapist has two choices. One is to work with the patient and family to effect a change in environment. A new environment would mean the absence of the provoking threat. In many cases, this may not be possible. A second response to threat is to develop changes in cognitive assessment of threat — that is, beliefs — followed by new behavioral responses to threat. Cognitive reappraisal of other persons' motives and behaviors is a useful technique with this type of violence. An excellent example of behavioral response change is given in Prothrow-Stith's book, in which an individual was assisted in a behavior change program to use humor as a diffusing technique. The individual used this most effectively and was able to end aggression and violence as a way of life.[192]

A second cause of violence is the personal need for power. For individuals who are using aggression toward others as a way to enhance self, they need help in discovering and using alternative sources for personal power. There are as many alternative sources for power as there are human activities in which individuals gain respect and honor. These include academic achievement at school, a variety of athletic and cultural activities, part-time work settings, and community activities, including volunteer service and political action. As a counselor, you can work with a team to explore and experiment with ways to achieve self-esteem and personal power through any of these activities.

Individuals who are addicted to "power highs" from violence need long-term addiction treatment programs (see Chapter 14).

Medication is often advocated as a therapeutic technique to control acting out by adolescents. Tranquilizers, antianxiety drugs, antidepressants, and neuroleptic drugs are all used in attempts to reduce aggressive behavior. My personal experience is that none of these drugs is therapeutically efficacious. In order to show behavior control, all of these drugs have to be raised to geometric multiples of the normal therapeutic dose. The individual is ultimately reduced to a zombie-like state, in which not only acting out is controlled, but also all other normal human activities. The patient becomes physically dysfunctional. The sad result is that the individual never deals with the primary problem underlying aggressive and violent behavior. As soon as the individual is taken off the medication, he returns to use of violence as a technique to deal with threat or to enhance personal power. I believe cognitive and behavioral interventions are the most appropriate treatment strategies for adolescent aggression and violence.

For victims and witnesses of violence, whether it is continual physical or sexual abuse or a single traumatic event, treatment is most important. Generally, treatment follows the process outlined in Chapter 8 for sexually abused patients. First, trust must be developed with the therapist, followed by willingness to work on the traumatic event or events of violence. The therapeutic work then proceeds abreactively through talking about events and details with the onset of the frightening feelings that went with the moment of trauma. A safe place or object is necessary if the abreaction becomes too intense or frightening for the patient during this process. Finally, cognitive work occurs, correcting dysfunctional and irrational beliefs that have resulted from the trauma. For individuals who have developed a phobic, high anxiety reaction to certain situations as a result of the original trauma, desensitization work may be helpful.

SUGGESTED READINGS

Feindler, Eva L., and Ecton, Randolph C., *Adolescent Anger Control: Cognitive Behavioral Techniques*, New York: Pergamon Press, 1986.
A very readable book that offers usable cognitive and behavioral techniques to help adolescents in therapy learn to control their anger and aggressive responses.

Prothrow-Stith, Deborah with Weissman, Michaele, *Deadly Consequences: How Violence Is Destroying Our Teenage Population and a Plan to Begin Solving the Problem*, New York: Harper Collins Publishers, 1991.
This book, by the former Commissioner of Public Health for the state of Massachusetts, who is now an assistant dean at the Harvard School of Public Health, is written in lay terms outlining the nature of the adolescent

violence problem with particular reference to the vulnerability of African-American males. Chapters at the end suggest formats for school programs, including several that the author personally designed.

Straus, Martha B., *Violence in the Lives of Adolescents*, New York: W. W. Norton and Company, 1994.
Straus writes primarily about adolescent victims of violence, combining case studies with helpful information about diagnosis and treatment.

Chapter 13

Suicide

The newspaper headlines read "Four Teens Take Their Lives." In the late 1980s, in Bergenfield, New Jersey, four adolescents, two boys and two girls, pulled a car into a garage, put a hose from the exhaust pipe into the car and proceeded to commit joint suicide. The community watched with horror as the postmortem delved into the lives of four young people who found life too heavy and death easier. Adolescent suicide remains a growing and frightening topic for many of us in American society.

THE NUMBERS

Over the last 14 years, a little over 30% of the 1,800 plus young people I have worked with in my treatment program and its affiliates have made one or more suicide attempts. Completed suicides for adolescents have risen from approximately 1,200 a year to 5,200 a year in the last 30 years.[193] Homicide and suicide bounce back and forth as the second and third leading causes of adolescent and young adult death. In 1988, 15.4 deaths per 100,000 in the 15- to 24-year-old age range were homicides as compared to 13.2 deaths per 100,000, which were by suicide.[194]

In addition to the formal suicide statistics, in which the death was self-inflicted, often accompanied by a note of explanation, there may be a much larger number of young suicides. There are about 100,000 one-car accidents involving 16- to 24-year-old drivers, for which there is no vehicular failure, inclement weather, or road condition explanation. These accidents result in approximately 5,000 vehicular deaths.[195] While most of these deaths are classified as accidental, so as not to further burden grieving family members, most police and medical examiners know that these deaths are suicides in which the weapon is an automobile.

The highest completed suicide rates are among young white males, but the rate for non-white males has more than doubled in the past 28 years.[196] However, the suicide attempt rate by adolescent females is approximately three times that of white males.[197] In other words, teenage girls make more suicide attempts, but teenage boys are more successful.

Firearms are the most frequent method of completed suicide for both genders. The second most common method is hanging, and the third gassing. Males use firearms and hanging more often than do females. Females use gassing and ingestion of substances more than do males. The most common method for attempted suicide is ingestion or overdose of substances, either legal or illegal.[198]

What is really scary is that 31% of high achievers in the Who's Who in American High School study considered suicide, and 5% have made suicide attempts.[199]

"Happy Days" Are Gone

What's happened to growing up in America? My generation experienced the teen years as happy days. We had a few scrapes, got into a little trouble, but we look back with fond, bittersweet memories of our growing up. While adolescents of that day in northern urban ethnic villages and southern small town ghettos experienced discrimination, injustice, and economic deprivation, there was a basic structure to growing up that did not include suicidal thinking and extreme sadness. Today, many adolescents, both male and female, African-American, white, and Hispanic, experience growing up as a sad desperate period in which death seems a welcome relief from the perilous ordeal.

Suicide and Social Control

Emile Durkheim, in *Suicide,* published in 1897, compared suicide in postindustrial societies. He suggested that certain dimensions of the society defined the suicide rate. His thesis was that the suicide rate varies inversely with external constraint. External constraint had two dimensions, integration and regulation. Lack of integration, or egoistic lifestyle, meant a lack of meaningful family ties or social relationships. Anomie was broken relationship with society as a result of economic and social adversity. Altruism represented excess integration, like in a cultic group resulting in ritual suicide, and fatalism resulted in a fourth type of suicide. [200]

While Durkheim's specific categories may not exactly apply to contemporary adolescents, his concept of a social dimension related to suicide is suggestive. First and foremost, the romanticization of adolescence, tied with an early assumption of maturity, has resulted in adolescents being cast adrift without the protection of adult guidance for the growing-up period. This lack of structure, limits, and supervision has opened the door to adolescents developing problems and behaviors resulting in dysfunction and desperation. Extreme withdrawal from family in order to pursue autonomy in adulthood is tied with the "me first" philosophy of many in our society. This expresses Durkheim's egoistic lack of meaningful family ties. The failure of the adolescent peer group, minus effective mentors to guide the adolescent into mature adulthood with effective social and economic membership in the society, is kin to Durkheim's anomie. [201] Both dimensions seem to apply to some contemporary suicides.

DIMINISHED SELF-CONTROL

One clear element in adolescent suicide is diminished self-control. Self-control may not have developed as a result of prolonged immaturity in peer group. Drug and/or alcohol use may interfere with myelinization of the prefrontal cortex, resulting in impairment of executive function. The failure of adult supervision to help the adolescent understand consequences of inappropriate behavior may contribute. Diminished self-control involves problems with delayed gratification, the ability to control troubling behaviors, and the loss of control of feelings as a result of behavioral problems. All of these add up to a situation in which the young person can become "cornered."

DESPERATION AND NOT DEPRESSION

Current standards in psychology and counseling fields state that depression is the primary cause of both suicide attempts and suicide completions. These standards add "acting out" and "rage" as special symptoms of adolescent depression. These symptoms have a neuro-chemistry of excess monoamines, while depression involves a mono-amine deficit. Having dealt with large numbers of young people who have made suicide attempts, as well as some postmortem recon-struction of successful adolescent suicides, I have not found many that qualify as real sadness-drenched, monoamine deficit cases of immobilizing depression.

More often I find a "down" or negative feeling that has an "ac-tive temper" to it. This feeling is best expressed with the word "desperation." Desperation describes someone who experiences frustration, sadness, and an element of anger as a result of being "cornered" by life's situations. The cornering may have resulted from family conflict or restriction, problems with school, the disa-bling effects of drug and alcohol dependence, or desperate angry sadness about failure of an intimate relationship. The suicide at-tempt or completion, in this case, is an angry and desperate act by an individual who cognitively sees no alternatives.

Drug and Alcohol Use

When the Bergenfield suicides occurred, I received calls from sev-eral networks and news departments asking for my comment as a professional with some reputation for working with adolescents. I proposed drug and alcohol dependence as a possible cause and was quickly told, "Thank you very much. We'll get back to you if we need anything." The networks rejected the drug and alcohol hypoth-esis out of hand because there was no immediate evidence of intoxi-cation. Subsequently, the toxicology section of the autopsy indi-cated that all four were under the influence of cocaine at very high levels, and that two of the four were legally drunk at the time of death.

Most adolescent suicides by regular drug and alcohol users do not occur during the chemical "high" phase of use, but rather when the individual is on the backswing down into a dull, "gray-sky," "the world sucks" pain. It is during this dull painful period that the ado-lescent in desperation says to herself, "The world sucks; I'm a piece of crap. Why not go out in a blaze of glory and overdose or drive my car into a tree?" Many adolescent suicides are misclassified in terms of cause because they do not occur during the active intoxication period. A study in South Carolina of high school students found alcohol use to be the single most important factor in suicidal ideation, suicide attempts, and actual suicides.[202] Drug and alcohol use is followed by aggression as the second most important factor.[203] The aggression factor in adolescent suicide thoughts, attempts, and completions points to desperation rather than depression as the primary mood.

TYPES OF ADOLESCENT SUICIDES

In approximately 85% of adolescent suicide attempts and completions, drug and alcohol dependence, causing distorted chemistry in the brain resulting in distorted feelings, lack of behavior control, and immature cognitive processes, is the primary cause.[204] Second, and often overlapping with drug and alcohol use, is anger toward a parent or a boy or girlfriend whose rejection, punishment, or anger has left the subject desperate. Third is failure in academic performance or sports activity or rejection by social group.

Martha Straus suggests a different typology which I also find very useful in evaluating adolescent patients.[205]

1. *Anger turned inward*: This is an act based on rage toward someone else, such as a family member, friend, or boyfriend/girlfriend, but which is turned inward toward self. This enactment of hostility is intended to be a punishment toward someone else.
2. *Manipulation*: Some adolescents make suicide attempts for attention-getting purposes or to gain power in a situation with family or friends.
3. *A cry for help*: Sometimes a troubled adolescent who becomes increasingly desperate will use a suicide attempt as a signal to the adult world that he or she needs help.
4. *Psychosis*: Straus suggests that 10 to 15% of suicidal adolescents make attempts as a means of relieving internal tension and confusion.
5. *The suicidal game*: Some adolescents play with death as a game, often for attention-getting purposes from peers.
6. *Reaction to loss*: Truly depressed adolescents, having trouble grieving the loss of a friend or relative, also make attempts.
7. *Life is too hard*: These adolescents, also suffering from

extreme distress or depression, will make a suicide attempt as a delusional attempt to end problems and stress.

8. *Rage and revenge*: Similar to the anger turned inward attempt, some adolescents consciously attempt to hurt others by a suicide attempt.

9. *Imitation and suggestibility*: There is much evidence that adolescents who are at risk for other reasons will see a news description of a suicide or a relative or friend's suicide as a trigger for their own attempts. I call these types of suicides "copy cat" suicides.

10. *Alienation*: These adolescents live in a chronically disengaged and self-destructive pattern that involves frequent risk taking which could end in death at any time. These suicides are similar to Durkheim's concept of anomie.

Signs and Symptoms

There are a number of potential signs and symptoms of an adolescent who is likely to make a suicide attempt or who is likely to complete suicide.

1. *Preoccupation with death or threat of suicide.* These are to be taken seriously. The old saying that "threatening suicide means the person will not do it" is simply not true. An adolescent who is preoccupied with death, death-related rock music, death symbols, or who talks about suicide is at high risk and should be taken seriously by family and therapist.

2. A young person who has a *clear history of drug and alcohol use and dependence.* Increasing substance use with decreasing performance in achievement arenas, family conflict, pushing limits, and visible intoxication are major concerns.

3. *Prior suicide attempt.* This is an indicator that another attempt may well occur.

4. Clear indication of *"down" feelings, especially desperation or depression.*

5. *Antisocial and aggressive behavior.*

6. A *family history of suicide.*

7. *Availability of a firearm.*

These factors in suicide attempts and completions have come out of psychological autopsies developing profiles of adolescents who completed suicide.[206]

ATTENTION-GETTING ATTEMPTS

Some suicide attempts by adolescents are clearly attention-getting behaviors. The direction of a cut in the wrist, the immediate announcement of pills taken, and other forms of "Hey, look at me" behavior indicate the attention-getting function of the attempt. However, these must be taken seriously, since these individuals may raise the ante if their attempt fails to achieve its goal. Since few adolescents are sufficiently knowledgeable about pharmacology or surgery, attention-getting attempts may result in accidental death because of their lack of knowledge. An example is the number of young people who use either over-the-counter or prescribed medication in suicide attempts. A seemingly innocuous medication like Tylenol may cause serious liver damage if it is not removed from the stomach before it is metabolized into the bloodstream.

TREATMENT

First and foremost, the potentially suicidal adolescent, or the adolescent who has made a suicide attempt, needs to be placed under tight supervision in order to prevent a second and successful attempt, while long-term therapy deals with underlying issues.

Second, if regular drug and/or alcohol use is present, this must be the primary treatment concern. Immediate cessation of all drug and alcohol use with appropriate therapy to initiate recovery and ongoing sobriety is in order.

Third, for adolescents without drug and alcohol dependence, whose primary problem is situational desperation, cognitive and behavioral therapy is called for in order to deal with self-defeating behaviors and cognitive appraisals. Effective short-term cognitive therapy will go a long way toward changing the individual's view of his or her current life situation. Keep in mind the importance of moving the suicidal individual, who is often externally directed in coping style, to an internal actor orientation, which will result in behavior change relieving the "cornered" situation.

Fourth, for those adolescents whose situational problem involves family conflict, family therapy may be an effective mode of treatment. The danger with family therapy is to maintain the adolescent's externalization of focus in coping style. The desperate adolescent who sees his problem as produced by parents and/or siblings and feels impotent to effect change will remain suicidal. The therapist needs to work with the adolescent, notwithstanding family resistance, to become internally focused, in charge of self, and to find self-initiated solutions, as well as family system solutions.

Fifth, in the case of the adolescent who is resistant to treatment and continues to have obsessive suicidal thoughts, hospitalization or some other form of institutional care that provides adequate suicide supervision is necessary to prevent risk of death. The resistant adolescent may also need a temporary course of mood-elevating medication in order to be available for cognitive, affective, and family therapy. Medication should be limited to the acute period in order not to interfere with neurochemical factors in adolescent brain development. The use of mood-altering medication will be effective only with truly depressed adolescents. Those who are unhappy and act out tend to experience an increase in acting out as a result of antidepressant medication.

Most adolescent suicide attempters who receive effective cognitive and behavioral therapy move quickly from desperation to a sense of efficacy about their lives and relationships. In a few months, they will have trouble making sense out of their suicide attempt in terms of their current life situation.

SUGGESTED READINGS

Straus, Martha, B., "Suicidal Adolescents" in Martha B. Straus, *Violence in the Lives of Adolescents*, New York: W. W. Norton & Company, 1994, pp. 31–53.
This is an excellent and relevant chapter on adolescent suicide which is helpful in understanding adolescent suicide as well as treating it.

While there are no great books on adolescent suicide, since most books emphasize depression and view adolescent suicide through an adult paradigm, the following two provide some help.

Joan, Polly, *Preventing Teenage Suicide: The Alternative Living Book*, New York: Human Sciences Press, Inc., 1986.

Peck, Michael L., Farberow, Norman L. and Litman, Robert E., (Eds.) *Youth Suicide*, New York: Springer Publishing Company, 1985.

Chapter 14

Drug and Alcohol Use

Drug and alcohol use remains a major plague for American adolescents. We have mounted a "war against drugs." A First Lady told children to "just say no." A variety of entertainment and sports figures have gone public about their drug use, gone into treatment, and become part of the chorus telling kids that drugs and drinking are dangerous. Millions of dollars have been spent publicly and privately, thousands of kids have gone through treatment, yet the plague remains the number one health problem for American young people.

The three major causes of death for adolescents and young adults (accidents, homicides, and suicides) are suggestive of drug and alcohol use as a primary cause. The continuing problem with school achievement across the board in America is also suggestive of the neuropsychological effects of drug and alcohol use. Rock videos, the rock music culture, and images of the high life in movies and on television continue to portray a simplistic view of good living, involving excessive use of alcohol and use of marijuana and cocaine.

Nation's Health reported the National Institute on Drug Abuse survey of high school seniors in 1992, finding that 40.7% admitted to using an illicit drug once in their lifetime. This was down from 65.5% in 1981. However, the same graduating class of 1992 admitted a 17% experimentation rate with inhalants and a 29.8% rate of binge drinking within the two weeks prior to the survey. Also alarming in the 1992 survey was an increase in cocaine use, up from 2% to 2.9%, and marijuana use, from 10.2% to 11.2%. LSD use for this group rose from 1.7% to 2.1%.[207] The 1993 survey of 50,000 high school seniors, tenth graders, and eighth graders from 400 schools was even more alarming. "Any use of" marijuana increased by 3 to

4 percentage points for these age groups since 1992. Daily cigarette smoking increased for all three groups. (Both cigarettes and marijuana are considered "entry drugs.") Also, use of inhalants, amphetamines, and LSD increased with all three age groups. African-American teens showed a decline in cigarette use and only a moderate increase in LSD use.[208]

A caution should be observed about reading these statistics as accurate. Those of us who work with adolescents who have drug and alcohol problems know that they seldom admit their total use to themselves, much less to other people. Even on anonymous surveys, such as the one behind the data reported above, they minimize their use. The strategy of minimization is designed to protect their use from intervention by parents and adult authorities. Part of the minimization is denial to self of the extent of use. Denial is characteristic of all of substance users, including adult alcoholics.

Andrew Malcolm suggests problems for a society when use of substances escapes the tight controls of religious and medical usage systems. Alcohol as a recreational drug historically has been subject to relatively tight control.[209] American adolescents use alcohol and other substances with almost no societal control.

Myths about Teenage Drug Use

One myth many parents hold about teenage drug use is that "All kids use drugs. It's part of growing up." The facts are that many kids do not experiment, particularly those kids who are among the high achieving group. The 1992 survey of Who's Who in American High Schools found that 95% of the real winners in high school not only do not smoke, but that 81% do not use alcoholic beverages or any other substance. This statistic may reflect denial and minimization of use. However, corrected statistics would still show a substantial group of non-users. Kids who become involved in drinking and using drugs tend to progress in their use and then to progressively fail in sports, extracurricular activities, academic work, and healthy socialization.[210]

A second myth is that many kids use occasionally with no harm. Occasional use is generally not true, because the tolerance property of mood-altering drugs requires increased use to get the original high. Also, young people who become involved in the partying crowds increase the frequency of their party behavior to regular weekend use, which produces detrimental consequences in other areas of their lives.

A third myth is that smoking a little marijuana is harmless. After all, the parents smoked pot in the 1970s and "outgrew" it. Factually, the marijuana that the parents smoked is not the same drug that is available today. As a result of hybridization in America, delta-9-tetrahydrocannabinol, the intoxicant in pot, has increased from 0.36% to 4.43% (in 1993). Today's marijuana is a far more potent drug.[211]

The fourth myth is "not my kid." Many parents think that kids in certain religious groups or socioeconomic groups or activities are protected from exposure to drugs. Drug and alcohol use in America is an equal opportunity problem for adolescents. Kids from all backgrounds in all parts of the country are exposed and even pressured by their peers to become part of the using group.

Fifth, "No problem. My kid only drinks." Most adults equate adolescent drinking to their own patterns of using alcoholic beverages as beverages. Most teenagers use beer, wine, and whiskey as drugs to get high. They chug-a-lug five or six cans of beer in a row in order to produce intoxication. They use booze as dope.

A FRAMEWORK FOR UNDERSTANDING TEEN SUBSTANCE USE

Most kids begin experimenting out of sight of parents with "adult substances" during the withdrawal substage. For most kids this involves cigarettes.[212] Nicotine use is usually followed by alcohol as another way to experiment with being an adult. Some kids bypass smoking and begin with alcohol.

Over the years, while working with many adolescents from different backgrounds who have become involved with and dependent upon alcohol and other drugs, I have seen a pattern emerge. The concept of progressive involvement goes back to E. M. Jellinek and his original progression curve for adult alcoholism.[213] Subsequently, Vernon Johnson, the founder of the Johnson Institute in Minneapolis, developed the four-stage concept of adult alcoholism.[214]

In my early days of working with adolescent users, I began to use ethnographic observation techniques in order to make sense out of their use, their deteriorating behavior, and their cognitive and affective problems. Out of this work emerged a four-stage concept that will be described below.[215] The stages are based on progression, which I believe is caused by the tolerance property of almost all mood-altering chemicals. The limbic system, the center of the feeling system of the brain, becomes accustomed to the effect of the drug, requiring an increase in amount of the drug to produce the original high. For some substances, like alcohol and marijuana, tolerance builds slowly. For other substances, like speed, cocaine, and heroin, tolerance builds rapidly.

Individuals take varying amounts of time to go through the four stages of progression. Some go very quickly, others more slowly. Some individuals use only one substance, such as alcohol or a combination of alcohol and marijuana, while others follow the progression of substances shown in the four stages. Kandel and Yamaguchi have documented staged progression in terms of different substances. They see nicotine, alcohol, and marijuana as entry drugs, followed by other substances, including cocaine and hallucinogens. Finally, crack and heroin constitute the final stage.[216] Ellickson, Hays, and Bell, in a prospective study of teenagers from the seventh to tenth grades, document similar stages.[217]

Stage One: Learning the Mood Swing

Most kids today are exposed to tobacco and alcohol or marijuana some time between ages 10 and 14. They say "no" at least one or two times. Having internalized their family's value system, they know that alcohol and drug use for kids is incompatible with achievement. The problem is that they are in the withdrawal phase of adolescent development, requiring them to distance from their families and "hang tight" with their peer group as a place of support for individualization. If the peer group is involved in drinking and smoking marijuana, they are caught in a dilemma. They want to say no, but the peers laugh and put them down. Since they need to

Table 14.1 Stage 1 Drug Use

Stage	Drugs	When	Behavior	Feelings
1. Learning	alcohol, pot	occasional	none	pleasure

belong to the peer group, they eventually try it. Often, they avoid real involvement the first couple of times that they use. They puff instead of deeply inhaling the marijuana joint. They sip the can of beer instead of chug-a-lugging several cans of beer until the "buzz" hits. Pushed by relentless teasing and laughter, they use it "correctly" on the fourth or fifth time and find themselves soaring up into a warm, wonderful euphoria. Given their age, always tired from fast growth, awkward because of the fast-growing hands, feet, knees, elbows, and nose, they experience life at this point as "terminal harassment." In the midst of this difficult time, the drug "high" represents a chance to feel good, unharried, and secure. Nothing goes wrong the first time. The horrors we adults warn about, such as being caught, going crazy, messing up in activities, or failing school, do not happen. They experience good feelings with no negative consequences, so why not keep using?

This first use stage involves learning that entry drugs can change your mood or feelings from okay to wonderful. Because early users use drugs only occasionally and spontaneously when someone else has booze or pot to share, there tend to be no negative consequences. Since there are no behavioral consequences, it is unlikely that parents will discover use during this experimentation period. If you notice the feeling chart, the substance moves feelings up to the edge of wonderful and then back down to okay or neutral, so that there are no feeling consequences of use.

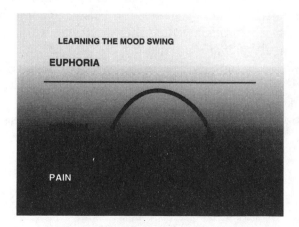

Figure 14.1 Stage I Feeling Chart

Stage 2: Seeking the Mood Swing

At some point, the early teen, now in the isolation period, decides that she likes the "high" enough that she does not want to wait until some friend happens to have some beer or pot to share. So she takes the initiative and begins to find her own money and her own source of substances so she can get high when she wants to. This is the beginning of the second period of drug use, in which individuals take initiative and control of their use. Because they can get high when they want to now, they begin to want to every Friday and Saturday night. They become regular "partyers." The base diet of drugs remains pot and alcohol, but their tolerance builds slightly and their fear of other drugs declines, so they try "harder" substances like hash, hash oil, and pills (prescriptions and over-the-counter). During this period, kids begin to lose control. The use slips over into week-nights, a limit the kids promise themselves they will never break. They find themselves unable to say no when a situation triggers unconscious buttons about being high. This initial inability to say "no" begins to cause problems when getting high interferes with studying for a class or preparation for an extracurricular activity.

There are some behavioral consequences. I usually describe this period as the period of "Visine and whorehouse cologne or perfume," since the young people are still enough in control of themselves not to let their drug use "hang out." They use eyedrops to take the red out of bloodshot eyes so their parents will not know they are smoking marijuana. And they use outrageous scents to cover the aromas of pot smoke in the clothes and booze on the breath. This is the period of a dual lifestyle, where they are able to maintain the facade of being straight and nonusing in front of parents and other important adults. But, out of sight of parents, they develop a second lifestyle oriented toward the drug use culture in their area. This may involve friends that they meet elsewhere and whom parents never meet. Kids tend to become more argumentative at home and to have trouble finding creative solutions to parental no's. This trouble in finding creative solutions is based in declining prefrontal cortex executive functions as a result of chemical insult to the brain. They become caught in lies occasionally, and money may be missing from around the house. They may begin to steal from parents and siblings to support their tolerance-increased drug use. Kids usually begin to drop peripheral hobbies and activi-

Table 14.2 Stage 2 Drug Use

Stage	Drugs	When	Behavior	Feelings
1. Learning	alcohol, pot	occasional	none	pleasure
2. Seeking	pot/alcohol, hash, pills	regular weekend weeknights	"dual life," mood swings	pleasure/ minor pain

ties, but not the main one. "Hobbies and sports are not cool anymore." Toward the very end of Stage 2, most kids have an average one-letter drop in school grades. Most of the time, caring parents jump on it, and the grades come up one more time. But they will soon fade into the pit, never to rise again.

Noticing the feeling curve, the adolescent user now reaches true euphoria as a result of developed competence in using drugs (Figure 14.2). However, on the downswing, as the chemical high wears off, his feelings approach the pain line. This negative backswing in feelings is the result of the tired, "burn-out" from drugs, causing alterations in metabolic processes in the body and from increased guilt about use itself, failed activities and a strained family relationship.

Sometime during Stage 2, most kids self-medicate for the first time. They find themselves in some difficulty with ensuing bad feelings and then use the drug high to make themselves feel good again. This is the beginning of true loss of control. Being high to

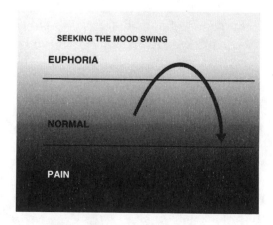

Figure 14.2 Stage II Feeling Chart

solve a problem often creates new problems with more bad feelings. Soon, they are getting high to deal with the bad feelings created by problems caused by drug use itself. At this point, progression is swift. Soon, drug use takes center stage in their lives. All else, including family, nonusing friends, school grades, sports, and activities, fade offstage into the shadows. Their use and lives are like a snowball going downhill, building up size and speed. This leads into the third stage. They may have their first blackout, that is, temporary amnesia to cover up embarrassing behavior.

Stage 3: Preoccupation with the Mood Swing

During the third stage, adolescent users become preoccupied with getting high. They start to use almost every day, between 5 to 7 days a week. Their use slips over into the school day, and involves skipping school to use and getting high at school or on the way to school. This corresponds to the adult alcoholic drinking on the job. At this point, they experiment with harder drugs, like hallucinogens and cocaine. Their use is still mainly marijuana and alcohol. Tolerance, however, is building rapidly, and they begin to overdose. Overdoses are episodes of miscalculating how much it takes to get high and crossing a higher threshold, called the toxic line, which produces some form of sick body response. During Stage 3, blackouts increase, and many hallucinogen users have a flashback for the first time.

Behaviorally, the effects of increasing distortion of chemistry of the brain cause diminishing behavioral control. Most mood-altering drugs are analogs of the neurotransmitters (natural brain chemicals). Regular use begins to distort the communication between brain cells involving a number of visible lost functions. One major loss is in the executive skills area in the prefrontal cortex, which is necessary for cognitive control of behavior. The third-stage drug user is increasingly impulsive and lacks behavior control. One result is that the individual drops the pretense of being straight. The dual lifestyle is gone. At this point, most parents know the kid is in trouble, but may not attribute the problems to drug and alcohol dependence. Kids begin skipping school, failing at school, getting suspended, and talking about dropping out. The family becomes a battleground. The user is perceived as a pathological liar. Stealing leaves home and hits the street in the form of shoplifting and often breaking and entering. Stealing combined with small time drug deal-

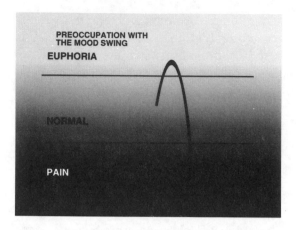

Figure 14.3 Stage III Feeling Chart A

ing is necessary to support the increased cost of higher tolerance. Often a school suspension or an arrest is the first news to the family that the kid is in trouble.

In the feeling area, you notice the chart shows the user still getting euphoric highs, but now on the backswing, plunging down into "gray skies," dull pain (Figure 14.3). This pain is made up principally of masses of guilt over out-of-control behavior and increasing shame, that is, negative feelings about self. The result is immediate self-medication to get rid of the pain and to produce pleasurable feelings again (Figure 14.4).

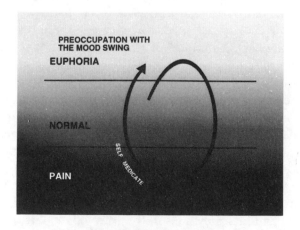

Figure 14.4 Stage III Feeling Chart B

Table 14.3 Stage 3 Drug Use

Stage	Drugs	When	Behavior	Feelings
1. Learning	alcohol, pot	occasional	none	pleasure
2. Seeking	pot/alcohol, hash, pills	regular weekend weeknights	"dual life," mood swings	pleasure/ minor pain
3. Preoccupied	pot/alcohol, hash, pills, LSD, PCP, cocaine	regular weekdays	openly a drug user	euphoria/pain

As the third stage continues, the young user loses the normal range of feelings. His whole life is a radical pendulum swing between the chemically induced, shimmering high and the dull, "gray" low. Most kids walk around in a cocoon looking at their friends, who seem to be handling it, and thinking that they are defective because they have so much pain and difficulty. They fail to see objectively that all of their peers who use at the same level have the same level of pain and problems.

Stage 3, looked at from a neuropsychological point of view, adds up to a prefrontal brain syndrome. Characteristic of a prefrontal syndrome is impulsive, aggressive, and disinhibited behavior, difficulty with attention and concentration, and emotional lability. Drug dependency at this stage results in affective and behavioral disregulation based in disturbance of the prefrontal structures of the brain.[218]

Stage 4: Using to Function

Now the user begins to have trouble "getting off," meaning that the tolerance has become so high that many drugs no longer produce euphoria (Figure 14.5). They begin to use less pot and alcohol and more speed, cocaine, and hallucinogens.

In time, the high from these drugs caps off and they find themselves in a desperate pursuit, "chasing the high." They now turn to shooting up, which avoids the filtering effect of the linings of the nose, lungs, and stomach, and gets more of the drug into the bloodstream and brain faster. They turn to crack, which reduces the particles of cocaine in a steam form to such a small size that they

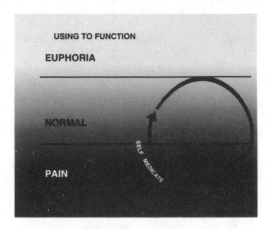

Figure 14.5 Early Stage IV Feeling Chart

easily pass through the lining of the lungs. At this point, the user wakes up in pain and desperately pursues enough drugs just to feel functional and get through the day (Figure 14.6).

Behaviorally, the user has become a zombie, a burnout, the walking dead. The fourth-stage user cannot sustain any activity or relationship and is subject to volcanic swings in mood, including suicidal depression and volcanic anger and aggression.

In the chart below (Table 14.4), you clearly see the progression in terms of increased use and decreased functioning. The disease is

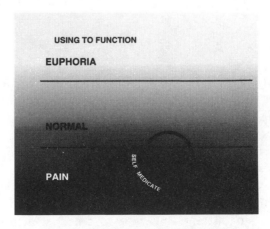

Figure 14.6 Stage IV Feeling Chart

Table 14.4 Stage 4 Drug Use

Stage	Drugs	When	Behavior	Feelings
1. Learning	alcohol, pot	occasional	none	pleasure
2. Seeking	pot/alcohol, hash, pills	regular weekend weeknights	"dual life," mood swings	pleasure/ minor pain
3. Preoccupied	pot/alcohol, hash, pills, LSD, PCP, cocaine	regular weekdays	openly a drug user	euphoria/pain
4. Using to Function	shooting up, crack	all the time everyday	"burnout," suicidal	pain

explained by the dynamic interaction of two sets of feelings. The first set are the chemically produced euphoric highs. The second set of feelings are those negative feelings that occur as a result of life's problems. As teenage users go through the drug use progression, the bad feelings grow because of increased debilitation of behavior. They use more, they have more problems, they feel worse, and therefore, the drug use becomes increasingly urgent to cope with those bad feelings. Most young people would stop, given the consequences that occur during Stage 3, but by then it's too late. They have to have the drugs to feel good enough to go through life. Alcohol/drug use is a developmental trap that may involve foreclosure in several areas of adolescent growth.

GENDER AND ETHNIC DIFFERENCES

There are some gender differences in drug use patterns. For example, females tend to start with cigarettes often for the purpose of appetite suppression, in order to maintain the artificially thin body ideal of our day.[219] Second, there is a tendency on the part of female users to spend less money until late in the use period. Males buy drugs for females as part of the mating ritual and in order to gain sexual access to females.

There are also some ethnic differences in use. For example, Mexican-American young people often start their use with hallucinogens, which include aerosol bottles, kerosene, gasoline, and other inhalable substances. Asian-American adolescents delay heavy drinking until Stage 3. Native Americans tend to use alcohol more than other substances.[220] There are also some regional variations, not only in substances, but in street nicknames for substances. Death rates from substance use are higher among males than females and among African-Americans than whites.[221] Notwithstanding the differences described above, the basic progressive involvement with drugs appears to follow the four-stage model.

WHO'S AT RISK?

The simple answer to this question is that all teens in America are at risk. Drugs are available in almost every community and school in North America. The delivery system for the drug world is better than the delivery system from Sears. In rural corners of Iowa, you can get the same list of drugs that you can in New York or Los Angeles. The speed at which crack traveled across America was an incredible example of drug availability all over the country.

After giving a generic answer of "every teen" to the question "Who's at risk?" there are some groups that are more vulnerable to drug use than others. First and foremost are those young people who have grown up in alcoholic or drug-using families. Research has documented, over and over again, the tendency of substance use to travel through families. There is a high contagion rate between an older child and younger siblings. Tarter suggests a nonspecific genetic influence is one factor in family vulnerability.[222] Second, those young people who have difficulty finding acceptance with an appropriate peer group during the withdrawal phase and the isolation phase of adolescent development are at risk. These young people include those with special physical handicaps, with learning disabilities, and with other problems that make them less than the norm in their school and community. Third, there is debate about minority groups and their level of risk based upon socioeconomic stress. There are some differences in use among African-American and Hispanic Americans on one side and white Americans on the other. However, the lowest use level is among Asian ethnic groups.[223] Fourth, some individuals appear to have a temperament trait called "sensation seeking."[224] These individuals seek high levels of emotional arousal through a variety of behaviors. Substance use is one more route to high levels of arousal.

Neuropsychologically, young people with other disorders that reflect a prefrontal brain syndrome are also at risk. This includes adolescents with attention deficit disorder, attention deficit disorder with hyperactivity, and conduct disorders. Finally, children (particularly male children) of adult alcoholics also appear in EEG studies as well as neuropsychological studies to have the characteristics of a prefrontal syndrome, therefore putting them at risk for personal chemical dependency.[225]

WHO STOPS?

Many young people stop after trying substances once or twice. Others stop after entering the first phase of use or continuing into the second phase. A smaller proportion stops after continuing progression to the third phase. Many observers simply see this as growing up experimentation. My experience is that those who stop do so because of some bad experience. They either have a negative reaction to the first high or an early high in the process of their use. Their curiosity is satisfied. Or they may have an experience of getting caught, having a friend get caught, or someone in their school die in an automobile accident or commit suicide at a time while they are still sufficiently in control to stop without formal treatment intervention. In addition, other factors influence progression or nonprogression through the stages, including peer group, environment, temperament, social class, expectancy, intelligence, and family.[226]

Does their regular use of substances at a level short of dependence cause harm? Based on current research, the commonly held view is that these adolescents escape harmful consequences. Current knowledge is based on cross-sectional studies. These studies show regular users, who cut down their use, falling in the normal range of cognitive abilities. However, many of these young adults may have suffered significant losses when measured against a pre-use baseline. My intuition suggests that regular use during the adolescent growth spurt may cause problems for the chemically guided process of new neuron network development. Prospective longitudinal neuropsychology research is needed to resolve this important question. This type of research would follow individuals from a childhood pre-use baseline through their use period into early adulthood.

A third group of people appear to stop in their early 20's. They reach their early 20's, having dropped out of high school or early college, and begin to see the problematic nature of their use. They first knock off the harder substances like crack, cocaine, hallucinogens, and speed. Later on, still impaired, they knock off marijuana. Usually at this point, they change their appearance, return to school, and make an attempt to reestablish a healthy life trajectory. We are now seeing many of these young people turn up at alcoholism treatment clinics in their mid to late thirties as full-blown adult alcoholics. Their failure to stop total use and to go through a rehabilitation process to deal with damaged areas of behavior, feelings, and personality leave them vulnerable to continued progress of the disease through the single substance, alcohol.

Young people who begin "party" drinking during high school may not be affected by excessive drinking until later. They go on to college and begin to drink frequently and heavily with peers, often to the detriment of good grades and activities. Some of this group go on to develop full-blown chemical dependency, resulting in interruption of their college education. Others in this group stop the excessive drinking in order to successfully negotiate university education and later graduate education. Some young people in this group also occasionally use marijuana and cocaine in a party situation. Again, a subgroup of these becomes progressively involved in the use of illicit substances to the point of dependence.

DIAGNOSTIC ASSESSMENT

Discovering adolescent drug use before the patient is totally out of control is difficult. Denial and various forms of manipulative behavior are used by most alcoholics and drug users to cover up the real source of their behavior. We have found that diagnostic assessment requires 4 to 6 hours of intensive interviewing by skilled individuals. We often use patients further along in treatment to help interview the new individual, since they have used many of the same denial and avoidance mechanisms.

We first build a picture of all of the troubling behaviors in the individual's life, including school, work, sports, and activities problems. We survey family relationship problems and problems in the legal area, including traffic-related charges. The Teen-Addiction Severity Index (T-ASI) surveys similar areas.[227] We always talk to other family members to secure additional information and attempt to have available to us school records and other records.

The last part of diagnosis is always a give-and-take process of pointing out incongruities in the information given to us by the individual, returning over and over again to his or her descriptions of use in the last week, or the week before, or the month before. As we pick up the inconsistencies, we are able to get slow, but sure, admission of increasing levels of use. The ultimate purpose is to place the individual within the four stages of drug use. Stage location gives us excellent information about the type of intervention and treatment needed.

DUAL DIAGNOSIS

Much has been made in recent years about dual diagnosis patients. The term dual diagnosis refers to another mental health problem in combination with substance dependence. Unfortunately, untrained, unskilled clinicians have misunderstood the DSM-IV diagnostic system and see many primary chemical dependency patients as dual-diagnosis patients. Any Stage 3 adolescent drug user will qualify for a conduct disorder diagnosis. The loss of control of behavior is a natural consequence of chemical insult to the brain through regular drug and alcohol use. Qualifying for a conduct disorder diagnosis, an adjustment disorder diagnosis, and parent-child problem in no way constitutes dual diagnosis. Dual diagnosis is limited to those patients who have a serious psychological disorder, such as schizophrenia or bipolar disorder, that is separate from the primary chemical dependency disorder.

An example of a dual diagnosis patient is an adolescent-onset schizophrenic who at the same time uses street drugs as a way to self-medicate. While this seems easy to detect, some adolescent drug users actually have schizophreniform episodes as a result of intense and mixed drug use. We have found it necessary to totally detox the individual and wait several months for the chemistry of the brain to move toward normal, before we are certain that there is a separate schizophreniform disorder present. The same concept applies to some young people who have been diagnosed with bipolar disorder.

Depression, the great diagnosis of our time, is often considered dual diagnosis with drug-using patients. All third- and fourth-stage drug users show signs of serious depression as a result of the shambles of their lives at that point. Situational depression resulting from life problems during drug use cannot be considered endogenous depression, and therefore does not mean a dual diagnosis.

For most substance dependent patients, conduct, depressive, and anxiety disorders resolve as a result of addiction treatment. However, a small number of these patients, who have primary disorders other than addiction, need appropriate treatment for their basic problem.

TREATMENT

Chronic Disease

Drug dependence and alcoholism are chronic, noncurable diseases. There is a tendency for relapse to occur, and the temptation to return to the euphoric high is always present. Any effective treatment is based on helping the individual reach acceptance of his or her disease and willingness to live a special lifestyle in order to minimize recurrence of the disease. From the early days of Alcoholics Anonymous, the analogy has been drawn between diabetes mellitus and alcoholism as chronic diseases.

The disease model is currently the predominant approach for treating drug and alcohol dependence. I believe it has great heuristic value for the treatment of addictions.

Nonuse

No treatment is possible while an individual is under the influence of drugs. The influence of drugs occurs not only during the visible intoxication period, but also in general life when chemical insult to the brain causes impulsivity and lack of behavior control. Immature and concrete reasoning is another characteristic of a brain altered by regular drug and alcohol use. If the individual cannot stop on his own with some controls by family members, it is necessary to place him in a totally controlled environment for a minimum period of time in order to ensure that he is drug-free and that the brain is recovering from these effects. Only then is treatment possible. For regular marijuana users, this period should be a minimum of a hundred days, because delta-9-tetrahydrocannabinol tends to remain in the lipid tissue of the brain for a long time.

12-Step Recovery

While many models have been proposed for recovery from alcohol and substance dependence, I have found treatment based on the

12-step recovery program of Alcoholics Anonymous to be comprehensive and effective.[228] Therefore, outpatient treatment for drug use should be accompanied by regular attendance at Alcoholic Anonymous. The recommendation of A.A. is 90 meetings in the first 90 days of sobriety in order to help the person not use during that period. When referring a patient to an inpatient program, I always make sure that it is a truly 12-step based program. Some programs claim to be A.A. oriented when they have A.A. meetings at night in the facility. However, their day treatment proceeds along traditional mental health lines without the 12-step focus. This type of program focuses more on group and individual counseling around problem-solving and self-actualization rather than applying the step recovery process to the actual alcohol/drug problem.

Reverse Peer Influence

Our own treatment at KIDS of North Jersey is based heavily on the use of reverse peer pressure. Peer influence is an important variable in initial adolescent drug use. Therefore, it makes sense to use recovering adolescents to help new individuals in treatment take their first steps toward sobriety. The principle of someone who has the problem and is recovering helping the new person is at the center of the success of Alcoholics Anonymous.

Acceptance of the Problem

The foundation of recovery is acceptance of the problem, which is the first step of Alcoholics Anonymous. Acceptance of the problem involves breaking the patient's denial of the fact and extent of substance dependence. This process requires patient use of his or her own life data, including amount and frequency of use, behavior, and the trouble he or she has in a variety of life arenas. The result is a self-accepted coherent picture of life "under the influence" and acceptance of responsibility for the choice to use and the consequences of use.

Lifestyle Change

Lifestyle change is another crucial principle for treatment and recovery from substance dependence. Lifestyles of users have been shaped around themselves, other users, and the excitement-oriented pattern of use. We have found that adolescents have to redesign their lifestyles in order to avoid not only the use itself, but becoming emotionally or physically close to use. This is the old A.A. adage of avoiding "wet people and places." This means avoiding people, places, and things associated with use, which trigger the urge to get high. The recovering adolescent needs to take responsibility for maintaining a sober lifestyle.

Developmental Repair

Given the troubled development caused by chemical insult to the brain, effective treatment needs to include repairing the developmental damage. This involves helping the individual in areas of identity, sexual identity, social relationships, family relationships, and cognitive processes to reach an age-appropriate maturity level.

Reducing Thrill-Seeking

Long-term sobriety and constructive living require a change in perception of pleasurable feelings. Substance use attunes the individual's pleasure perception to a high, exotic level. He becomes a "feeling junkie," needing thrills and highs to feel good. This disharmony persists into recovery. True sobriety involves moving from thrills and highs to "serenity," a quiet, warm, good feeling. Therapy for this problem focuses on helping the patient to stop pursuing thrills while at the same time learning to experience quieter good feelings.

Related to pursuit of thrills and highs is a series of cognitive frames that equates "good times" with excitement and extremes. Cognitive therapy can assist the patient to detect these cognitive frames and question them in terms of their outcomes. Next, the patient is helped to build replacement frames that are consistent with a sober lifestyle.

Types of Treatment

Parental supervision plus counseling may be enough to help a young adolescent caught using during the first stage or the first part of the second stage. Parental supervision will have to be strict to help the young person avoid the urge to use while the counseling process unfolds.

Failing this simple intervention, a more intensive intervention calls for outpatient counseling, often twice a week, plus regular attendance at Alcoholics Anonymous. This requires tighter parental supervision, in which the young person is not allowed time alone, either at home, after school, or with peers. Since all good treatment requires becoming drug-free, parents have the primary responsibility under this level of intervention. Experience shows that only 5 to 10% of using young people find and maintain sobriety with this level of help.

The next level of help calls for short-term inpatient treatment. The Minnesota model, 28-day, Alcoholics Anonymous based program was developed for middle-age alcoholics. Some programs extend treatment by a week or two to give the adolescent patient more time for recovery. Again, 5 to 10% of adolescent patients find and maintain sobriety through this treatment option.

Long-term treatment is necessary for an overwhelming majority of adolescent users. This has to involve several features. One is a relatively long residential period, from 3 to 6 months, in order to outlast the effects of drugs with a long residual presence in the brain. Second, the program must use a developmental rehabilitation model that involves assisting the young person in rebuilding his or her life, arena by arena. My own program features a second phase in which the young person remains in day-care treatment 7 days of the week, while going to his or her own home at night. The time at home is used to rebuild the family relationship. As the family relationship stabilizes, the patient moves into third phase, which is the return to the achievement arena, meaning school or work. Here patients develop the ability to be disciplined in the achievement activity and to resist negative peer pressure for return to drug use. As they stabilize this arena of life, they earn free time in order to pursue friendships and constructive use of leisure time.

Family Treatment

Family treatment is necessary for all adolescent patients. Family members cannot live with a teenager acting out as a result of drugs without getting a little crazy themselves. In order to cope with the threat to self-esteem of the drug user's behavior, each family member experiments with, and then chooses, a style of behavior in order to survive and bolster self-esteem. A parent may choose to be an enabler and become enmeshed in the user's disease, cleaning up her messes, or may choose to distance and withdraw, becoming a passive adult. The passive parent leaves the responsibility for the family, and particularly the troubled user, on the other parent. Siblings of the user may choose a variety of roles. One sibling may choose the "family hero" role, attempting to fix the family by super-achievement. Unfortunately, no matter how great the achievement, the family remains painful, therefore the achievement is experienced as a failure. A second sibling may choose to be a "family scapegoat," imitating the acting-out behavior of the user in order to get attention. After all, negative attention is better than no attention at all. A third sibling may withdraw into distant silence as a "lost child" in order to avoid family pain. A fourth child may take the role of a "clown or mascot," using humor to diffuse approaching conflict. Conflicts are frightening to small children and come with increasing frequency in the family of a drug user.[229]

Family treatment is necessary to support not only the primary user in recovery but every family member. Because siblings are highly at risk for joining the user in substance dependence, treatment for them becomes a return to healthy development and avoidance of drug use. In addition, parents and all family members need a chance to work through the pain they have experienced and the anger they feel, in order to become healthy again.

Some families of adolescent users include an alcoholic or drug dependent parent. In those cases, recovery of the adolescent is problematic because the family continues to experience all of the painful, angry, and "walking on eggs" feelings that go with chemical dependency. Effective treatment of the family involves intervening with the using parent. This parent needs treatment in order for the adolescent and family to progress in recovery.

Intervention

Two myths seem to inhibit clinicians from strong action with a using adolescent patient. First, clinical folk wisdom has been that alcoholics and drug users cannot be helped unless they want help. This is not true. Almost all users who enter treatment are there under duress. Someplace in the shadows is a "cocked, pointed gun" in terms of force by spouse, parent, judge, or employer. It appears that chemically dependent patients who are in treatment under force do a little better in terms of completion of treatment and long-term sobriety than those who appear to volunteer.[230]

The second myth is the old idea that all adolescents try drugs or alcohol and outgrow it. Research indicates that substance use involves chemical insult to the brain. This results in interference with psychosocial development and potential interference with development of the mature brain. Many young users may ultimately curtail or stop their use, but they remain seriously impaired in one or more areas of adult maturity.

The responsible clinician needs to act quickly to find appropriate treatment for the adolescent user.

SUGGESTED READINGS

Newton, Miller, *Gone Way Down: Teenage Drug-Use Is a Disease*, Tampa, FL: American Studies Press, 1981.
A short book designed to help parents understand the nature and progression of adolescent drug use.

Newton, Miller, and Polson, Beth, *Not My Kid*, New York: Arbor House, 1984.
A longer popular book with many vignettes about kids and families related to drug use. It covers drug use, prevention, parent action, and treatment.

DuPont, Robert L., *Getting Tough on Gateway Drugs: A Guide for the Family*, Washington, DC: American Psychiatric Press, 1984.
This book by the founder of the National Institute of Drug Abuse is another excellent manual for parents about kids and drugs.

Johnson, Vernon, *I'll Quit Tomorrow* (rev. ed.), San Francisco: Harper and Row, 1980.
A primary resource about chemical dependency and middle-aged adult alcoholism.

TREATMENT CENTERS

Short-Term Centers

Betty Ford Center
P.O. Box 1560
Rancho Mirage, CA 92270
Phone: (800) 854–9211
Length of stay: average is 24 days

Marworth
Lily Lake Road
Waverly, PA 18471
Phone: (800) 442–7722
Length of stay: 28 days

Sierra Tucson
(18 years old and over)
16500 North Lago del Oro Parkway
Tucson, AZ 85737
Phone: (800) 624–9001
Length of stay: 5–30 days

Long-Term Centers

Growing Together
1013 Lucerne Avenue
Lake Worth, FL 33460
Phone: (407) 585-0892
Length of stay: 2 weeks to 6 months,
partial hospitalization and/or outpatient treatment

Kids Helping Kids
P.O. Box 75148
Cincinnati, OH 45275
Phone: (606) 689-5437
Length of stay: approximately 1 year

KIDS of North Jersey, Inc.
P.O. Box 2455
Secaucus, NJ 07096-2455
Phone: (201) 863-0505
Length of stay: individual

Pathway Family Center
22180 West Ninemile Road
Southfield, MI 48034
Phone: (313) 356-0373
Length of stay: 1 month to 1 year

Second Chance, Inc.
P.O. Box 751090
Memphis, TN 38175-1090
Phone: (901) 368-5683
Length of stay: individual

Chapter 15

A Cluster of Risk Behaviors

While some young people are involved in a single problem, such as sexual or violent acting out, there is a tendency for problem behaviors to cluster together in many troubled adolescents. Jessor states, "By now, a fair amount of evidence has accumulated on this question, and there is considerable support for co-variation perspective. The evidence for co-variation is strongest for those risk behaviors that are also problem behaviors, for example, drug use, delinquency, alcohol abuse, and sexual precocity."[231] My experience with troubled adolescents confirms the data on the clustering of drug and alcohol dependence, violent acting out, sexual acting out, delinquency, including theft, vandalism, and running away, and suicide attempts.

The clustering of these behaviors provokes the question as to their cause. In my experience, I have seen two patterns in adolescents who exhibit this cluster of behaviors.

First are those adolescents who appear to have normal development up until some time in the early teen years. They come from relatively normal families, perform within the normal to superior range at school, have normal activities and interests, and socialize in healthy ways. Sometime approximately two years after initial substance use, they begin to exhibit mild troubling behaviors. As their use of alcohol and illicit drugs increases, they begin to visibly exhibit two or more of the cluster behaviors. They associate with peers who engage in similar risk behaviors. In this case, I believe that the drug and alcohol use insults the brain and interrupts normal development. Substance use is causal to lack of behavior control and lack of normal sexual development. Problem adolescents in this trajectory are usually in the third stage of drug and alcohol use. Suicide attempts come out of down, desperate feelings that are a result of multiple problems in their lives and the distorted feeling system caused by drug use.

A second trajectory that results in the same cluster of problem behaviors begins in early childhood. These adolescents come from troubled families, often headed by single parents, under enormous financial and environmental stress. They tend to be troubled in behavior from early childhood onward. Many of these young people have been classified by child study teams early in elementary school either as learning disabled or emotionally handicapped. For this group, drug and alcohol use becomes a natural next step in their pathological developmental pathway. Their peers, who share similar family environment and disability stressors, engage in similar risk behaviors. At the third stage of drug use, they appear on the surface to be the same as those young people from healthy families with normal developmental pathways who deteriorate as a result of drug use.

Some professionals suggest a third trajectory involving adolescents who have been subject to physical abuse and/or sexual abuse for long periods of time, therefore constituting a group of kids who suffer from post-traumatic stress disorder and in theory use drugs to self-medicate. My personal clinical experience suggests that a number of kids with these kinds of problems do end up with the cluster of risk behaviors. However, in this case, their abuse is part of a generally stressful environment, as suggested in the second trajectory above. Like other teenagers who use substances, adolescents in this group tend to use substances to join a peer group and "for the fun of it" long before they begin self-medicating. There are other adolescents who have suffered from abuse and have some of the symptoms of post-traumatic stress disorder who require special treatment for their abuse experiences but do not use drugs and are not involved in violence or sexual abuse. These adolescents appear to cope with school, peers, and others well until some event triggers difficulty.

Many clinicians propose different treatment strategies for the two groups. My experience, however, suggests that the same intensive, total intervention treatment is necessary for both groups. The second group is developmentally troubled from the start. The first group becomes developmentally troubled as a result of drug use. In both cases, there are major missing pieces of healthy growing up. In both cases, they are cognitively, affectively, and behaviorally out of control.

TREATMENT

First and foremost, these patients must be placed in a secure, drug and alcohol-free environment. Before any developmental habilitation can be done, the individual must be drug and alcohol-free and a period of time must elapse to allow the chemistry of the brain to slowly return to normal. Subjectively, the patient experiences this period as calming down from the panicky, chaotic internal state experienced at the height of acting-out behavior.

Second, patients must be helped to reach acceptance and admission of their problematic lives. Without admission of problems, there is no possibility of facing those problems and facilitating change.

Third, treatment must be cognitive in nature, helping patients to use the consequences of their behavior to make sense out of their problems and to develop increasing abilities to reason about behavior and consequences.

Fourth, the treatment must include progressive developmental habilitation. It is impossible to deal with all developmental problems at the same time. A good model deals with one developmental arena at a time. When the individual patient has mastered one area, it becomes the foundation for attacking the next area. (See the treatment section of Chapter 14 for a description of the habilitation model at KIDS of North Jersey, Inc.)

Fifth, some adolescents with the cluster of risk behaviors suffer from post-traumatic stress disorder resulting from physical or sexual abuse. In addition to primary treatment cited above, they need to deal with their history of abuse through abreactive work as described in Chapter 8.

Sixth, a family component is a necessary part of effective intervention and treatment. According to McCord, "Strong family control appeared to reduce the likelihood of juvenile deviance and delinquency in both intact and mother alone families."[232] Not only does family control act as a preventive measure, but it is a necessary insulation after treatment until adult autonomy and maturity for these troubled young people. The treatment program must include a component assisting parents to develop stronger family coherence and parental supervision of children.

Chapter 16

Eating Disorders
and Body Image

There are gender differences in growing up in America. Males are rewarded more for performance in activities including school and sports. While young women are increasingly rewarded for activities, the greater emphasis is on their appearance. They are treated as if their identity is how they look. Obviously, this is in part sexual in terms of attracting a member of the opposite sex for dating, commitment, and ultimately marriage and reproduction. However, this emphasis on identity as body appearance leads to skewed development for many female adolescents in America, deemphasizing other aspects of personality and other abilities during the developmental process. Some improvement has occurred as a result of the women's movement. However, this remains a problem area in development.

For some girls, this self-identification with body shape is especially problematic. As they go through the early pubertal growth period involving "terminal" awkwardness, large hands, feet, nose, knees, and elbows, they become increasingly "obsessed" with their body appearance. Their obsession involves hips, thighs, stomach, and breasts. If somehow they can improve their body appearance, they think they will feel better inside. These young women have merged their identity and self-worth with appearance and body shape. Seeing body as self leads these young women into problematic behavior with food.

DIETING TO RESTRICTING: ANOREXIA NERVOSA

Many young women experiment not only with hair, makeup, and dress, but also with dieting as a way to improve appearance and, therefore, self-worth. For some young women, the flirtation with dieting becomes a compulsive pattern. Dieting moves to serious restricting of food intake. They become obsessed with avoiding the kinds of food they equate with the production of body fat. They move from normal, healthy exercise to obsessive exercise as a way to take off any accrued weight from recent meals. As these young women move from 10% to 15% to 20% below normal body weight, they become anorexic. They acquire a disease called anorexia nervosa, literally meaning starvation from nervous or psychological causes.

These young women tend to be high achievers and to come from overenmeshed families. Steven Levenkron calls this type of young woman *The Best Little Girl in the World*, which is the title of his book about an anorexic girl. [233]

Ten percent of young women with anorexia nervosa die from their disease. The general prevalence of the disease is estimated to be between 0.5% and 2% of the female population. [234] One other key characteristic of anorexia nervosa is distorted body image. The anorexic girl who looks like a concentration camp refugee sees herself as fat. In the past, anorexia nervosa has tended to be a white, middle- and upper-class disease, but in the last decade clinicians have been seeing African-American and Hispanic girls with the disease.

FAILING TO RESTRICT: BULIMIA

Some young women start out restricting, but fail. They cannot maintain the discipline of extremely low food intake and self-starvation. Failure results in bingeing. Severe starvation builds intensive hunger, which results in overeating binges. Subsequent to the binge, the girl feels guilty about losing control and putting so much food into her body. She compensates by purging. Purging may involve self-induced vomiting, inappropriate use of laxative pills, diuretics, and purgatives such as ipecac. She may also engage in intense exercise. This eating disorder is called bulimia. Since it tends to *originate* in anorexia nervosa, I call this form of bulimia the

AB or anorexic/bulimia form. There are several other etiological patterns for bulimia.

These young women tend to fluctuate widely in weight because of the alternating compulsive bingeing followed by compulsive purging. As the disorder develops, the frequency and size of binges progress. The increased amount of eating forces increased purging. Between putting too much food into the body and desperately getting it out, the life of this young woman becomes emotional torture.

There is a second form of bulimia, which I usually call by the simple title of the disorder. The young women with this form do not start out restricting and fail. They usually acquire the purging part of the disorder through peer contact in the locker room. In talking with peers, they complain about diets not working, only to receive the advice of a friend, who suggests purging as a way to keep the weight down. As the disease develops, these young women vary from slightly over normal weight to heavy. Their disorder is as driven and compulsive in bingeing and purging as the AB form.

Like anorexia nervosa, both forms of bulimia tend to be overwhelmingly female disorders. Halmi estimates the incidence in the female adolescent and young adult population to be between 3% and 9%.[235]

OVEREATING

A third eating disorder follows a somewhat different trajectory. This eating disorder is called overeating and it results in the condition of obesity, which is significant overweight. Estimates suggest that between 10% and 15% percent of all adolescents are truly obese.[236] This is determined by skinfold measures as well as weight compared to normal for the age, size, and body frame. While some young people with obesity have physiologically based problems such as tumors, malfunctioning glands, and neurologically based problems, the overwhelming majority of obese adolescents are overeaters. They have become hooked on the taste and feeling of a full stomach. If one listens to many of them describe the warm feeling they get when filling up with enjoyed foods, it sounds like they are "hugging themselves from within." For some obese adolescents this is an individual process. For others, it is learned in their family system.

Overeating tends to be more of a female problem than a male problem. Some experts suggest this has to do with difference in activity amounts and rates between adolescent males and females in American culture.

Overeating resembles drug self-medication in many ways. Overeaters tend to binge when experiencing fear, anxiety, or loneliness. They tend to correct bad feelings with food instead of mood-altering substances.

THEORETICAL PERSPECTIVES AND TREATMENTS

A variety of theories have been put forward to describe eating disorders. Hilde Bruch, a psychodynamic psychiatrist, suggested that anorexia is a response to becoming an adult woman through pubertal growth. She sees anorexia nervosa as resistance to physically and psychologically becoming an adult woman, since lowered body weight prevents or stops the menstrual cycle. This resistance to pubertal development is rooted in defective resolution of the first oedipal crisis. Bruch treated a number of young anorexic girls, using analysis to deal with their resistance to resolving the oedipal crisis during the pubertal period.[237] Remaining a "little girl" keeps sexual maturity and feelings from occurring. Self-starvation produces amenorrhea (nonmenstruation).

Salvador Minuchin and associates approached anorexia as a family systems disorder. They saw the anorexic girl as a symptom-bearer attempting to deal with issues within the family system through her behavior and disorder. Overenmeshment was seen as a major family symptom in these cases. The patient's enmeshment and systems role have a function in maintaining family stability, given other family problems.[238]

Pope and Hudson discovered a relationship between bulimia and endogenous depression in family trees. They suggest that bulimia may have a genetic base related to depression. They experimented with use of antidepressant medication to deal with bingeing and purging. While their study shows success, subsequent studies have failed to replicate their findings.[239]

A variety of other approaches have been used to understand and treat various eating disorders. A number of cognitively oriented therapists have used cognitive behavioral therapy with some success.[240] They see anorexia nervosa and bulimia as expressions of faulty cognitive beliefs and behavior based on those beliefs.[241]

In my own therapeutic career focused on adolescent drug and

alcohol users, I discovered a minority of girls who swung back and forth between alcohol and drug use on the one hand, and bingeing and purging on the other. Subsequent literature has suggested some connection between chemical dependency and bulimia. Alcoholism produces a chaotic family system which seems to be the origin of bulimia.[242]

More recently, a number of clinicians have suggested a connection between childhood sexual abuse of females and the subsequent development of one of the eating disorders.[243]

EATING DISORDERS AS ADDICTIVE

Clinically and practically, I have found all three eating disorders to respond to adolescent addiction treatment. Listening to eating disorder patients with an ethnographic ear, I have heard them discuss the feelings related to a full stomach for overeaters, the shimmery feeling of self-starvation, and the relief of purging, as mild "highs." These young women seem to experience a pleasurable reward in the brain as a result of their food-related behaviors. Observing their behavior, one sees a progression in terms of frequency and amount of their eating-related behaviors. This progression appears to resemble tolerance in drug use.

During the period I was developing an addictive treatment model for the three eating disorders, Hans Huebner and others were doing hard research concerning the involvement of neurochemistry in anorexia nervosa and bulimia. Huebner makes a strong case for self-starvation producing increased adrenocorticotropic hormone (ACTH) which in turn is involved in stimulating an increase in endorphins. Endorphins are the neurotransmitters that produce relief from pain and a pleasurable mood state. Endorphins are the body's natural counterpart to opiates. Increased endorphins would give the psychological reward of an opiate-like high. This psychological reward would increase the ability of the anorexic girl to cope with life and would reduce her anxiety and depression. In addition, Huebner documents an increase in endorphins as a result of bingeing, both in bulimia and overeating. Finally, he speculates about a potential increase in endorphins as a result of various purging behaviors. His work goes a long way to substantiate the potential for an addictive pattern in the three eating disorders.[244]

Related to the subjective high from self-starving, bingeing, and purging is an apparent withdrawal syndrome with attendant craving that occurs with abstinence from all three eating disorders. My own clinical experience coincides with Huebner's experience as to the importance of preparing the eating disorder patient for this withdrawal and craving period.

One problem for many eating disorder patients treated in other modalities is subsequent relapse. Having experienced termination of treatment as cure, they experience relapse as failure. The chronic/addictive disease model sees relapse as part of the disease. No cure is possible. Only an altered lifestyle permits the individual to live with the chronic disease in a healthy way. The change of lifestyle with healthy behaviors maintained on a continuing basis seems to be an effective approach for these young women.

TREATMENT

While it is possible to treat adolescents with anorexia nervosa, bulimia, or overeating in outpatient counseling, it is difficult.

First and foremost, it is necessary to stop addictive food-related behavior by external control. A short- to long-term eating disorder treatment program effectively stops the compulsive behaviors by close supervision. It is almost impossible to do therapy with a girl who is obsessing about eating or avoiding food. The "abstinence" (from addictive behaviors) period lays the groundwork for subsequent therapy about the disorder and other related issues in the individual's identity development, sexual development, and family system.

Unlike drugs and alcohol, food cannot be given up. Central to the treatment of eating disorders is the food plan. This is a structured approach that includes three meals plus an evening snack on a regulated basis. In the beginning, the treatment center and/or family administers the food plan, relieving the girl of the anxiety about choice. As she progresses in recovery, she takes over management of her own food plan. The goal is to reduce eating from a tense, obsessive business, to an automatic behavior, as a necessary practice to sustain life. Many eating disorder patients who participate in Overeaters Anonymous turn over their meals for the day to a sponsor. This practice relieves anxiety and obsession with food.

There are certain foods that trigger anxiety and/or bingeing for eating disorder patients. Those foods, including foods made with refined sugar, are excluded from the food plan. The food plan provides balanced nutrition, thereby combating gnawing hunger and the urge to binge.

Denial of the problem is characteristic of eating disorder patients. Work on a reality-based picture of eating behavior and its general behavioral consequences is the foundation of therapy and recovery. This is acceptance of the first step of Overeaters Anonymous. Step work and participation in O.A. are an important part of recovery. Acceptance of the first step also means taking personal responsibility for the early choices that led to the disorder, for the consequences to others, and for maintenance of a healthy lifestyle.

The eating disorder patient needs to develop a healthy lifestyle in all areas of life in order to minimize the urge to correct negative feelings by avoidance of food, overeating, or excessive exercise. This lifestyle also involves continuing the "food plan" to reduce food and weight from an obsessive issue to a routine behavior.

SUGGESTED READINGS

Agras, W. Stewart, *Eating Disorders: Management of Obesity, Bulimia and Anorexia Nervosa*, New York: Pergamon Press, 1987.
This is a brief and technical introduction to treatment of all three eating disorders using cognitive behavioral and other therapeutic techniques.

Boskind-White, Marlene, and White, William C., *Bulimarexia: The Binge/Purge Cycle*, New York: W. W. Norton, 1983.
The Whites write from their experience treating bulimics. The book includes an excellent description of the disorder as well as an approach to treatment based on bulimia as learned behavior.

Bruch, Hilde, *The Golden Cage: The Enigma of Anorexia Nervosa*, Cambridge: Harvard University Press, 1978.
This is a well-written book on the problem of anorexia nervosa.

Haskew, Paul, and Adams, Cynthia H., *When Food Is a Four-Letter Word*, Englewood Cliffs, NJ: Prentice-Hall, 1984.
This is a middle level book orienting the articulate layman and the average professional therapist to the whole business of eating disorders. It is an excellent start for an orientation about food addiction.

Huebner, Hans F., *Endorphins, Eating Disorders and Other Addictive Behaviors*, New York: W. W. Norton, 1993.
Huebner writes an excellent book from the viewpoint of both research and clinical experience documenting addictive patterns for anorexia nervosa and bulimia. He gives helpful suggestions for treatment based on this theory.

Levenkron, Steven, *The Best Little Girl in the World*, Chicago: Contemporary Books, 1978.
A case story that effectively introduces laymen and professionals to anorexia nervosa.

Minuchin, Salvador, et al., *Psychosomatic Families: Anorexia Nervosa in Context*, Cambridge: Harvard University Press, 1978.
An excellent introduction, with case material, to family therapy as a tool to treat anorexia nervosa.

Root, Maria P. P., Fallon, Patricia, and Friedrich, William N., *Bulimia: A Systems Approach to Treatment*, New York: W. W. Norton, 1986.
The authors describe bulimia from a family systems viewpoint and then produce an approach to assessment and treatment based on family systems theory. They include excellent case material.

Chapter 17

Depression

Depression is the hot, trendy diagnosis of our day for a variety of reasons, including the development of several generations of effective medication for the disorder. Not only are many adults in our society on Prozac or its analogues, Zoloft and Paxil, but an even larger number go for regular therapy for depression. This increase may result from a variety of factors, including improved clinician awareness, increased environmental stress, and/or increased patient awareness via the media.

There is a tendency to see many people as having biologically based depression. While there are some good arguments for the concept of biological depression as opposed to reactive depression, research in this area is equivocal. In a recent study, Rende and associates found significant environmental influence, but no significant genetic influence, in depressive symptomatology among 707 pairs of siblings (including twins).[245] The distorted brain chemistry profile, that is depression, is similar for someone who is diagnosed as having biological depression and for someone who has situational depression from some form of loss.[246] Since this is a great bag in which to place many patients with negative feelings, it is natural that this diagnosis should spill over to adolescents.

THE NUMBERS

Petersen et al., writing about "Depression and Adolescence," describe three levels of depression. First, they describe brief depressed moods, which almost all human beings have at one time or another. Second, they describe depressive syndromes, a constellation of behaviors and emotions that are found to statistically occur together.

Third, they cite clinical depression as a mood disorder, in which they include major depressive disorder and dysthymic disorder. They propose a series of symptoms for clinical depression, including depressed or irritable moods, decreased interest in pleasurable activity, changes in weight, sleep problems, psychomotor agitation or retardation, fatigue or loss of energy, feelings of worthlessness or abnormal guilt, reduced concentration and decision-making ability, and repeated suicidal ideation attempts or plans. Five or more of these symptoms must be experienced for two weeks or longer.[247]

Using the above criteria, Petersen et al. cite an average of 7% clinical depression in the general population. They cite a figure of 3% of adolescents with major depressive disorder in the general population.[248] Klerman suggests an increase in depression among adolescents in recent decades.[249] My experience, based on conversations with therapists of various schools, attendance at a variety of professional meetings, and conversations with other professional practitioners, suggests a much higher number of teenagers are being labeled as depressed and treated as such.

Gender Differences

Several studies indicate that gender differences in depression emerge by age 14 to 15 and appear to persist into adulthood. Females tend to be classified as depressed more frequently than males.[250]

WITH OTHER DISORDERS

Depression is cited as causal to, or coinciding with, a variety of disorders, including anorexia nervosa, bulimia, overeating, drug dependence, alcoholism, physical abuse, sexual abuse, learning disabilities, gender confusion, and others. Based on my own experience, I suggest that situational depression is often a natural result of third-stage drug and alcohol dependence. By that time, the normal range of feelings has been erased, leaving the adolescent user swinging between radical extremes, the shimmering chemical high and the dull, gray, "the world sucks" down. The user at this stage has turned the family into a battleground, is messing up in school, has given up activities, is involved in criminal activity, and has given up normal peer relationships. Each of these problems alone is a good reason to feel down. Added together, these facts are the foundation of intense clinical depression. Underlying situational depression is disturbed neurochemistry as a result of regular infusion of mood-altering substances, disturbed cognitive evaluations, and losses.

PROBLEM DIAGNOSIS FOR TEENS

Depression is a problematic diagnosis for teenagers. Popular observation sees teens as subject to mercurial mood swings. Rapid change in mood is a hallmark particularly of the early adolescent period.

Rapid change in feelings is based on several facts about adolescent development. First and foremost is the acute self-consciousness involved in a higher level of self-awareness as a result of neurological maturation. The early adolescent is always "on" before "the imaginary audience." This involves microscopic examination of self. Most early teenagers, given the fact of physical awkwardness as a result of disproportionate growth, find themselves wanting. This negative self-evaluation results in down feelings.

The early adolescent's body is in a period of rapid change triggered by major shifts in hormone levels in the body. Several of the hormones involved have correlates in terms of mood change and feelings. The rapid swing of feelings from up and enthusiastic to sad and distressed is another natural cause for down feelings.

A third area of normal adolescent growth contributing to a misdiagnosis of clinical depression is the conscious awareness of one's own feelings that is characteristic of the early adolescent period. For the first time, the young person not only feels but is conscious of the feelings and examines the feelings. This consciousness and self-examination of feelings tends to exaggerate the ups and downs of mood changes.

Another issue in down feelings for teens is the identity development process. Adolescents are exploring a variety of aspects of self, using role-taking and experimentation. Some of the experiments fail, others are inconclusive, all leading to not-so-happy feelings.

Additionally, many adolescents pick up the lingo of depression from the media and use it to present complaints to clinicians.

Since the advent of serotonin reuptake blockers as a new generation of antidepressant medication, I find an increasing number of teenage patients who have been diagnosed as depressed and are on Prozac, Zoloft, or Paxil. These prescriptions are written most often by psychiatrists, but occasionally by family practitioners. The reason for treatment and medication has been unhappiness with acting out on the part of these adolescents to the point of trouble in the family, at school, and in the community. Since definitions and criteria for depression among adolescents have been widened to include irritability, acting out, and anger as symptoms, this diagnosis *appears* to be appropriate. The attempt to solve acting out by serotonin reuptake blockers universally fails. The reason is neurochemical. Depression appears to be an inadequate amount of monoamines (serotonin and norepinephrine) present in the synaptic gaps in the brain. On the other hand, behavioral excess and acting out appear to result from excessive monoamines in the synaptic gap.[251] Antidepressant medication increases monoamine availability in the brain, therefore increasing acting out behavior rather than extinguishing it. This suggests a clear difference between true, sadness–based depression and adolescent unhappiness.

Adding up the above factors in the early adolescent period, it is not surprising that teenagers are moody and often moody in a down or negative way. I believe it is dangerous to label natural moodiness or unhappiness and acting out in the teenage passage as clinical depression. The suggestive label at a time of affective and cognitive vulnerability can create major depressive disorder where only moodiness existed before.

THE FUNCTION OF NEGATIVE FEELINGS

Randolph Nesse suggests that we in the therapeutic professions in America are too quick to give medication that shuts off negative feelings. He goes on to develop a series of discussions of the positive function of negative feelings for human beings. He points out that almost all qualities and characteristics of human beings are "adaptive" in the sense that they have a function related to our survival and well-being as biological creatures. Anxiety functions as a form of arousal to deal with threat in the "fight or flight" response and system.[252]

Nesse suggests that sadness and depression, while a more complicated issue, are a programmed slow-down of the human body in order to allow and force a reorientation in terms of new strategies to solve a major life problem. He goes on to suggest that immediately medicating negative, but normal, feeling states interferes with the life-enhancing function of these negative emotions. Antidepressant medication, by aborting the reorientation process, may keep the individual stuck in a faulty life strategy.

DEPRESSION OR DISTRESS

I believe most adolescent depression is not clinical depression, but one or another form of distress signaling the need for change. Distress is frustration with current moods, situations, or relationships. Distress is a down feeling that may express itself as sadness, irritability, or frustration. Distress is a functional feeling, in the sense that it creates the energy for change. Distress is an evaluation of a current situation as not good. The not-good evaluation suggests the need for change. The combination of unpleasant feelings and the negative evaluation become the driving force for healthy changes during the experimentation with identity, behavior, socialization, and relationships that are the main tasks of adolescence.

Given the fact that the adolescent period is a period of spurt growth and rapid change, it is not surprising to find frequent episodes of distress signaling the need to develop better strategies for particular problems. Offer and associates, in a self-image survey, found that approximately 20% of teens report feelings of emotional distress.[253] Approaching this distress as depression, in a classical biological sense, causes the clinician to seek immediate relief for the feelings, rather than discovering which strategies and behaviors are not working for the individual. Medication, at this point, shuts down not only the distress, but also the urgency and energy for change.

DEALING WITH DISTRESS

Before rushing to a diagnosis, or even an operating diagnosis, of depression or dysthymia, the clinician needs to approach the negative mood as distress. Procedurally, this means looking for the area or strategy of life that is failing the individual teenager at the moment. Often, these failing strategies are experiments with identity, with male/female relationships leading toward intimacy, with family relationships, with larger socialization issues, or with educational preparation and choice.

Differential diagnosis procedures require eliminating drug and alcohol use with resulting life area failures as a likely cause of teenage distress. Discovering an area of dysfunction leading to the distress clearly eliminates depression as an appropriate diagnosis for the particular teenager.

The Depressed Adolescent

After sorting out distressed adolescents by using the criteria suggested above, including the presence of acting out, anger, rage, or an active mode of unhappiness, there remains a much smaller group of genuinely depressed teenagers. These young people have been the victims of sexual or physical abuse, have a debilitating physical illness, or have been subject to a major loss such as a parent figure, sibling, or grandparent. They display the nonactive symptoms of major depression, including depressed moods, decreased interest in pleasurable activity, often weight loss or gain, sleep problems, fatigue or loss of energy, feelings of worthlessness, abnormal guilt, reduced concentration and decision-making ability, and sometimes repeated suicidal ideation, attempts, or plans.

This group of adolescent patients should be treated for major depression using a cognitive approach. The grieving adolescent will need help in working through the stages of grief to resolve the loss. The sexually abused adolescent will need to do abreactive work in order to resolve the abuse incidents of the past and begin to develop healthy self-esteem and sexuality for the future. If abuse is continuing, the therapist will need to take protective steps to end the abuse immediately. Adolescents with suicidal ideations or plans will need immediate supervision until the intensity of the depression resolves itself to the point of no self-danger.

Medication?

Many therapists follow the current standard wisdom about depression, which is that medication is the faster and more appropriate approach. Even when using cognitive therapy, an equally efficacious therapy over the long term, therapists often seek medication for their patients during the interim to produce relief and faster response to cognitive therapy. This is a problem for adolescent patients.

Research shows that tricyclic antidepressants have made no real difference between treated and control adolescent subjects.[254] In addition, the package instructions for physicians with Prozac and Zoloft indicate that these serotonin reuptake blockers are not for use with patients under 18 years of age.

If you remember, the earlier discussion in Chapter 5 suggested that mood-altering medication is contraindicated for adolescents. Adolescence is a period not only of spurt growth in the body, but also of high velocity change in the brain involving breaking of old synaptic connections and the making of new synaptic connections with chemical guidance as part of the new connection process. Any drug that interferes with synaptic chemistry has the potential of interfering with normal and healthy development. I suggest that antidepressant medication should be used only in the most extreme circumstances, after distress has been eliminated as a finding and all other techniques for depression therapy have been exhausted.

TREATMENT

First and foremost, as stated earlier, the counselor needs to approach the adolescent with down feelings as having "distress." This means exploring sources of the sad, irritated, or frustrated feelings. Substance use needs to be investigated as a possible cause.

Second, having found the area of problem in the teen's life that is the source of the sad feelings, the therapist then moves to help the adolescent explore that area in a cognitive way. This means dealing with the tendency to exaggerate and awfulize. It means leading the adolescent patient beyond black-and-white valuative statements into areas of gray that suggest other options.

Third, as the distressing situation is seen from other angles and perspectives, the therapist can help the individual become aware of his or her coping strategy. Awareness of the strategy brings with it the chance to examine how and why the strategy is failing.

Fourth, the therapist then leads the teen into exploration of alternative strategies. This should result in experimentation with other strategies as homework, followed by discussion of the results in subsequent sessions.

Fifth, for the teen who appears to be so down as not to respond to therapy, the therapist should work with family members to help the teen, even by physical assistance, to do aerobic speed exercises. Fast walking, calisthenics, aerobic dance exercise, or any speeded-up exercise will increase the endorphin level in the brain, producing a feeling of equanimity that counteracts the sadness and distress. Exercise produces immediate relief and availability for therapy.

Sixth, the small group of adolescents with major depression will need to be treated for that depression, including use of cognitive therapy, assistance in the grief process for those suffering a loss, and abreactive work for those who have been abused. Medication should be used only if the adolescent is not available for therapy due to the intensity of the depression and the suggestions for exercise in the above paragraph fail. The course of pharmacological therapy should be extremely brief, helping the adolescent become available for therapy. Prolonged antidepressant medication may seriously interfere with normal neurological development during adolescence.

Seventh, suicidal adolescents should be hospitalized or otherwise placed in residential treatment with adequate suicide supervision until suicidal ideations abate.

Chapter 18

Chronic Diseases

Chronic diseases are those diseases for which there is no cure. The subject faces a lifetime of living with the disease. In many cases, it is possible for a patient to live a relatively normal, healthy life, given the fact of the disease. He must develop a special lifestyle oriented toward keeping the disease under control. For diabetes, the lifestyle involves regular testing of blood or urine for glucose and a combination of insulin use, special diet, adequate rest, and exercise. Young epilepsy patients must take one or more medications to control seizures and avoid certain kinds of activities that trigger seizures. Asthma victims must pursue a medication regimen and avoid allergenic substances and stress, which provoke asthma attacks. Finally, head injury patients often need medication to control seizures, and a variety of cognitive, compensatory, and substitution techniques in order to pursue work, socialization, and family life.

Chronic disease is the predominant form of illness in our day. Later in life, individuals acquire heart disease and, in other cases, cancer. Even cancer in remission is subject to return. In both cases, changes in lifestyle are critical as a health regimen to cope with the possibility of recurrence.

Turk and Speers cite diabetes mellitus as the tenth leading cause of death in the United States across all age groups, and sixth among adolescents.[255] The most serious and prevalent type of diabetes is called Type 1, juvenile-onset or insulin-dependent. This is one of several chronic diseases that beset adolescents. Others include asthma, epilepsy, and head injuries.

Until recently, I was unaware of the fact that a large percentage of traumatic brain injury that results in ongoing impairment occurs to young men 30 years of age or under.[256] Young men tend to be risk takers and users of mood-altering substances that cause more accidents in automobiles and other settings.

Historically, our medical paradigm has been based on treating acute diseases that are of short duration and are relatively curable. Chronic diseases are noncurable, but they are manageable.

THE ADOLESCENT: "INVULNERABLE SELF"

Adolescents appear to have more difficulty with chronic disease management than adults. The problems with adolescents and juvenile-onset diabetes are legend. The same is true of teenagers with asthma, epilepsy, and head injuries.

Most adolescents have a sense of invulnerability, seeming to believe that nothing negative can happen or harm them. This "invulnerable self" has been suggested as a possible cause of risk-taking on the part of adolescent males. This sense of personal fearlessness not only involves a lack of reasonable self-protection, but results in denial about limits and handicaps. This denial is particularly difficult for individuals with chronic diseases, who need to accept their problem in order to manage it.

For adolescents, denial is rooted in their need to be normal, particularly with reference to peer group. Adolescents, especially during the early period, have a strong and overwhelming need to blend with a peer group. Any abnormality is perceived as a giant stigma, potentially causing rejection by peers.

According to Peter Blos, "any serious distortion of the body image will become manifest in some specific ego impairment."[257] Chronic diseases as body distortions frequently cause adolescents to turn up in a therapist's office.

COMPLIANCE

According to Turk and Speers, "the levels of adherence to diabetic self-care regimens are notoriously low."[258] Compliance levels for diabetics have been reported to be as low as 48%.

Kaplan and Simon state "failure to adhere to therapeutic regimens is a major problem hampering the quality of medical care." They go on to suggest that rates of noncompliance vary between 15% and 93% depending on the patient population and the definition of nonadherence.[259] Adolescent nonadherence or noncompli-ance is on the high end of those percentages.

Compliance or adherence involves following the prescribed health regimen and lifestyle changes. A number of interventions have been tried to raise levels of compliance: education, warnings by medical personnel, reporting-back systems, and family assistance. Compliance problems continue to fill behavioral medicine and chronic disease literature.

ACCEPTANCE OF DISEASE

Alcoholics Anonymous and chemical dependency treatment have something to offer in this area. The foundation of recovery for an alcoholic or drug addict is acceptance of the disease as chronic in terms of A.A.'s first step which is "admitting powerlessness over alcohol." Subsequent to acceptance of and surrender to the disease, new health regimens are learned and lifestyle changes are made.

Harry Tieboult, who treated Bill W. (a cofounder of A.A.) for depression and was an observer of the development of Alcoholics Anonymous, suggests that a personality reorganization around the fact of alcoholism is central to recovery.[260] Tieboult went on to see this personality reorganization as similar to religious conversion but without any religious content. The personality reorganization in this case was around deep-level acceptance of the chronic disease as defining self. Based on this foundation, lifestyle change can occur.

My own experience with adolescent diabetics, asthmatics, drug/alcohol dependent individuals, and individuals with other chronic diseases has shown this to be true. However, with teens, the urge to be normal makes acceptance of the disease and the personality reorganization process much more painful and difficult.

OTHER PROBLEMS

An adolescent with a chronic disease, having accepted her primary ongoing disease, still faces other major problems during the develop-mental passage. The identity development process, based so heavily on the enlarged body and adult reproductive capability, becomes problematic for the adolescent with a less than normal and healthy body. Special help is needed for this adolescent to develop role experimentation and interest in activities that promote a healthy sense of self, notwithstanding the chronic disease.

Second and of equal importance is the problem of sexuality. Adolescence is a period in which sexual identity, orientation, and behavior is developed as a result of physical maturation and increasing interaction with peers. Adolescents with chronic diseases face a series of special problems. At a time when they are seeking to be more independent, their disease often keeps them dependent on parents and other caregivers. In addition, their mobility may be restricted because of legal rules limiting access to a driver's license. Also, they face difficulty in terms of peer acceptance or rejection as a result of their chronic disease problems. And if this were not enough, their disease and treatment regimens, including medication, may physically interfere with sexual arousal and sexual performance. [261]

Adolescents with chronic diseases need special help in developing identity, sexual identity, and gender orientation, based on acceptance of their chronic disease condition.

TREATMENT

The foundation of treatment for chronic diseases is "midwifing" acceptance of and surrender to the chronic disease. This involves a reorganization of personality around the fact of the disease. In my experience, this is facilitated by traumatic failure events related to problems caused by the disease. Using these traumatic events makes it somewhat easier for the adolescent to move from denial to acceptance and surrender.

Second, adolescents usually go through a grief process about loss of normalcy. This process begins with denial, moves to anger, then to depression, and finally acceptance and surrender. Sometimes, adolescents jump back and forth between denial and anger or between depression and anger. Therapists must be persistent and patient in pushing and moving them toward the therapeutic crisis that results in deep level-acceptance.

Third, the adolescent patient's perception about social success and well-being plays a role in compliance. Conflict between this perception and the behavior required for compliance to a chronic disease health regimen causes noncompliance. The therapist needs to explore the patient's perception and help the patient resolve conflicts.

Fourth, the therapist needs to be informed about the nature of each of the chronic diseases, the individual's particular case, and appropriate health regimens. The therapist can assist the adolescent patient in developing behavior change and the health regimen after acceptance and surrender.

Fifth, the therapist needs to assist the adolescent chronic disease patient in pursuing activities and role experimentation that leads to identity development. Both healthy and handicapped role models and mentors may be useful in this process.

Sixth, the therapist needs to assist the adolescent patient in grappling with sexual development issues. This requires working knowledge of the special problems of individuals with a variety of handicaps and chronic illnesses with relationship to sexuality and sexual performance. Having a medically trained expert in the area of the handicapped and sexuality is a critical resource for treatment in this area.

Chapter 19

Conclusion

We have taken a journey through the adolescent development period. We have looked at theories of adolescence, particularly a rite-of-passage theory involving movement through withdrawal from family as a child, an isolation period involving preparation for adulthood, and finally reentry to family and society as an adult. We have looked at neurological development, general physical development, and reproductive system development during the adolescent period. I have put forward a series of suggestions about the stance therapists need to take when working with adolescents and their families.

In addition, a number of specific areas of adolescence, including identity development, spirituality and values, development of social relations and skills, development of sexual role and behaviors, and education as well as vocational choice, have been considered. We have also looked at a number of problems areas including aggression and violence, teenage suicide, drug and alcohol use and dependence, a common cluster of risk behaviors, family conflict, eating disorders, depression, and the problem of adolescent-onset chronic diseases.

Two facts emerge. First, most adolescents go through the adolescent passage in healthy ways. They reach adulthood prepared for intimacy and sexuality, economic autonomy, and adult participation in society. At the same time, a growing minority of teens find the passage a "perilous ordeal." They stumble developmentally along the way. Due to drugs and alcohol, sexual precocity, aggression and violence, eating disorders, distress, and other problems, they foreclose early on development in one or more major areas. They enter adulthood arrested in personal growth, troubled in behavior, and unprepared for adult participation in society.

This second group is troubled in part because of personal and family choices along the way, but also because of societal problems with the adolescent passage. The lack of mentoring during the isolated preparatory period is one problem. A second problem is the lack of a clear reentry process into family and society with adult self-concept and societally recognized adult status. This second problem is based in part on the confused pseudoadult period from 18 to 23, in which we give the late teen expectations of adult status, but the complexity of our society and economy limits the ability of the teen to function as an autonomous adult. Solutions can be societal or individual.

SUGGESTIONS FOR SOCIAL CHANGE

First and foremost, I believe we need to reduce the long period of ambiguity about adult status, pseudoadulthood. This means raising the age of majority to 21 in all fifty states. I realize that this is a controversial proposal. However, there is no way to develop total adult status at 18, 19, and 20. The complexity of our society requires a longer educational period or a family-supported early work period in order to establish financial independence. Voting, jury service, and signing legal and financial contracts should all occur at 21 years of age. Raising the legal age to 21 does not make legal age exactly coincide with total adult status in society. That occurs around ages 23 to 24. However, raising the legal age to 21 will reduce the current 5- to 6-year period from legal majority to actual adult status, thereby reducing the period of confusing ambiguity.

The carnage on our highways, including maiming and death that resulted from lowering the drinking age to 18, forced American society to raise the legal drinking age to 21. This was done in spite of the previous "hurrah" that military service at 18 should bring with it the right to drink at 18. A few states still have a lower age. This needs to be corrected.

Second, I believe we need a clear ritual of adult status in American society. This ritual could be a year's mandatory national service requirement of all young people that must begin between the ages of 18 and 22. It should begin after completion of high school and should involve either one or two years of required service to the society, prior to entering full adult status. Norwegian society requires universal military service for all young men. Israel requires military service for both men and women. I believe we should require national service in a variety of formats. Army, Navy, Marine Corps, and Air Force is one form of service. Peace Corps, Vista, or a Conservation Corps are other existing possibilities for national service. I suggest that we add a new possibility given the increased aging of our population: the creation of a lower level in the National Health Service for individuals to serve as ambulance attendants, nursing aides, and hospital attendants in a variety of institutions served by the National Health Corps. A tuition voucher for a year of higher education could be given for successful completion of a year of service. This service would provide a clearer ritual of reentry to society in adult status. It would clearly demarcate the end of adolescence with a period spent away from home. In addition, the service itself would create a sense of adult responsibility for American society as a whole. National service could become the reentry ritual for young Americans.

Third, we need to provide adequate preparation for adulthood during the isolation period of adolescence. Despite attempts to make education neutral, our public education system needs to become the formal preparation for adulthood. This means a reinvestment of values in American education. Values need to occur in teaching of history and civics, in health and biology with regard to sexual behavior, and in public and civic responsibility in a whole variety of educational areas. We cannot prepare young people for responsible adult life if we do not teach them the expectations and rules of appropriate adult behavior in American society. In order to include values in the educational process, communities, states, and the nation will have to go through the process of hammering out a consensus on a variety of value issues. This process toward consensus can be initiated at the federal level as a condition for states and local districts to receive federal funds. States, through legislature and departments of education, can initiate the process. Finally, local school boards can begin the process for their own districts.

The Rewards of Guiding Youth

A second area of solutions for pitfalls along the "perilous ordeal" resulting in early developmental foreclosure is individual and/or family therapy.

In order to guide adolescents through the perilous ordeal, the therapist has to be a healthy adult with an effective, age-appropriate lifestyle. A number of the negative countertransference issues cited in Chapter 5 result from unresolved family-of-origin issues, current relationship or family issues, or life trajectory issues of the therapist. Growing professionally, growing personally, and growing interpersonally are all part of the necessary foundation for effective work with adolescents. The troubled teen is not seeking an aging peer but rather a stable adult for guidance through this difficult transition.

Many therapists and counselors complain about difficulties in working with the troubled minority of adolescent patients. I find this work exhilarating and rewarding. First, I find young people far more capable of change in cognition, behavior, and even personality. While there is neural plasticity in the brain that remains throughout the lifespan, this is particularly true during the adolescent passage, given spurt growth in changing the organization of the brain through the making of new synapses, new networks, and higher level associational functions. Working with adolescents is rewarding because they change. As a guide, you can make a real difference in their development. You make a difference in development by not only altering the course of their adolescent trajectory but by correcting developmental problems from childhood. Working effectively with adolescents means offering teenage patients the opportunity to enter adulthood as full and healthy human beings.

Peggy

Peggy[262] came to treatment in the KIDS program straight out of a county mental hospital. She had previously been hospitalized in the psychiatric unit of a noted private hospital after a suicide attempt. The psychiatrist and staff found her resistant to treatment and recovery. The parents, unwilling to give up, had tried a second time. This resulted in a second suicide attempt, hospitalization in a county mental facility, and ultimately a judgment by the staff that she was intractable and schizophrenic. The staff recommended that the family initiate proceedings to have her custodially hospitalized in a long-term state institution as a hopeless psychotic. They gave up on her.

By luck or by accident, at a parent self-help group, her parents met some other parents who had adolescents in the KIDS of North Jersey program. Her family came to look and decided to make one more attempt to help Peggy before giving up. The county hospital had labeled Peggy as a hopeless adolescent schizophrenic patient. Often a quick single diagnosis is given to adolescents in treatment units where treatment focuses on fast relief for acting out and dangerous symptoms. We discovered in the course of her admission that her primary problem was adolescent alcohol and drug dependence. Our approach is aimed at teasing out all appropriate problems and diagnoses in order to develop an effective treatment plan for the patient. When I saw her the first time, she was a thin, angry, hurting 15-year-old. First we had to wait out and extinguish her hospital-developed behavior. Then real treatment could begin. Over the course of a two-year period, we patiently helped Peggy face her problem and connect her failure at school, her family conflict, her suicidal ideations and attempts, and her defiant behavior to increasing drug and alcohol use. She accepted her disease. Then she began building a new lifestyle in order to live healthily with her chronic disease. With ups and downs, she slowly moved through the process of returning to her family and building a successful relationship with her adoptive parents and sister.

Later in treatment, she worked through issues about her adoption and religion. Then, she moved back to the education arena and learned how to focus on schoolwork and achievement and how to reject the advances of her old drug-using peer group. She had a real struggle with peer pressure, especially with males from the drug-using group. Patient work on her self-esteem, being internally validated, got her through this problem. She ultimately graduated from high school on the honor roll, went to community college, graduated on the dean's list, and then pursued her dream of a musical career in a fine arts oriented college. Recently, Peggy graduated, having been on the dean's list her entire college career, and much to her surprise, her diploma read magna cum laude. She could not believe that she had been among the academic elite of her school.

After Peggy's graduation from formal treatment, she faced several other developmental crises with help. The first had to do with dating and intimacy. She continued to be excited by "punk, druggie image" males. This was a recurrence of the problem first encountered during her return to school while in treatment. Her drug use period had produced a correlation between this image and sexual excitement. She kept pursuing relationships with newly sober individuals who used her, abused her, and moved on. It took some heavy cognitive work over a brief period of time to help her look at her dream for relationship, marriage, and family. Then we looked at the path that her image of an exciting male would lead to in terms of intimacy and family. She slowly rebuilt her dream image with a future orientation, looking for a different kind of male. In the process, she met a young man at her school who shared her dreams and her values for a future. They became engaged and were married.

A subsequent crisis involved a period of high pressure at school when she began to have thoughts of giving up the college of her dreams because the requirements appeared to be overwhelming. She wanted, impulsively, to transfer to a lesser institution and take the minimal requirements for music teacher certification. Instead of trying to resolve all of the issues at once, I helped her decide on a respite period during which she would lower her course load, perhaps extending her college career by a semester. In addition, we did some work on organizing life and study in order to make the most out of the time available to her without totally crippling her life. The result was that she got through the period of high stress, decided to stay with college, and ultimately graduated with a real sense of achievement and success. Today, when I hear from Peggy, it is not with problems that require therapy, but rather sharing the good things of her healthy adult life. She talks about pursuing music education jobs for herself and her husband, and their future lifestyle, including location and type of home, things that constitute their dream for the future. Contact with Peggy and other former patients provides moments of real happiness for me; I have seen that they are capable of changing from "walking disaster areas" to healthy young adults with a future.

Change Is Possible

For those therapists who are intimidated by acting-out adolescent patients, real change can occur. Adolescents have a high level of plasticity and potential for change, since it is a period of experimenting with roles, experimenting with behaviors, and deciding what kind of adults they are going to be. If you understand the adolescent passage and the various paths and possible developmental traps involved in growing up, it is possible to work effectively with adolescent patients. The key to adolescent therapy is a framework of belief about healthy growing-up. This includes value decisions about healthy adult lifestyles and healthy adolescent developmental paths. Finally, good therapists for adolescents constantly demand change and movement from their adolescent patients.

Notes

INTRODUCTION

1. Bullough, V. L. (1981). Age at menarche: A misunderstanding. *Science*, 213, 365–366.

2. National Center for Health Statistics. (1991).

3. National Center for Health Statistics. (1990, November 28). Supplement, Advance report of final mortality statistics, 1988. *Monthly vital statistics report*, 39(7) (Table 7).

4. National Center for Health Statistics. (1991).

5. *Nation's Health* (1993, May–June), p. 7.

6. U.S. Department of Commerce. (1961). *Current population reports* (Series P-20, No. 110) (Tables 2 & 5). Washington, DC: Bureau of the Census.

U.S. Department of Commerce. (1990). *Current population reports* (Series P-20, No. 443) (Table 1). Washington, DC: Bureau of the Census.

7. U.S. Department of Justice (1990). *Age-specific arrest rates and race-specific arrest rates for selected offenses: 1965–1988.* Washington, DC: Federal Bureau of Investigation.

8. Centers for Disease Control. (1990, October 5). Summary of notifiable diseases, United States: 1989. *Morbidity and mortality weekly report*, 38(54), pp. 10–11.

9. Henshaw, S. K., Kenney, A. M., Somberg, D., & Van Vort, J. (1989). *Teenage pregnancy in the United States: The scope of the problem and state responses* (Table 5). New York: The Alan Guttmacher Institute.

CHAPTER 1

10. Based on a summary of Hall's theory in R. E. Muuss (1962), *Theories of adolescence* (5th ed.) (pp. 20ff). New York: Random House.

11. Ausubel, D. P. (1954). *The theory and problems of adolescent development.* New York: Grune & Stratton.

12. Muuss, R. E. (1962). *Theories of adolescence* (5th ed.) (pp. 24ff). New York: Random House.

13. Freud, A. (1980). Adolescence as a developmental disturbance. In Caplan & Lebovici (Eds.), *Adolescence: Psychosocial perspectives* (pp. 5–10). New York: Basic Books.

14. Blos, P. (1979). *The adolescent passage: Developmental issues.* New York: International Universities Press.

15. Kaplan, L. J. (1984). *Adolescence: The farewell to childhood.* New York: Simon & Schuster.

16. Elson, M. (Ed.). (1987). *The Kohut seminars on self psychology and psychotherapy with adolescents and young adults* (pp. 305ff). New York: W. W. Norton.

17. Mead, M. (1961). *Coming of age in Samoa.* New York: Quill.

18. Sullivan, H. S. (1953). *The interpersonal theory of psychiatry.* New York: W. W. Norton.

19. Erikson, E. H. (1968). *Identity: Youth and crisis.* New York: W. W. Norton.

20. Gesell, A., Ilg, F. L., & Ames, L. B. (1956). *Youth: The years from ten to sixteen,* New York: Harper & Row.
   Ames, L. B., Ilg, F. L., & Baker, S. M. (1988). *Your ten- to fourteen-year-old.* New York: Dell Publishing.

21. Piaget, J. (1972). Intellectual evolution from adolescence to adulthood. *Human Development, 15,* 1–12.

22. Kohlberg, L. (1984). Moral stages and moralization: The cognitive-developmental approach. In L. Kohlberg, *Essays on moral development: Volume II, The psychology of moral development: The nature and validity of moral stages* (pp. 170–211). San Francisco: Harper & Row.

23. Rebok, G. W. (1987). *Life-span cognitive development.* New York: Holt, Reinhart & Winston.

24. Muuss, R. E. (1962). Selman's stage theory of social cognition. In R. E. Muuss, *Theories of adolescence* (5th ed.) (pp. 245ff). New York: Random House.

25. Muuss, R. E. (1962). David Elkind's theory of adolescent egocentrism. In R. E. Muuss, *Theories of adolescence* (5th ed.) (pp. 264ff). New York: Random House.

26. Block, J. (1971). *Lives through time.* Berkeley: Bancroft Books.

27. Offer, D., & Sabshin, M. (1984). Patterns of normal development. In D. Offer & M. Sabshin (Eds.), *Normality and the life cycle: A critical integration* (pp. 393–425). New York: Basic Books.

28. Thomas, A., & Chess, S. (1989). Temperament and personality. In G. A. Kohnstamm, J. E. Bates, & M. K. Rothbart (Eds.), *Temperament in childhood* (pp. 249–261). Chichester, England: John Wiley.

CHAPTER 2

29. Richards, M., & Petersen, A. C. (1987). Biological theoretical models of adolescent development. In V. B. Van Hasselt & M. Hersen (Eds.), *Handbook of adolescent psychology* (pp. 34–52). New York: Pergamon Press.

30. Gilligan, C. (1982). *In a different voice: Psychological theory and women's development.* Cambridge: Harvard University Press.

CHAPTER 3

31. Feldman, S. S., & Elliott, G. R. (Eds.). (1990). *At the threshold: The developing adolescent.* Cambridge: Harvard University Press.

32. Epstein, H. T. (1974). Phrenoblysis: Special brain and mind growth periods, Part 2, Human mental development. *Developmental Psychobiology, 7,* 217–224.

Epstein, H. T. (1986). Stages in human brain development. *Developmental Brain Research, 30*(1), 114–119.

33. Cowan, W. M. (1990). The development of the brain. In R. R. Llinás (Ed.), *The workings of the brain: Development, memory and perception: Readings from Scientific American Magazine* (pp. 39–57). New York: W. H. Freeman.

34. Kandel, E. R., Schwartz, J. H., & Jessell, T. M. (1991). Development, critical periods, and the emergence of behavior. In E. R. Kandel, J. H. Schwartz, & T. M. Jessell, *Principles of neural science* (3rd ed.) (pp. 884–983). New York: Elsevier.

35. Epstein, H. T. (1986). Stages in human brain development. *Developmental Brain Research, 30*(1), 114–119.

36. Huttenlocher, P. R. (1993). Synaptogenesis in human cerebral cortex. In G. Dawson & K. W. Fischer (Eds.), *Human behavior and the developing brain* (pp. 137ff). New York: Guilford Press.

37. Fischer, K. W., & Rose, S. P. (1993). Dynamic development of coordination of components in brain and behavior: A framework for theory and research. In G. Dawson & K. W. Fischer (Eds.), *Human behavior and the developing brain* (pp. 3–22). New York: Guilford Press.

38. Gibson, K. R. (1991). Myelination and behavioral development: A comparative perspective on questions of neoteny, altriciality and intelligence. In K. R. Gibson & A. C. Petersen (Eds.), *Brain maturation and cognitive development* (pp. 29–63). New York: Aldine De Gruyter.

39. Yakovlev, P., & Lecours, A. (1967). The myelogenetic cycles of regional maturation of the brain. In A. Minkowski (Ed.), *Regional development of the brain in early life* (pp. 3–7). Oxford: Blackwell Scientific Publication.

Fox, N. A., & Davidson, R. J. (1984). *The psychobiology of affective development* (p. 381). Hillsdale, NJ: Lawrence Erlbaum.

40. Fox, N. A., & Davidson, R. J. (1984). *The psychobiology of affective development* (pp. 95ff). Hillsdale, NJ: Lawrence Erlbaum.

41. Liederman, J., Merola, J. L., & Hoffman, C. (1986). Longitudinal data indicate that hemispheric independence increases during early adolescence. *Developmental Neuropsychology, 2*(3), 183–201.

42. Thatcher, R. W. (1991). Maturation of the human frontal lobes: Physiological evidence for staging. *Developmental Neuropsychology, 7*(3), 397–419.

Thatcher, R. W. (1993). Cyclic cortical reorganization: Origins of human cognitive development. In G. Dawson & K. W. Fischer (Eds.), *Human behavior and the developing brain* (pp. 232–266). New York: Guilford Press.

43. Dennis, M., & Kohn, B. (1985). The active-passive test: An age-referenced clinical test of syntactic discrimination. *Developmental Neuropsychology, 1*(2), 113–137.

44. Dennis, M. (1991). Frontal lobe function in childhood and adolescence: A heuristic for assessing attention regulation, executive control, and the

intentional states important for social discourse. *Developmental Neuropsychology*, 7, 327–358.

45. Ryan, C. M. (1990). Age-related improvement in short-term memory efficiency during adolescence. *Developmental Neuropsychology, 60*(3), 193–205.

46. Tarter, R. E. (1994). *N.E.E.M. study of youth at risk.* Unpublished proposal.

47. Dennis, M. (1991). Frontal lobe function in childhood and adolescence: A heuristic for assessing attention regulation, executive control, and the intentional states important for social discourse. *Developmental Neuropsychology*, 7, 327–358.

48. Welsh, M. C., Pennington, B. F., & Groisser, D. B. (1991). A normative-developmental study of executive function: A window on prefrontal function in children. *Developmental Neuropsychology, 7*(2), 131–149.

49. Piaget, J., (1972). Intellectual evolution from adolescence to adulthood. *Human Development, 15,* 1–12.

Kagan, R. (1992). Minding the curriculum: Student epistemology and faculty conspiracy. In A. Garrod (Ed.), *Emerging themes in moral development.* New York: Teachers College Press.

50. Fischer, K. W. (1980). A theory of cognitive development: The control and construction of hierarchies of skills. *Psychological Review, 87,* 477–531.

51. Fischer, K. W., & Rose, S. P. (1993). Dynamic development of coordination of components in brain and behavior: A framework for theory and research. In G. Dawson & K. W. Fischer (Eds.), *Human behavior and the developing brain* (pp. 3–56). New York: Guilford Press.

52. Keating, D. (1990). Adolescent thinking. In S. S. Feldman & G. R. Elliott (Eds.), *At the threshold: The developing adolescent* (pp. 54–89). Cambridge: Harvard University Press.

53. Sacks, O. (1985). *The man who mistook his wife for a hat and other clinical tales.* New York: Harper & Row.

54. Elkind, D. (1967). Egocentrism in adolescence. *Child Development,* 38, 1025–1034.

55. Stuss, D. (1991). Self, awareness, and the frontal lobes: A neuropsychological perspective. In G. Goethals & J. Strauss, *The self: Interdisciplinary approaches* (pp. 255–278). New York: Springer-Verlag.

56. Kimura, D. (1992). Sex differences in the brain. *Scientific American,* 118–125.

CHAPTER 4

57. Richards, M., & Petersen, A. C. (1987). Biological theoretical models of adolescent development. In V. B. Van Hasselt & M. Hersen (Eds.). *Handbook of adolescent psychology* (pp. 34–52). New York: Pergamon Press.

58. Katchadourian, H. (1977). *The biology of adolescence.* (pp. 111ff). San Francisco: W. H. Freeman.

59. Feldman, S. S., & Elliott, G. R. (Eds.). (1990). *At the threshold: The developing adolescent* (p. 33). Cambridge: Harvard University Press.

60. Katchadourian, H. (1977). Somatic changes of puberty. In H. Katchadourian, *The biology of adolescence* (pp. 22–53). San Francisco: W. H. Freeman.

61. Katchadourian, H. (1977). Somatic changes of puberty. In H. Katchadourian, *The biology of adolescence* (pp. 22–53). San Francisco: W. H. Freeman.

Dusek, J. B. (1991). Biological change in adolescent development. In J. B. Dusek, *Adolescent development and behavior* (2nd ed.) (pp. 41–71). Englewood Cliffs, NJ: Prentice-Hall.

62. Katchadourian, H. (1977). *The biology of adolescence* (pp. 35–36). San Francisco: W. H. Freeman.

63. Bullough, V. L. (1981). Age at menarche: A misunderstanding. *Science, 213,* 365–366.

64. Katchadourian, H. (1977). Reproductive maturation and factors affecting puberty. In H. Katchadourian, *The biology of adolescence* (pp. 52–86). San Francisco: W. H. Freeman.

65. Katchadourian, H. (1977) *The biology of adolescence.* (pp. 79–80). San Francisco: W. H. Freeman.

66. Katchadourian, H. (1977). *The biology of adolescence* (p. 140). San Francisco: W. H. Freeman.

67. Tanner, J. M. (1973). Growing up. *Scientific American, 229*(3), 34–43.

Chart: Petersen, A. C., & Taylor, B. (1980). The biological approach to adolescence: Biological change and psychological adaptation. In J. Adelson (Ed.), *Handbook of adolescent psychology* (pp. 117–155). New York: John Wiley.

68. Katchadourian, H. (1977). *The biology of adolescence* (p. 123). San Francisco: W. H. Freeman.

69. Katchadourian, H. (1977). *The biology of adolescence* (pp. 32, 35). San Francisco: W. H. Freeman.

70. Katchadourian, H. (1977). *The biology of adolescence* (pp. 122–126). San Francisco: W. H. Freeman.

71. Katchadourian, H. (1977). *The biology of adolescence* (pp. 122–123, 126–128). San Francisco: W. H. Freeman.

72. Diamond, F., Jr., Ringenberg, L., Macdonald, D., Barnes, J., Shi Hu, C., Duckett, G., Sweetland, M., & Root, A. (1986). Effects of drug and alcohol abuse upon pituitary-testicular function in adolescent males. *Journal of Adolescent Health Care, 7*(1), 28–33.

73. Richards, M., & Petersen, A. C. (1987). Biological theoretical models of adolescent development. In V. B. Van Hasselt & M. Hersen (Eds.), *Handbook of adolescent psychology* (pp. 34–52). New York: Pergamon Press.

74. Richards, M., & Petersen, A. C. (1987). Biological theoretical models of adolescent development. In V. B. Van Hasselt & M. Hersen (Eds.). *Handbook of adolescent psychology* (pp. 34–52). New York: Pergamon Press.

75. Coren, S. (1992). *The left-hander syndrome: The causes and consequences of left-handedness.* New York: Free Press.

CHAPTER 5

76. Carrillo, J. E. (1992). Providing primary care to the adolescent. In D. E. Rogers & E. Ginzberg (Eds.), *Adolescents at risk: Medical and social perspectives* (pp. 122–127). Boulder: Westview Press.

77. Newton, M. (1990). *Getting straight: Out of a drug distorted adolescent passage* (p. 26). Secaucus, NJ: KIDS Centers of America.

78. Newton, M. *Rap therapy*. Unpublished paper.

79. Meichenbaum, D. (1977). *Cognitive-behavior modification: An integrative approach*. New York: Plenum Press.

80. Meichenbaum, D. (1977). *Cognitive-behavior modification: An integrative approach* (pp. 31ff). New York: Plenum Press.

81. Nezu, A. (1985). *Treatment manual: Social problem-solving for depression*. Unpublished paper.

82. Meichenbaum, D. (1977). *Cognitive-behavior modification: An integrative approach* (pp. 107ff). New York: Plenum Press.

83. Kendall, P. C., & Hollow, S. D. (Eds.). (1979). *Cognitive-behavioral interventions: Theory, research and procedures*. San Diego: Academic Press.

84. Lazarus, A. A. (1989). *The practice of multimodal therapy: Systematic, comprehensive and effective therapy*. Baltimore: Johns Hopkins University Press.

85. Elster, A. B., & Kuznets, N. J. (1994). *AMA guidelines for adolescent preventive services (GAPS): Recommendations and rationale* (pp. 29–39). Baltimore: Williams & Wilkins for The American Medical Association.

86. Ausubel, D. P. (1954). *The theory and problems of adolescent development*. (p. 507). New York: Grune & Stratton.

87. Seligman, M. E. P. (1975). *Helplessness: On depression, development, and death*. New York: W. H. Freeman.

CHAPTER 6

88. Fischer, K. W. (1980). A theory of cognitive development: The control and construction of hierarchies of skills. *Psychological Review, 87*, 477–531.

89. Harter, S. (1990). Self and identity development. In S. S. Feldman & G. R. Elliott (Eds.), *At the threshold: The developing adolescent* (p. 377). Cambridge: Harvard University Press.

90. Block, J. (1971). *Lives through time*. Berkeley: Bancroft Books.

91. Thomas, A., & Chess, S. (1989). Temperament and personality. In G. A. Kohnstamm, J. E. Bates, and M. K. Rothbart (Eds.), *Temperament in Childhood* (pp. 249–261). Chichester, England: John Wiley.

92. Bowen, M. (1985). *Family therapy in clinical practice*. Northvale, NJ: Jason Aronson.

93. Blos, P. (1979). *The adolescent passage: Developmental issues* (pp. 118ff, 142ff). New York: International Universities Press.

94. Fischer, K. W. (1980). A theory of cognitive development: The control and construction of hierarchies of skills. *Psychological Review, 87*, 477–531.

95. Erikson, E. H. (1968). *Identity: Youth and crisis* (p. 160). New York: W. W. Norton.

96. Dusek, J. B. (1991). *Adolescent development and behavior* (2nd ed.) (pp. 332–334). Englewood Cliffs, NJ: Prentice-Hall.

97. Gilligan, C. (1982). *In a different voice: Psychological theory and women's development*. Cambridge: Harvard University Press.

98. McGoldrick, M. (1989). Women and the family life cycle. In B. Carter & M. McGoldrick (Eds.), *The changing family life cycle: A framework for family therapy* (2nd ed.) (pp. 29–68). Boston: Allyn & Bacon.

99. Harter, S. (1990). Self and identity development. In S. S. Feldman & G. R. Elliott (Eds.), *At the threshold: The developing adolescent* (pp. 381ff). Cambridge: Harvard University Press.

100. Leman, K. (1985). *The birth order book*, Old Tappan, NY: Fleming H. Ravel.

101. Toman, W. (1993). *Family constellation: Its effects on personality and social behavior* (4th ed.). New York: Springer Publishing.

102. Blos, P. (1979). *The adolescent passage: Developmental issues* (pp. 74–77). New York: International Universities Press.

103. Kiell, N. (1964). *The universal experience of adolescence* (pp. 246ff). New York: International Universities Press.

104. Kiell, N. (1964). *The universal experience of adolescence* (p. 490). New York: International Universities Press.

105. Marcia, J. E. (1980). Identity and adolescence. In J. Adelson (Ed.), *Handbook of adolescent psychology* (pp. 159ff). New York: John Wiley.

106. Sugar, M. (1993). Adolescent motherhood and development. In M. Sugar (Ed.), *Female adolescent development* (2nd ed.) (pp. 213ff). New York: Brunner/Mazel.

CHAPTER 7

107. Gesell, A., Ilg, F. L., & Ames, L. B. (1956). *Youth: The years from ten to sixteen*, New York: Harper & Row.

108. Kohlberg, L. (1981). The six stages of moral judgement. In L. Kohlberg, *Essays on moral development: Volume I, The philosophy of moral development: Moral stages and the idea of justice* (pp. 409–412). San Francisco: Harper & Row.

109. Power, F. C., Higgins, A., & Kohlberg, L. (1989). *Lawrence Kohlberg's approach to moral education.* New York: Columbia University Press.

110. Power, F. C., Higgins, A., & Kohlberg, L. (1989). *Lawrence Kohlberg's approach to moral education.* New York: Columbia University Press.

CHAPTER 8

111. Kaplan, L. J. (1984). *Adolescence: The farewell to childhood.* New York: Simon & Schuster.

112. Brooks-Gunn, J., & Reiter, E. O. (1990). The role of pubertal processes. In S. S. Feldman & G. R. Elliott (Eds.), *At the threshold: The developing adolescent* (pp. 41ff). Cambridge: Harvard University Press.
Rosenbaum, M. (1993). Changing body image of the adolescent girl. In M. Sugar (Ed.), *Female adolescent development* (2nd ed.) (pp. 62–80). New York: Brunner/Mazel.

113. Brooks-Gunn, J., & Reiter, E. O. (1990). The role of pubertal processes. In S. S. Feldman & G. R. Elliott (Eds.), *At the threshold: The developing adolescent* (pp. 16–53). Cambridge: Harvard University Press.

114. Rosenbaum, M. (1993). Changing body image of the adolescent girl.

In M. Sugar (Ed.), *Female adolescent development* (2nd ed.) (pp. 62–80). New York: Brunner/Mazel.

115. Blos, P. (1979). *The adolescent passage: Developmental issues.* New York: International Universities Press.

116. Sullivan, H. S. (1953). *The interpersonal theory of psychiatry.* New York: W. W. Norton.

117. Schwartz, M. (1993, January 22). *Sexually traumatized adolescents.* Lecture presented at Masters and Johnson Sexual Trauma Program, New Orleans, LA.

118. Maltz, W. (1991). *Sexual healing journey: A guide for survivors of sexual abuse.* New York: Harper Perennial.

119. Katchadourian, H. (1990). Sexuality. In S. S. Feldman & G. R. Elliott (Eds.), *At the threshold: The developing adolescent* (pp. 330ff). Cambridge: Harvard University Press.

120. Irwin, C., Jr., & Schafer, M. (1992). Adolescent sexuality. In D. E. Rogers & E. Ginzberg (Eds.), *Adolescents at risk: Medical and social perspectives* (pp. 36ff). Boulder: Westview Press.

121. Newton, M. (1986). *Kids, drugs, and sex.* Tampa: American Studies Press.

122. Newton, M. (1986). *Kids, drugs, and sex.* Tampa: American Studies Press.

123. Irwin, C., Jr., & Schafer, M. (1992). Adolescent sexuality. In D. E. Rogers & E. Ginzberg (Eds.), *Adolescents at risk: Medical and social perspectives* (p. 46). Boulder: Westview Press.

124. Irwin, C., Jr., & Schafer, M. (1992). Adolescent sexuality. In D. E. Rogers & E. Ginzberg (Eds.), *Adolescents at risk: Medical and social perspectives* (p. 43ff). Boulder: Westview Press.

125. Katchadourian, H. (1990). Sexuality. In S. S. Feldman & G. R. Elliott (Eds.), *At the threshold: The developing adolescent* (pp. 330–351). Cambridge: Harvard University Press.

126. Irwin, C., Jr., & Schafer, M. (1992). Adolescent sexuality. In D. E. Rogers & E. Ginzberg (Eds.), *Adolescents at risk: Medical and social perspectives* (p. 52). Boulder: Westview Press.

127. Irwin, C., Jr., & Schafer, M. (1992). Adolescent sexuality. In D. E. Rogers & E. Ginzberg (Eds.), *Adolescents at risk: Medical and social perspectives* (p. 53). Boulder: Westview Press.

128. Irwin, C., Jr., & Schafer, M. (1992). Adolescent sexuality. In D. E. Rogers & E. Ginzberg (Eds.), *Adolescents at risk: Medical and social perspectives* (p. 53). Boulder: Westview Press.

129. Irwin, C., Jr., & Schafer, M. (1992). Adolescent sexuality. In D. E. Rogers & E. Ginzberg (Eds.), *Adolescents at risk: Medical and social perspectives* (p. 53). Boulder: Westview Press.

130. Who's Who among American High School Students. (1992). *23rd annual survey of high achievers: Attitudes and opinions from the nation's high achieving teens.* Lake Forest, IL: Educational Communications.

131. Irwin, C., Jr., & Schafer, M. (1992). Adolescent sexuality. In D. E. Rogers & E. Ginzberg (Eds.), *Adolescents at risk: Medical and social perspectives* (p. 54ff). Boulder: Westview Press.

132. Irwin, C., Jr., & Schafer, M. (1992). Adolescent sexuality. In D. E. Rogers & E. Ginzberg (Eds.), *Adolescents at risk: Medical and social perspectives* (p. 60–61). Boulder: Westview Press.

133. Courtois, C. A. (1988). *Healing the incest wound: Adult survivors in therapy* (pp. 28–85). New York: W. W. Norton.

134. Courtois, C. A. (1988). *Healing the incest wound: Adult survivors in therapy* (p. 276). New York: W. W. Norton.

135. Courtois, C. A. (1988). *Healing the incest wound: Adult survivors in therapy* (pp. 90–91). New York: W. W. Norton.

136. Courtois, C. A. (1988). *Healing the incest wound: Adult survivors in therapy* (pp. 115–116). New York: W. W. Norton.

137. Blos, P. (1979). *The adolescent passage: Developmental issues* (p. 204). New York: International Universities Press.

138. Carnes, P. (1983). *Out of the shadows*. Minneapolis: CompCare Press.

139. Meyer, J. K. (1985). Ego-dystonic homosexuality. In H. I. Kaplan & B. J. Sadock, *Comprehensive textbook of psychiatry/IV* (4th ed.) (pp. 1056–1065). Baltimore: Williams & Wilkins.

140. Byne, W., & Parsons, B. (1993). Biology and human sexual orientation. *The Harvard Mental Health Letter*, 10(8), 5–7.

141. Horgan, J. (1993). Eugenics revisited: Trends in behavioral genetics. *Scientific American*, 120–131.

142. Berenstein, F. (1995). Benjamin L. In *Lost Boys*. New York: W. W. Norton.

143. Blos, P. (1979). *The adolescent passage: Developmental issues* (pp. 247–249). New York: International Universities Press.

144. Elster, A. B., & Kuznets, N. J. (1994). *AMA guidelines for adolescent preventive services (GAPS): Recommendations and rationale*, Baltimore: Williams & Wilkins for The American Medical Association.

145. Westhead, V. A., Olson, S. J., & Meyer, J. K. (1990). Gender identity disorders in adolescence. In M. Sugar (Ed.), *Atypical adolescence and sexuality* (pp. 87–107). New York: W. W. Norton.

CHAPTER 9

146. Combrinck-Graham, L. (1985). A developmental model for family systems. *Family Process*, 24(2), 139–150.

147. Carter, B., & McGoldrick, M. (1989). Overview: The changing family life cycle—A framework for family therapy. In B. Carter & M. McGoldrick (Eds.), *The changing family life cycle: A framework for family therapy* (2nd ed.) (pp. 3–28). Boston: Allyn & Bacon.

148. Combrinck-Graham, L. (1985). A developmental model for family systems. *Family Process*, 24(2), 139–150.

149. Toman, W. (1993). *Family constellation: Its effects on personality and social behavior* (4th ed.). New York: Springer Publishing.

150. Visher, E. B., & Visher, J. S. (1979). *Step-families: A guide to working with stepparents & stepchildren* (pp. 195ff). New York: Brunner/Mazel.

151. Rutter, M., Quinton, D., & Hill, J. (1990). Adult outcome of institu-

tion-reared children: males and females compared. In L. Robins & M. Rutter (Eds.), *Straight and devious pathways from childhood to adulthood* (pp. 142ff). Cambridge: Cambridge University Press.

152. Maughan, B., & Pickles, A. (1990). Adopted and illegitimate children growing up. In L. Robins & M. Rutter (Eds.), *Straight and devious pathways from childhood to adulthood* (pp. 36–61). Cambridge: Cambridge University Press.

153. Newton, M. (1981). *Gone way down: Teenage drug-use is a disease.* Tampa: American Studies Press.

DuPont, R. L. (1984). *Getting tough on gateway drugs: A guide for the family.* Washington, DC: American Psychiatric Press.

154. McCord, J. (1990). Long-term perspectives on parental absence. In L. Robins & M. Rutter (Eds.), *Straight and devious pathways from childhood to adulthood* (pp. 128–129). Cambridge: Cambridge University Press.

155. Maccoby, E., & Martin, J. (1983). Socialization in the context of the family: Parent-child interaction. In E. M. Hetherington (Ed.), *Handbook of child psychology: Socialization, personality, and social development* (Vol. 4). New York: John Wiley.

156. Bowen, M. (1985). *Family therapy in clinical practice.* Northvale, NJ: Jason Aronson.

CHAPTER 10

157. Elkind, D. (1967). Egocentrism in adolescence. *Child Development,* 38, 1025–1034.

158. Elkind, D. (1967). Egocentrism in adolescence. *Child Development,* 38, 1025–1034.

159. Elkind, D. (1967). Egocentrism in adolescence. *Child Development,* 38, 1025–1034.

160. Gesell, A., Ilg, F. L., & Ames, L. B. (1956). *Youth: The years from ten to sixteen,* New York: Harper & Row.

161. Muuss, R. E. (1962). *Theories of adolescence* (5th ed.) (pp. 270ff). New York: Random House.

162. Sullivan, H. S. (1953). *The interpersonal theory of psychiatry* (p. 45). New York: W. W. Norton.

163. Selman, R. (1980). *The growth of interpersonal understanding: Development and clinical analyses.* New York: Academic Press.

164. McCord, J. (1990). Problem behaviors. In S. S. Feldman & G. R. Elliott (Eds.), *At the threshold: The developing adolescent* (pp. 414–430). Cambridge: Harvard University Press.

CHAPTER 11

165. Ausubel, D. P. (1954). *The theory and problems of adolescent development* (p. 471). New York: Grune & Stratton.

166. Dusek, J. B. (1991). *Adolescent development and behavior* (2nd ed.) (pp. 339ff). Englewood Cliffs, NJ: Prentice-Hall.

167. Eccles, J. S., Midgley, C., Wigfield, A., Buchanan, C. M., Reuman, D., Flanagan, C., & McIver, D. (1993). Development during adolescence: The impact of stage-environment fit on young adolescents' experiences in schools and family. *American Psychologist, 48*(2), 90–101.

168. Kiell, N. (1964). *The universal experience of adolescence* (p. 827). New York: International Universities Press.

169. Flowers, D. L. (1993). Brain basis for dyslexia: A summary of work in progress. *Journal of Learning Disabilities, 26*, 575–582.

170. Friedman, S. (1993, June 13). Where teen-agers care for the elderly. *New York Times.*

CHAPTER 12

171. Prothrow-Stith, D., with Weissman, M. (1991). *Deadly consequences: How violence is destroying our teenage population and a plan to begin solving the problem* (p. 14). New York: Harper Collins.

172. Prothrow-Stith, D., with Weissman, M. (1991). *Deadly consequences: How violence is destroying our teenage population and a plan to begin solving the problem* (p. 15). New York: Harper Collins.

173. Prothrow-Stith, D., with Weissman, M. (1991). *Deadly consequences: How violence is destroying our teenage population and a plan to begin solving the problem* (p. 16). New York: Harper Collins.

174. U.S. Department of Justice. (1991). *Criminal Victimization, 1990* (Special Report No. NCJ-122743). Washington, DC: Bureau of Juvenile Statistics.

175. Christoffel, K. K. (1990). Violent death and injury in U.S. children and adolescents. *American Journal of Diseases of Childhood, 144*, 697–706.

176. Who's Who among American High School Students. (1992). *23rd annual survey of high achievers: Attitudes and opinions from the nation's high achieving teens.* Lake Forest, IL: Educational Communications.

177. Christoffel, K. K. (1990). Violent death and injury in U.S. children and adolescents. *American Journal of Diseases of Childhood, 144*, 697–706.

178. Children's Safety Network. (1991). *A data book of child and adolescent injury.* Washington, DC: National Center for Education in Maternal and Child Health.

179. Christoffel, K. K. (1990). Violent death and injury in U.S. children and adolescents. *American Journal of Diseases of Childhood, 144*, 697–706.

Harlow, C. (1989). *Injuries from crime* (Special Report No. NCJ-116811). Washington, DC: U.S. Department of Justice.

180. Children's Safety Network. (1991). *A data book of child and adolescent injury.* Washington, DC: National Center for Education in Maternal and Child Health.

181. Wilson, W. J. (1987). *The truly disadvantaged.* Chicago: University of Chicago Press.

Centerwall, B. (1984). Race, socioeconomic status and domestic homicide, Atlanta, 1971–72. *American Journal of Public Health, 74*, 813–815.

182. Elliott, F. A. (1992). Violence, the neurologic contribution: An overview. *Archives of Neurology, 49*, 595–603.

183. Elliott, F. A. (1992). Violence, the neurologic contribution: An overview. *Archives of Neurology, 49*, 595–603.

184. Prothrow-Stith, D., with Weissman, M. (1991). *Deadly consequences: How violence is destroying our teenage population and a plan to begin solving the problem* (p. 182). New York: Harper Collins.

185. Collins, J. J., & Messerschmidt, P. M. (1993). Epidemiology of alcohol related violence. *Alcohol Health and Research World, 17(2)*, 93–100.

186. Pihl, R. O., & Peterson, J. B. (1993). Alcohol, serotonin and aggression. *Alcohol Health and Research World, 17(2)*, 113–116.

187. Who's Who among American High School Students. (1992). *23rd annual survey of high achievers: Attitudes and opinions from the nation's high achieving teens*. Lake Forest, IL: Educational Communications.

188. Fuster, J. M. (1989). *The prefrontal cortex: Anatomy, physiology and neuropsychology of the frontal lobe* (p. 70). New York: Raven Press.

189. Elliott, F. A. (1992). Violence, the neurologic contribution: An overview. *Archives of Neurology, 49*, 595–603.

190. Elliott, F. A. (1992). Violence, the neurologic contribution: An overview. *Archives of Neurology, 49*, 595–603.

191. Carroll, A. H., & Lichtenberg, P. A. (1994). Post-traumatic stress disorder and its implications for rehabilitation populations. *Advances in Medical Psychotherapy, 7*, 145–152.

192. Prothrow-Stith, D., with Weissman, M. (1991). *Deadly consequences: How violence is destroying our teenage population and a plan to begin solving the problem*. New York: Harper Collins.

Chapter 13

193. National Center for Health Statistics. (1991).

194. Simons, J. M., Finlay, B., & Yang, A. (1991). *The adolescent and young adult fact book* (p. 64). Washington, DC: Children's Defense Fund.

195. Source: National Center for Health Statistics, *Vital Statistics of the United States: 1988, Vol. II—Mortality, Part A* (1991), Table 1–9.

196. Garland, A. F., & Zigler, E. (1993). Adolescent suicide prevention: Current research and social policy implications. In *Adolescence*, Special Issue of *American Psychologist, 48(2)*, 169–182.

197. Garland, A. F., & Zigler, E. (1993). Adolescent suicide prevention: Current research and social policy implications. In *Adolescence*, Special Issue of *American Psychologist, 48(2)*, 169–182.

198. Garland, A. F., & Zigler, E. (1993). Adolescent suicide prevention: Current research and social policy implications. In *Adolescence*, Special Issue of *American Psychologist, 48(2)*, 169–182.

199. Who's Who among American High School Students. (1992). *23rd annual survey of high achievers: Attitudes and opinions from the nation's high achieving teens*. Lake Forest, IL: Educational Communications.

200. Travis, R. (1990). Halbwachs and Durkheim: A test of two theories of suicide. *The British Journal of Sociology, 41(2)*, 225–243.

201. Bongar, B. (1991). *The suicidal patient: Clinical and legal standards of care* (pp. 3ff). Washington, DC: American Psychological Association.

202. Garrison, C. Z., McKeown, R. E., Valois, R. F., & Vincent, M. L. (1993). Aggression, substance use, and suicidal behaviors in high school students. *American Journal of Public Health*, 83(2), 179–184.

203. Garrison, C. Z., McKeown, R. E., Valois, R. F., & Vincent, M. L. (1993). Aggression, substance use, and suicidal behaviors in high school students. *American Journal of Public Health*, 83(2), 179–184.

204. Garrison, C. Z., McKeown, R. E., Valois, R. F., & Vincent, M. L. (1993). Aggression, substance use, and suicidal behaviors in high school students. *American Journal of Public Health*, 83(2), 179–184.

Newton, M. (1985, December 1). Some experts only obscure problems of teen suicide. *New York Times*.

Newton, M. (1982). *Adolescent suicide in Plano and substance use*. Unpublished study.

Newton, M. (1990). *The Bergenfield adolescent suicides*. Unpublished study.

205. Straus, M. B. (1994). Suicidal adolescents. In M. B. Straus, *Violence in the lives of adolescents* (pp. 31–53). New York: W. W. Norton.

206. Garland, A. F., & Zigler, E. (1993). Adolescent suicide prevention: Current research and social policy implications. In *Adolescence*, Special Issue of *American Psychologist*, 48(2), 171.

CHAPTER 14

207. *Nation's Health* (1993, May–June).

208. Johnston, L., O'Malley, P., & Bachman, J. (1994). *Monitoring the future study: The national high school senior survey*. Rockville, MD: National Institute on Drug Abuse.

209. Malcolm, A. I. (1975). *The craving for the high* (pp. 1–14). New York: Pocket Books.

210. Who's Who among American High School Students. (1992). *23rd annual survey of high achievers: Attitudes and opinions from the nation's high achieving teens*. Lake Forest, IL: Educational Communications.

211. National Study on Drug Abuse. *The 1993 report of the potency monitoring project*. (1993). Bethesda: Author.

212. Kandel, D., & Yamaguchi, K. (1993). From beer to crack: Developmental patterns of drug involvement. *American Journal of Public Health*, 83, 851–855.

213. Jellinek, E. M. (1960). *The disease concept of alcoholism*. New Haven: College University Press.

214. Johnson, V. E. (1960). *I'll quit tomorrow* (rev. ed.). New York: Harper & Row.

215. This work is based on previous work and publications.

Newton, M. (1981). *Gone way down: Teenage drug-use is a disease*. Tampa: American Studies Press.

Newton, M., & Macdonald, D. I. (1981). The clinical syndrome of adolescent drug-use. In L. A. Barness (Ed.), *Advances in Pediatrics*, Vol. 28 (pp. 1–25). Chicago: Yearbook Medical Publishers.

Newton, M., & Polson, B. (1984). *Not my kid*. New York: Arbor House.

Newton, M. (1984). *Adolescent drug-use as a disease.* Secaucus, NJ: KIDS of North Jersey.

216. Kandel, D., & Yamaguchi, K. (1993). From beer to crack: Developmental patterns of drug involvement. *American Journal of Public Health, 83,* 851–855.

217. Ellickson, P. L., Hays, R. D., & Bell, R. M. (1992). Stepping through the drug use sequence: Longitudinal scalagram analysis of initiation and regular use. *Journal of Abnormal Psychology, 101,* 441–451.

218. Tarter, R. E. (1994). *N.E.E.M. study of youth at risk.* Unpublished proposal.

219. Mezzich, A. C., et al. (undated). *Gender differences in the pattern and progression of substance use in conduct disordered adolescents.* Unpublished manuscript, University of Pittsburgh School of Medicine, Western Psychiatric Institute and Clinic, Pittsburgh.

220. Ellickson, P. L., Hays, R. D., & Bell, R. M. (1992). Stepping through the drug use sequence: Longitudinal scalagram analysis of initiation and regular use. *Journal of Abnormal Psychology, 101,* 441–451.

221. Horgan, C., et al. (1993). *Substance abuse: The nation's number one health problem, key indicators for policy.* Boston: Institute for Health Policy, Brandeis University, with The Robert Wood Johnson Foundation.

222. Tarter, R. E. (1991). Developmental behavior-genetic prespective of alcoholism etiology. In M. Galanter (Ed.), *Recent developments in alcoholism,* 9 (pp. 66–85). New York: Plenum Press.

223. U. S. Department of Health and Human Services. (1993). *National survey results on drug use from the monitoring the future study, 1975–1992, Vol. I.* Rockville, MD: National Institute on Drug Abuse.

224. Rothbart, M. K. (1989). Biological process in temperament. In G. A. Kohnstamm, J. E. Bates, & M. K. Rothbart (Eds.), *Temperament in childhood* (p. 93). Chichester, England: John Wiley.

225. Tarter, R. E. (1994). *N.E.E.M. study of youth at risk.* Unpublished proposal.

226. Bates, M. (in press). Psychology. In M. Galanter, *Recent developments in alcoholism,* 11, New York: Plenum Press.

227. Kaminer, Y., Bukstein, O., & Tarter, R. E. (1991). The teen-addiction survey severity index: Rational reliability. *The International Journal of Addiction, 26*(2), 219–226.

228. Gilbert, F. S. (1991). Development of a "steps questionnaire". *Journal of Studies on Alcohol, 52,* 353–360.

229. Wegscheider, S. (1981). *Another chance: Hope and help for the alcoholic family.* Palo Alto, CA: Science & Behavior Books.

230. Anderson, D. J. (1981). *Perspective on treatment: The Minnesota experience.* Center City, MN: Hazelden.

CHAPTER 15

231. Jessor, R. (1992). Risk behaviors in adolescents: A psychosocial framework for understanding and action. In D. E. Rogers & E. Ginzberg (Eds.),

Adolescents at risk: Medical and social perspectives (p. 24). Boulder: Westview Press.

232. McCord, J. (1990). Long-term perspectives on parental absence. In L. Robins & M. Rutter (Eds.), *Straight and devious pathways from childhood to adulthood* (p. 127). Cambridge: Cambridge University Press.

CHAPTER 16

233. Levenkron, S. (1978). *The best little girl in the world.* Chicago: Contemporary Books.

234. Halmi, K. A. (1987). Anorexia nervosa and bulimia. In V. B. Van Hasselt & M. Hersen (Eds.). *Handbook of adolescent psychology.* New York: Pergamon Press.

235. Halmi, K. A. (1987). Anorexia nervosa and bulimia. In V. B. Van Hasselt & M. Hersen (Eds.). *Handbook of adolescent psychology.* New York: Pergamon Press.

236. Dusek, J. B. (1991). *Adolescent development and behavior* (2nd ed.) (p. 387). Englewood Cliffs, NJ: Prentice-Hall.

237. Bruch, H. (1978). *The golden cage: The enigma of anorexia nervosa.* Cambridge: Harvard University Press.

238. Minuchin, S., et al. (1978). *Psychosomatic families: Anorexia nervosa in context.* Cambridge: Harvard University Press.

239. Pope, H. G., Jr., & Hudson, J. I. (1984). *New hope for binge eaters: Advances in the understanding and treatment of bulimia.* New York: Harper & Row.

240. Agras, W. S. (1987). *Eating disorders: Management of obesity, bulimia and anorexia nervosa.* New York: Pergamon Press.

241. Garner, D. M., & Beamis, K. M. (1982). A cognitive-behavioral approach to anorexia nervosa. *Cognitive Therapy and Research, 6*(2), 133–150.

242. Root, M. P. P., Fallon, P., & Friedrich, W. N. (1986). *Bulimia: A systems approach to treatment* (p. 89). New York: W. W. Norton.

243. Root, M. P. P., Fallon, P., & Friedrich, W. N. (1986). *Bulimia: A systems approach to treatment* (pp. 58–59). New York: W. W. Norton.

244. Huebner, H. F. (1993). *Endorphins, eating disorders and other addictive behaviors* (pp. 49–77, 139–144). New York: W. W. Norton.

CHAPTER 17

245. Rende, R. D., Plomin, R., Reiss, D., & Hetherington, E. M. (1993). Genetic and environmental influences on depressive symptomatology in adolescence: Individual differences and extreme scores. *Journal of Child Psychology and Psychiatry, 34,* 1387–1398.

246. Kruk, Z. L., & Pycock, C. J. (1983). *Neurotransmitters and drugs* (2nd ed.) (pp. 65–67). Baltimore: University Park Press.

247. Petersen, A. C., Compas, B. E., Brooks-Gunn, J., Stemmler, M., Ey, S., & Grant, K. E. (1993). Depression and adolescence. *American Psychologist, 48,* 155–168.

248. Petersen, A. C., Compas, B. E., Brooks-Gunn, J., Stemmler, M., Ey, S., & Grant, K. E. (1993). Depression and adolescence. *American Psychologist*, 48, 155–168.

249. Klerman, G. L. (1988). The current age of youthful melancholia: Evidence for increase in depression among adolescents and young adults. *British Journal of Psychiatry*, 152, 4–14.

250. Petersen, A. C., Compas, B. E., Brooks-Gunn, J., Stemmler, M., Ey, S., & Grant, K. E. (1993). Depression and adolescence. *American Psychologist*, 48, 155–168.

251. Cooper, J. R., Bloom, F. E., & Roth, R. H. (1986). *The biochemical basis of neuropharmacology* (5th ed.) (pp. 304–308). New York: Oxford University Press.

252. Nesse, R. M. (1991). What good is feeling bad? The evolutionary benefits of psychic pain. *The Sciences*, 30–37.

253. Offer, D., Ostrov, E., & Howard, K. I. (1987). Epidemiology of mental health and mental illness among adolescents. In J. D. Call et al. (Eds.). *Basic handbook of child psychiatry*. New York: Basic Books.

254. Petersen, A. C., Compas, B. E., & Brooks-Gunn, J. (1991). *Depression in adolescence: Implications of current research for programs and policy, Report prepared for the Carnegie Council on Adolescent Development*. Washington, DC.

CHAPTER 18

255. Turk, D. C., & Speers, M. A. (1983). Diabetes mellitus: A cognitive-functional analysis of stress. In T. P. Burish & L. A. Bradley (Eds.). *Coping with chronic disease: Research and applications* (pp. 191–192). New York: Academic Press.

256. Sachs, P. R. (1991). *Treating families of brain-injury survivors* (p. 2). New York: Springer Publishing.

257. Blos, P. (1979). *The adolescent passage: Developmental issues* (p. 448). New York: International Universities Press.

258. Turk, D. C., & Speers, M. A. (1983). Diabetes mellitus: A cognitive-functional analysis of stress. In T. P. Burish & L. A. Bradley (Eds.). *Coping with chronic disease: Research and applications* (pp. 195). New York: Academic Press.

259. Kaplan, R. M., & Simon, H. J. (1990). Compliance in medical care: Reconsideration of self-predictions. *Annals of Behavioral Medicine*, 12(2), 66.

260. Tieboult, H. M. (1949). *The act of surrender in the therapeutic process*. New York: National Council on Alcoholism.

261. Greydanus, D. E., Gunther, M. S., Demarest, D. S. & Sears, J. M. (1990). Sexuality of the chronically ill adolescent. In M. Sugar, *Atypical adolescence and sexuality* (pp.147–157). New York: W. W. Norton.

CHAPTER 19

262. This case study, under a fictitious name, is described with permission.

Bibliography

Ackerman, S. (1992). *Discovering the brain*. Washington, DC: National Academy Press.

Adolescence (1993). Special Issue of *American Psychologist*, 48(2).

Black, C. (1971). *Double duty: Sexually abused*. New York: Ballantine Books.

Block, J. (1971). *Lives through time*. Berkeley: Bancroft Books.

Blos, P. (1979). *The adolescent passage: Developmental issues*. New York: International Universities Press.

Boskind-White, M., & White, W. C. (1983). *Bulimarexia: The binge/purge cycle*. New York: W. W. Norton.

Bowen, M. (1985). *Family therapy in clinical practice*. Northvale, NJ: Jason Aronson.

Bruch, H. (1973). *Eating disorders, obesity, anorexia nervosa and the prison within*. New York: Basic Books.

Bruch, H. (1978). *The golden cage: The enigma of anorexia nervosa*. Cambridge: Harvard University Press.

Callahan, C. M., & Rivara, F. P. (1992). Urban high school youth and handguns: A school-based survey. *Journal of the American Medical Association, 267*.

Carnes, P. (1983). *Out of the shadows*. Minneapolis: CompCare Press.

Carskadon, M. A. (1990). Adolescent sleepiness: Increased risk in a high-risk population. *Alcohol, Drugs and Driving, 5/6*, 317–328.

Carter, B., & McGoldrick, M. (Eds.). (1989). *The changing family life cycle: A framework for family therapy* (2nd ed.). Boston: Allyn & Bacon.

Coren, S. (1992). *The left-hander syndrome: The causes and consequences of left-handedness*. New York: Free Press.

Courtois, C. A. (1988). *Healing the incest wound: Adult survivors in therapy*. New York: W. W. Norton.

Dawson, G., & Fischer, K. W. (Eds.). (1993). *Human behavior and the developing brain*. New York: Guilford Press.

DuPont, R. L. (1984). *Getting tough on gateway drugs: A guide for the family*, Washington, DC: American Psychiatric Press.

Dusek, J. B. (1991). *Adolescent development and behavior* (2nd ed.). Englewood Cliffs, NJ: Prentice-Hall.

Elster, A. B., & Kuznets, N. J. (1994). *AMA guidelines for adolescent preventive services (GAPS): Recommendations and rationale*, Baltimore: Williams & Wilkins for The American Medical Association.

Elkind, D. (1984). *All grown up & no place to go: Teenagers in crisis*, Reading: Addison-Wesley.

Ellis, A., & Dryden, W. (1987). *The practice of rational emotive therapy*. New York: Springer Publishing.

Elson, M. (Ed.). (1987). *The Kohut seminars on self psychology and psychotherapy with adolescents and young adults*. New York: W. W. Norton.

Erikson, E. H. (1968). *Identity: Youth and crisis*. New York: W. W. Norton.

Feindler, E. L., & Ecton, R. C. (1986). *Adolescent anger control: Cognitive behavioral techniques*. New York: Pergamon Press.

Feldman, S. S., & Elliott, G. R. (Eds.). (1990). *At the threshold: The developing adolescent*. Cambridge: Harvard University Press.

Freud, A. (1958). Adolescence. *Psychoanalytic Study of the Child, 13*, 255–278.

Freud, A. (1980). Adolescence as a developmental disturbance. In Caplan & Lebovici, (Eds.), *Adolescence: Psychosocial perspectives* (pp. 5–10). New York: Basic Books.

Gesell, A., Ilg, F. L., & Ames, L. B. (1956). *Youth: The years from ten to sixteen*, New York: Harper & Row.

Gibson, K. R., & Petersen, A. C. (Eds.). (1991). *Brain maturation and cognitive development*. New York: Aldine De Gruyter.

Gilligan, C. (1982). *In a different voice: Psychological theory and women's development*. Cambridge: Harvard University Press.

Gunnar, M. R., & Collins, W. A. (Eds.). (1988). *The Minnesota Symposia on Child Psychology: Vol. 21. Development during the transition to adolescence*. Hillsdale: Lawrence Erlbaum.

Harvard Graduate School of Education. (1991). Conference on *New perspectives on adolescent development*. Cambridge, MA.

Haskew, P., & Adams, C. H. (1984). *When food is a four-letter word*. Englewood Cliffs, NJ: Prentice-Hall.

Huebner, H. F. (1993). *Endorphins, eating disorders and other addictive behaviors*. New York: W. W. Norton.

Inhelder, B., & Piaget, J. (1958). *The growth of logical thinking from childhood to adolescence*. New York: Basic Books.

James, B. (1989). *Treating traumatized children: New insights and creative interventions*. Lexington: Lexington Books.

Joan, P. (1986). *Preventing teenage suicide: The alternative living book*. New York: Human Sciences Press.

Johnson, V. E. (1960). *I'll quit tomorrow* (rev. ed.). New York: Harper & Row.

Johnston, L., O'Malley, P., & Bachman, J. (1994). *Monitoring the future study: The national high school senior survey*. Rockville, MD: National Institute on Drug Abuse.

Kaplan, L. J. (1984). *Adolescence: The farewell to childhood*. New York: Simon & Schuster.

Katchadourian, H. (1977). *The biology of adolescence*. San Francisco: W. H. Freeman.

Kohlberg, L. (1988). *Moral education, justice and community: A study of three democratic high schools*. New York: Columbia University Press.

Kohlberg, L., & Gilligan, C. (1971). The adolescent as philosopher. *Daedalus, 100*, 1051–1086.

Kohnstamm, G. A., Bates, J. E., & Rothbart, M. K. (Eds.). (1989). *Temperament in childhood*. Chichester, England: John Wiley.

Lazarus, A. A. (1989). *The practice of multimodal therapy: Systematic, comprehensive and effective therapy*. Baltimore: Johns Hopkins University Press.

Levenkron, S. (1978). *The best little girl in the world.* Chicago: Contemporary Books.

Maltz, W. (1991). *Sexual healing journey: A guide for survivors of sexual abuse.* New York: Harper Perennial.

Maultsby, M. C., Jr., & Hendricks, A. (1974). *You and your emotions.* Lexington, KY: Rational Self Help Books.

Meichenbaum, D. (1977). *Cognitive-behavior modification: An integrative approach.* New York: Plenum Press.

Minuchin, S., et al. (1978). *Psychosomatic families: Anorexia nervosa in context.* Cambridge: Harvard University Press.

Moriarty, A. R. (1991). Adolescent satanic cult dabblers: A differential diagnosis. *Journal of Mental Health Counseling, 13*(3), 393–404.

Muuss, R. E. (1962). *Theories of adolescence* (5th ed.). New York: Random House.

Napier, A. Y., with Whitaker, C. A. (1978). *The family crucible.* Toronto: Bantam Books.

Newton, M. (1990). *Getting straight: Out of a drug distorted adolescent passage.* Secaucus, NJ: KIDS Centers of America.

Newton, M. (1981). *Gone way down: Teenage drug-use is a disease.* Tampa: American Studies Press.

Newton, M. (1986). *Kids, drugs, and sex.* Tampa: American Studies Press.

Newton, M., & Macdonald, D. I. (1981). The clinical syndrome of adolescent drug-use. In L. A. Barness (Ed.), *Advances in Pediatrics, Vol. 28* (pp. 1–25). Chicago: Yearbook Medical Publishers.

Newton, M., & Polson, B. (1984). *Not my kid.* New York: Arbor House.

National Study on Drug Abuse. *The 1993 report of the potency monitoring project.* (1993). Bethesda: Author.

Offer, D., & Offer, J. B. (1975). *From teenage to young manhood: A psychological study.* New York: Basic Books.

Offer, D., & Sabshin, M. (Eds.) (1984). *Normality and the life cycle: A critical integration.* New York: Basic Books.

Persons, J. B. (1989). *Cognitive therapy in practice: A case formulation approach.* New York: W. W. Norton.

Petersen, A. (1988). Adolescent development. In M. R. Rosenzweig & L. W. Porter (Eds.), *Annual Review of Psychology, Vol. 39* (pp. 583–607). Palo Alto, CA: Annual Reviews.

Petersen, A. C., & Taylor, B. (1980). The biological approach to adolescence: Biological change and psychological adaptation. In J. Adelson (Ed.), *Handbook of adolescent psychology* (pp. 117–155). New York: John Wiley.

Phillips, D. E., & Carstenson, L. L. (1986). Clustering of teenage suicide after television news stories about suicide. *New England Journal of Medicine, 315,* 685–689.

Piaget, J., (1972). Intellectual evolution from adolescence to adulthood. *Human Development, 15,* 1–12.

Pope, H. G., Jr., & Hudson, J. I. (1984). *New hope for binge eaters: Advances in the understanding and treatment of bulimia.* New York: Harper & Row.

Powell, D. H. (1986). *Teenagers: When to worry and what to do.* Garden City: Doubleday.

Prothrow-Stith, D., with Weissman, M. (1991). *Deadly consequences: How violence is destroying our teenage population and a plan to begin solving the problem.* New York: Harper Collins.

Richards, M., & Petersen, A. C. (1987). Biological theoretical models of adolescent development. In V. B. Van Hasselt & M. Hersen (Eds.). *Handbook of adolescent psychology.* (pp. 34–52). New York: Pergamon Press.

Robins, L., & Rutter, M. (Eds.). (1990). *Straight and devious pathways from childhood to adulthood.* Cambridge: Cambridge University Press.

Rogers, D. E., & Ginzberg, E. (Eds.). (1992). *Adolescents at risk: Medical and social perspectives.* Boulder: Westview Press.

Root, M. P. P., Fallon, P., & Friedrich, W. N. (1986). *Bulimia: A systems approach to treatment.* New York: W. W. Norton.

Seligman, M. E. P. (1975). *Helplessness: On depression, development, and death.* New York: W. H. Freeman.

Simons, J. M., Finlay, B., & Yang, A. (1991). *The adolescent and young adult fact book.* Washington, DC: Children's Defense Fund.

Sugar, M. (Ed.). (1990)., *Atypical adolescence and sexuality.* New York: W. W. Norton.

Sugar, M. (Ed.). (1993). *Female adolescent development* (2nd ed.). New York: Brunner/Mazel.

Tanner, J. M. (1973). Growing up. *Scientific American, 229*(3), 34–43.

Visher, E. B., & Visher, J. S. (1979). *Step-families: A guide to working with stepparents & stepchildren.* New York: Brunner/Mazel.

Wegscheider, S. (1981). *Another chance: Hope and help for the alcoholic family.* Palo Alto, CA: Science & Behavior Books.

Weiner, I. B. (1990). Distinguishing healthy from disturbed adolescent development. *Journal of Development and Behavioral Pediatrics, 11*(3), 151–154.

Who's Who among American High School Students. (1992). *23rd annual survey of high achievers: Attitudes and opinions from the nation's high achieving teens.* Lake Forest, IL: Educational Communications.

Wilson, W. J. (1987). *The truly disadvantaged.* Chicago: University of Chicago Press.

Woznica, J. G., & Shapiro, J. R. (1990). An analysis of adolescent suicide attempts: The expendable child. *Journal of Pediatric Psychology, 15,* 789–796.

Index